마이갓 5 Step 모의고사 공부법

1 ● **Vocabulary 필수 단어 암기 & Test**
① 단원별 필수 단어 암기 ② 영어 → 한글 Test ③ 한글 → 영어 Test

2 ● **Text 지문과 해설**
① 전체 지문 해석 ② 페이지별 필기 공간 확보 ③ N회독을 통한 지문 습득

3 ● **Practice 1 빈칸 시험 (w/ 문법 힌트)**
① 해석 없는 반복 빈칸 시험 ② 문법 힌트를 통한 어법 숙지
③ 주요 문법과 암기 내용 최종 확인

4 ● **Practice 2** **(w/ 해석)**
한글을 통한 내용 숙지

5 ● **Qui** ② 100% 자체 제작 변형문제 ③ 빈출 내신 문제 유형 연습

영어 내신의 끝
마이갓 모의고사 고1,2

1 등급을 위한 5단계 노하우
2 모의고사 연도 및 시행월 별 완전정복
3 내신변형 완전정복

영어 내신의 끝
마이갓 교과서 고1,2

1 등급을 위한 10단계 노하우
2 교과서 레슨별 완전정복
3 영어 영역 마스터를 위한 지름길

마이갓 교재
보듬책방 온라인 스토어 (https://smartstore.naver.com/bdbooks)

마이갓 10 Step 영어 내신 공부법

Vocabulary

필수 단어 암기 & Test
① 단원별 필수 단어 암기
② 영어 → 한글 Test
③ 한글 → 영어 Test

Grammar

단원별 중요 문법과 연습 문제
① 기초 문법 설명
② 교과서 적용 예시 소개
③ 기초/ Advanced Test

Text

지문과 해설
① 전체 지문 해석
② 페이지별 필기 공간 확보
③ N회독을 통한 지문 습득

Practice 3

빈칸 시험 (w/ 해석)
① 주요 내용/어법/어휘 빈칸
② 한글을 통한 내용 숙지
③ 반복 시험을 통한 빈칸 암기

Practice 2

빈칸 시험 (w/ 해석)
① 주요 내용/어법/어휘 빈칸
② 한글을 통한 내용 숙지
③ 반복 시험을 통한 빈칸 암기

Practice 1

어휘 & 어법 선택 시험
① 시험에 나오는 어법 어휘 공략
② 중요 어법/어휘 선택형 시험
③ 반복 시험을 통한 포인트 숙지

Quiz

객관식 예상문제를 콕콕!
① 수능형 객관식 변형문제
② 100% 자체 제작 변형문제
③ 빈출 내신 문제 유형 연습

Final Test

주관식 서술형 예상문제
① 어순/영작/어법 등
   주관식 서술형 문제 대비!
② 100% 자체 제작 변형문제

전체 영작 연습

직접 영작 해보기
① 주어진 단어를 활용한
   전체 서술형 영작 훈련
② 쓰기를 통한 내용 암기

학교 기출 문제

지문과 해설
① 단원별 실제 학교 기출
   문제 모음
② 객관식부터 서술형까지
   완벽 커버!

23년 고1
11월 모의고사

마이갓

연습과 실전 모두 잡는 내신대비 완벽
| workbook |

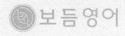보듬영어

2023 고1

11월

WORK BOOK

———

2023년 고1 11월 모의고사 내신대비용 WorkBook & 변형문제

CONTENTS

2023 고1 11월 WORK BOOK

보듬영어

Voca

| ❶ voca | ❷ text | ❸ [/] | ❹ ____ | ❺ quiz 1 | ❻ quiz 2 | ❼ quiz 3 | ❽ quiz 4 | ❾ quiz 5 |

18	so ~ that ...	아주 ~해서 ...하다		continue to V	계속 ~하다
	appreciate	진가를 알아보다, 이해하다, 감사하다		healthy	건강한, 건전한
	confident	확신하는, 자신에 찬		commit to	~하겠다고 약속하다
	in response to	~에 반응[응답]하여		devote	바치다, 헌신하다, 전념하다
	graduate	졸업하다; 대학원생, 졸업생		otherwise	그렇지 않으면, ~와 다르게
	assistant	보조의; 조수		be likely to V	~하기 쉽다, ~할 가능성이 있다
	develop	발달[개발]하다, (병에) 걸리다		progress	진보[발전]하다, 전진하다; 진보, 발전
	apply for	~을 지원[신청]하다		as a result	그 결과
	convenience	편의, 편리(성)	21	objective	목표, 목적; 객관적인
	look forward to -ing	~하기를 고대하다		property	재산, 부동산, 특성, 속성
19	shade	그늘, 가리개; 그늘지게 하다		bounce off	튀어 분리되다, ~에 대한 반응을 살피다
	set up	설치하다, 마련하다, 시작하다		reflect	반영하다, 나타내다, 숙고하다
	forward	전달하다, 전송하다; 앞으로		argue	논쟁[논의]하다, 주장하다
	exotic	이국적인, 진기한, 외래의, 이국의		physical	물리적인, 육체의
	point at	~을 가리키다		all but	거의, ~외에 모두
	track	철로, 선로; 추적하다, 탐지하다		exist	존재하다, 실존하다
	sink	가라앉다, 침몰하다; 싱크대		maintain	유지하다, 주장하다
20	unfortunately	불행하게도, 안타깝게도		correct	교정하다; 정확한, 올바른
	responsibility	책임; 해야 할 일		universe	우주, 은하계, 세계
	growth	성장, 발육, 발전		register	등록하다, 기재하다; 등록부, 명부
	keep -ing	계속 ~하다		interpret	해석하다, 통역하다, 설명하다
	manage to	(힘든 일을) 간신히 해내다	22	novel	소설; 새로운, 참신한
	end with	~로 끝나다		demand	요구하다, 필요로 하다; 요구, 수요
	lack	부족, 결핍; ~가 부족하다		detail	세부 (항목); 자세히 말하다, 열거하다
	describe	묘사하다, 기술하다, 설명하다		organize	정리하다, 체계화[구조화]하다

Voca

❶ voca	❷ text	❸ [/]	❹ ____	❺ quiz 1	❻ quiz 2	❼ quiz 3	❽ quiz 4	❾ quiz 5

	so that	~하기 위하여		entire	전체의, 완전한; 전부, 전체
	polite	예의 바른, 공손한		risk	위험; 위험을 무릅쓰다
	permission	허락, 허가	24	sooner or later	조만간, 머지않아
	particular	특정한, 개개의; 사항, 상세		bury	묻다, 매장하다
	discover	발견하다, 알다, 깨닫다		nerve	신경, 긴장, 담력, 정신력
	matter	문제, 사안, 물질; 문제가 되다, 중요하다		reduce	줄이다, 낮추다, 감소하다
	reveal	드러내다, 폭로하다		initial	최초의, 초기의; 머리글자(의)
	crucial	필수적인, 결정적인, 아주 중요한		response	대답, 응답
	finding	결과, 결론		stimuli	자극 (stimulus의복수형)
	tension	긴장, 팽팽함		occur	일어나다, 발생하다, 존재하다
	conflict	분쟁, 충돌, 갈등; 충돌하다, 다투다		at the same time	반면에, 동시에
23	nearly	거의, 대략, 간신히, 면밀하게		neuron	신경 단위, 뉴런
	go through	겪다, 경험[통과]하다, 자세히 조사[검토]하다		enhance	향상시키다, 강화하다, 높이다
	get to	~에 도착하다		probably	아마
	the rest	나머지		evolve	진화하다, (서서히) 발전하다
	prevent A from B	A가 B하지 못하게 하다		ancestor	조상, 선조
	adequate	적절한, 적당한, 충분한		survival	생존, 생존자; 생존을 위한
	prevent	막다, 예방하다, 방지하다		attend to	~에 주의를 기울이다, 집중하다
	harmful	해로운		reaction	반응, 반작용, 반발
	bloodstream	혈류		environment	환경, 주위(의 상황)
	affect	~에 영향을 미치다, ~인 척하다; 정서		turn down	거부[거절]하다, 낮추다, 쇠퇴하다
	aspect	측면, 면, 양상, 관점		neural	신경(계)의
	iceberg	빙산		threat	위협, 협박
	reflection	반영, 반사, 숙고, 반성		stand out	두드러지다, 눈에 띄다, 뛰어나다
	disease	질병, 질환		equivalent	동등한, 상당하는; 등가물, 상당하는 것

Voca

❶ voca   ❷ text   ❸ [/]   ❹ _____   ❺ quiz 1   ❻ quiz 2   ❼ quiz 3   ❽ quiz 4   ❾ quiz 5

	turn off	끄다, 잠그다, 흥미를 잃다, (길이) 갈라지다	receive	받다, 받아들이다
25	global	세계적인, 전 세계의, 전체적인	certificate	자격증, 증명서; 자격증[면허증]을 교부하다
	investment	투자	entry	참가, 출품(작), 입구, 참가자
	fossil fuel	화석 연료	participation	참여, 참가
	exceed	넘다, 초과하다, 초월하다	registration	등록 (서류), 기재
26	slavery	노예 제도, 노예의 신분	28	amazing	놀랄 만한, 굉장한
	successfully	성공적으로	urban	도시의
	escape from	~에서 달아나다	explore	탐구하다, 탐험하다
	escape	달아나다, 벗어나다; 탈출, 도망	solve	풀다, 해결하다
	assist	돕다, 거들다	clue	단서, 실마리
	slave	노예	complete	완성[완료]하다; 완전한
	spread	펴다, 퍼뜨리다, 퍼지다; 확장, 유포, 보급	limit	한정하다, 제한하다; 한계, 제한
	well-known	잘 알려진, 유명한	sign up	참가하다, 가입하다
	including	~을 포함하여	29	determine	결심[결정]하다, 알아내다
	immigrant	(타국에서 온) 이주민, 이민자	transfer	옮기다, 전하다; 이동, 환승
	autobiography	자서전	guideline	가이드라인, 지침, 지표
	in addition to	~뿐만 아니라, ~에 더하여	consideration	고려 (사항), 배려, 숙고
	candidate	후보자, 지원자	requirement	요건, 필요조건
	vice president	부사장, 부통령	specify	명시하다, 자세히 말하다
	state	상태, 국가, 주; 진술하다	diagnosis	진단, 분석 ((복수형 diagnoses))
27	outdoor	야외의, 실외의	in the case of	~에 관해서, ~의 경우에는
	competition	경쟁, 시합	potential	가능성이 있는, 잠재적인; 가능성, 잠재력
	performance	수행, 성과, 성적, 공연	strict	엄한, 엄격한, 엄밀한, 정확한
	match	경기, 시합, 호적수; 경쟁시키다, 어울리다	regulation	조절, 규제, 규정
	participant	참여자, 참가자	doubt	의심, 불확실성; 의심하다

Voca

❶ voca	❷ text	❸ [/]	❹ _____	❺ quiz 1	❻ quiz 2	❼ quiz 3	❽ quiz 4	❾ quiz 5

	purpose	목적, 의도; 의도하다			characteristic	특징, 특성, 특색; 독특한, 특징적인		
	obtain	얻다, 구하다, 획득하다, 행해지다			adapt	조정하다, 적응시키다, 개작하다		
	process	과정, 절차; 처리하다, 가공하다			psychologist	심리학자		
	consistency	일관성, 일치, 조화			impressive	인상적인, 감명 깊은		
	at least	적어도, 최소한			reverse	뒤바꾸다, 반전시키다; 반대(의), 뒤(의)		
	as for	~의 경우에는, ~에 대해서 말하자면			literally	말 그대로, 문자 그대로		
	immediate	즉각적인, 직접의, 인접한			turn ~ upside downt	~을 뒤집다		
	intend	~할 작정이다, 의도하다			put ~ in ...	~을 ...에 넣다		
30	term	기간, 용어, (-s) 조건, 관점; 말하다			adjust to	~에 맞추다, 적응하다		
	impression	인상, 감명, 흔적			normally	보통, 일반적으로, 정상적으로		
	sacrifice	희생하다, 헌신하다; 헌신, 희생, 제물			upright	똑바른, 수직의, 올바른, 정직한		
	possession	소유(권), (-s) 소지품, 재산			concentrate	집중하다, 농축하다; 농축액		
	naturally	자연스럽게, 본래			take off	벗다, 이륙하다, 없애다		
	stem from	~에서 생기다, 유래하다			confront	직면하다, 맞서다		
	distance	거리, 간격, 차이			fortunately	다행히, 운이 좋게(도)		
	emotional	감정의, 감정적인			perception	인식, 인지, 지각		
	assumption	가정, 추정, 생각			return	수익, 귀환, 반환; 돌아오다		
	get rid of	~을 제거하다[없애다]	32		phase	단계, 시기, 국면		
	useless	쓸모없는, 소용없는, 헛된			search for	~을 찾다		
	overcome	극복하다, (남을) 이기다			be allowed to	~하는 것이 허용되다		
	clarity	명료함, 명확함			present	제공하다, 주다; 현재의, 출석한; 현재, 선물		
	era	시대, 시기			unrelated	관련이 없는		
	eliminate	없애다, 제거하다, 실격시키다			advantage	이익, 이점; 이롭게 하다		
	stuff	물건, 물질, 재료; 채우다, 채워 넣다			equally	마찬가지로, 똑같이, 평등하게		
31	remarkable	놀랄 만한, 주목할 만한, 훌륭한			knowledgeable	지식이 있는, 정통한		

	search	찾다, 수색하다; 찾기	34	include	포함하다, 포괄하다
	suggest	제안하다, 암시하다, 시사하다		explain	설명하다, 해명하다
	access	접근, 이용; 접근하다, 이용하다		indicate	말하다, 나타내다, 표시하다
	improve	향상[개선]시키다, 향상하다		carve	조각하다, 새기다
	judgment	판단, 판결, 견해		draw	끌다, 그리다, 비기다; 끌기, 제비(뽑기)
33	anthropologist	인류학자		point out	지적하다, 언급하다
	tend to V	~하는 경향이 있다		indeed	실제로, 사실
	focus	집중하다, 초점을 맞추다; 중심, 초점		possess	소유하다, ~의 마음을 사로잡다
	feature	특징, 특집, 용모; 특집으로 하다, 특집으로 삼다		subject	주제, 과목, 대상; 지배하다, 복종시키다
	zoom in	확대하다		decay	쇠퇴, 부패; 부패[부식]하다, 쇠퇴하다
	object	~에 반대하다; 목표, 대상, 물체		extraordinary	비상한, 비범한, 특파의, 임시의
	individual	개인; 개인의, 개별적인, 독특한		form	형태, 모양, 양식; 형성하다, 만들다
	treat	대우하다, 다루다, 치료하다; 대접		universal	우주의, 보편적인, 광범위한
	species	종, 종류		chase	추격, 추구; 뒤쫓다, 추구하다
	ecosystem	생태계		sense	느끼다, 감지하다; 감각, 느낌, 분별
	perspective	관점, 시각, 전망, 경치, 원근법	35	statistic	통계학, (-s) 통계, 통계 자료
	additional	추가적인, 추가의		prediction	예측, 예상, 예언
	tool	도구, 연장		according to	~에 의하면, ~에 따라
	take up	차지하다, 시작하다, 계속하다		experiment	실험, 시험, 시도; 실험하다, 시도하다
	at a time	한 번에, 한꺼번에		conduct	~을 하다, 지휘하다, (전기 등을) 전도하다; 행동
	pay attention to	~에 주목하다		average	평균; 평균의; 평균이 ~가 되다
	varied	다양한, 다채로운		be expected to	~할 것으로 기대되다
	ecological	생태(학)의, 환경 친화적인		for instance	예를 들면
	involve	포함[수반]하다, 필요로 하다, 관련시키다		encounter	접하다, 마주치다; 마주침, (뜻밖의) 만남
	emphasize	강조하다, 두드러지게 하다		bet	내기하다, 단언하다; 내기

		❶ voca	❷ text	❸ [/]	❹ ____	❺ quiz 1	❻ quiz 2	❼ quiz 3	❽ quiz 4	❾ quiz 5

	repeat	되풀이하다, 반복하다; 반복		development	발달, 발전, 성장
	relative	상대적[비교적]인, 관련된; 친척, 동족		influence	영향을 미치다; 영향(력)
	frequency	빈번함, 빈도, 진동수		lead	인도하다, 이끌다, 안내하다, 지도하다
	loss	손실, 손해, 상실, 패배		factor	요인, 요소, 지수
	approach	접근하다; 접근(법)		decision	결정, 결심, 판결
	fade away	흐려지다, 사라지다	37	facial	얼굴의, 안면의
	similarly	유사하게, 마찬가지로		recognition	인정, 표창, 인식
	collect	모으다, 수집하다, 징수하다		in terms of	~ 면에서, ~에 관하여
	figure out	산출[계산]하다, 알아내다		identification	동일시, 공감
	depending on	~에 따라		relate to	~을 이해하다, ~와 관련이 있다
	region	지역, 지방		contain	포함[함유]하다, 억누르다, 억제하다
	insurance	보험		instance	사례, 경우
	rely on	~에 의존[의지]하다		decrease	감소; 감소하다
36	adolescent	청소년, 젊은이; 청소년기의		identify	알아보다, 확인하다, 동일시하다
	decision-making	의사 결정		enroll	등록하다, 입학[입회]시키다
	circuit	순회 (노선), 순환, 회로		texture	감촉, 질감, 결, 구조; ~을 짜서 만들다
	disadvantage	약점, 불리, 불이익; 불리하게 하다		particularly	특히, 상세히
	mature	성숙한, 원숙한; 성숙해지다		appearance	외모, (겉)모습, 출현, 등장
	task	일, 과업; ~에 과중한 부담을 주다		wrinkle	주름; 주름이 지다, 찌푸리다
	evaluate	평가하다, 감정하다		highlight	집중하다, 강조하다; 가장 중요한 부분
	consequence	결과, 영향(력), 중요성		weight	무게, 체중
	responsible	책임있는		be used to V	~하는 데 사용되다
	prevent A from -ing	A가 ~하지 못하게 하다[막다]	38	decline	하락[감소]하다, 거절하다; 감소, 하락
	modify	수정하다, 바꾸다		diversity	다양(성)
	on the other hand	한편, 반면에		crop	(농)작물, 수확(량)

Voca

❶ voca   ❷ text   ❸ [/]   ❹ _____   ❺ quiz 1   ❻ quiz 2   ❼ quiz 3   ❽ quiz 4   ❾ quiz 5

	attempt	시도; 시도하다		conservative	보존적인, 보수적인
	extreme	극단의, 극단적인; 극단		pant	숨을 헐떡이다; 헐떡임, (-s) 바지
	produce	생산[제조]하다, 초래하다; 농산물		athletic	운동 경기의
	grain	곡물, 낱알, 알갱이		superior	우수한, 상위의, 뛰어난; 상사, 윗사람
	wheat	밀, 소맥		opposing	상반된, 대립되는, 상대방의
	enormous	엄청난, 거대한, 막대한		alter	바꾸다, 변경하다, 고치다
	thousands of	수천의, 많은		modernize	현대화하다
	traditional	전통적인, 고풍의		keep up with	~을 따라잡다, 뒤처지지 않다, 알다
	variety	변화, 다양(성), 품종		abandon	버리다, 단념[포기]하다; 방종
	be replaced by	~에 의해 대체되다		neglect	무시[방치]하다; 소홀, 무시
	strategy	전략, 전술, 계획, 방법		root	뿌리, 근원; 뿌리를 내리다
	to begin with	우선, 첫째로		effect	결과, 영향, 효과; 초래하다, 이루다
	production	생산, 산출물, 연출, 제작, 상연		surface	표면, 외관; 표면의; 겉으로 드러나다
	population	인구, 개체 수	40	noticeable	주목할 만한, 두드러진
	contribution	(원인) 제공, 기여, 기고, 분담금		connection	연결, 접속, 연관(성), 인맥, 관계
	at risk	위험에 처한		apply	지원[신청]하다, 적용하다, 바르다
	when it comes to	~에 관한 한, ~라면		innovation	혁신, 쇄신
	disaster	재앙, 재난, 재해		account for	(~의 비율을) 차지하다, 설명하다
	depend on	~에 의존하다, ~에 달려 있다		trait	특성, 특색, 특징
	narrow	좁은, 편협한, 가까스로의; 좁히다		necessarily	반드시, 필연적으로
	selection	선택, 선별, 선발		acquire	얻다, 습득하다
	plant	식물, 공장; 심다, 이식하다, 설치하다		peer	또래, 동료; 자세히 들여다보다
	survive	살아남다, 생존하다		relevant	관련 있는, 연관된, 적절한
39	be known for	~로 알려져 있다		similarity	유사성, 닮음
	contrast	차이, 대조; 대조하다, 대비시키다		revise	수정하다, 고치다

Voca

❶ voca	❷ text	❸ [/]	❹ _____	❺ quiz 1	❻ quiz 2	❼ quiz 3	❽ quiz 4	❾ quiz 5

41 - 42	diverse	다양한, 여러 가지의		definitely	확실히, 틀림없이
	force	강요하다; 힘, 세력		arouse	불러일으키다, 자극하다, 깨우다
	movement	운동, 움직임, 행동		except	제외하고; 제외하다
	straight	똑바로, 일직선으로, 곧장, 솔직하게		isolation	고립, 격리, 분리
	constant	일정한, 지속적인, 변함없는		competitive	경쟁력이 있는, 경쟁하는
	gravity	중력, 만유인력, 심각성		opposite	반대(되는 사람[것]); 반대의
	A as well as B	B뿐만 아니라 A도		protective	보호하는, 방어적인
	resistance	저항(력), 반항, 반대	43 - 45	stop by	잠시 들르다, 잠깐 방문하다
	accordingly	그에 따라, 그래서		surrounded	~로 둘러싸인
	curved	굽은, 곡선 모양의		solution	해결(책), 용액
	path	(작은) 길, 진로, 보도, 경로		request	요청, 요구; 요청[요구]하다
	represent	표현하다, 나타내다		take care of	~을 돌보다, 보살피다
	combination	조합, 결합(물)		stand up	일어서다, 여전히 유효하다
	elementary	초보의, 기본의, 초등학교의		realize	깨닫다, 알아차리다, 인식하다, 실현하다
	mention	말하다, 언급하다; 언급		no matter how	어떻든간에, 어떻게 하든, ~하더라도
	isolated	외딴, 고립된, 격리된			
	namely	즉, 다시 말해			
	joint	공동의, 합동의; 관절, 연결 부위			
	arrangement	배열, 배치			
	attention	주의(력), 집중(력), 관심			
	separately	제각각, 각자, 따로따로			
	significance	중요성			
	greatly	크게, 몹시, 대단히, 위대하게			
	increase	(수량이) 늘다, 증가하다; 증가			
	tendency	경향, 추세, 성향, 체질			

Voca

❶ voca	❷ text	❸ [/]	❹ _____	❺ quiz 1	❻ quiz 2	❼ quiz 3	❽ quiz 4	❾ quiz 5

18	so ~ that …			continue to V	
	appreciate			healthy	
	confident			commit to	
	in response to			devote	
	graduate			otherwise	
	assistant			be likely to V	
	develop			progress	
	apply for			as a result	
	convenience		21	objective	
	look forward to -ing			property	
19	shade			bounce off	
	set up			reflect	
	forward			argue	
	exotic			physical	
	point at			all but	
	track			exist	
	sink			maintain	
20	unfortunately			correct	
	responsibility			universe	
	growth			register	
	keep -ing			interpret	
	manage to		22	novel	
	end with			demand	
	lack			detail	
	describe			organize	

Voca

❶ voca ❷ text ❸ [/] ❹ _____ ❺ quiz 1 ❻ quiz 2 ❼ quiz 3 ❽ quiz 4 ❾ quiz 5

	so that				entire	
	polite				risk	
	permission			24	sooner or later	
	particular				bury	
	discover				nerve	
	matter				reduce	
	reveal				initial	
	crucial				response	
	finding				stimuli	
	tension				occur	
	conflict				at the same time	
23	nearly				neuron	
	go through				enhance	
	get to				probably	
	the rest				evolve	
	prevent A from B				ancestor	
	adequate				survival	
	prevent				attend to	
	harmful				reaction	
	bloodstream				environment	
	affect				turn down	
	aspect				neural	
	iceberg				threat	
	reflection				stand out	
	disease				equivalent	

보듬영어

Voca

	❶ voca	❷ text	❸ [/]	❹ ____	❺ quiz 1	❻ quiz 2	❼ quiz 3	❽ quiz 4	❾ quiz 5
	turn off				receive				
25	global				certificate				
	investment				entry				
	fossil fuel				participation				
	exceed				registration				
26	slavery			28	amazing				
	successfully				urban				
	escape from				explore				
	escape				solve				
	assist				clue				
	slave				complete				
	spread				limit				
	well-known				sign up				
	including			29	determine				
	immigrant				transfer				
	autobiography				guideline				
	in addition to				consideration				
	candidate				requirement				
	vice president				specify				
	state				diagnosis				
27	outdoor				in the case of				
	competition				potential				
	performance				strict				
	match				regulation				
	participant				doubt				

	purpose				characteristic		
	obtain				adapt		
	process				psychologist		
	consistency				impressive		
	at least				reverse		
	as for				literally		
	immediate				turn ~ upside down		
	intend				put ~ in ...		
30	term				adjust to		
	impression				normally		
	sacrifice				upright		
	possession				concentrate		
	naturally				take off		
	stem from				confront		
	distance				fortunately		
	emotional				perception		
	assumption				return		
	get rid of			32	phase		
	useless				search for		
	overcome				be allowed to		
	clarity				present		
	era				unrelated		
	eliminate				advantage		
	stuff				equally		
31	remarkable				knowledgeable		

Voca

	search		34	include	
	suggest			explain	
	access			indicate	
	improve			carve	
	judgment			draw	
33	anthropologist			point out	
	tend to V			indeed	
	focus			possess	
	feature			subject	
	zoom in			decay	
	object			extraordinary	
	individual			form	
	treat			universal	
	species			chase	
	ecosystem			sense	
	perspective		35	statistic	
	additional			prediction	
	tool			according to	
	take up			experiment	
	at a time			conduct	
	pay attention to			average	
	varied			be expected to	
	ecological			for instance	
	involve			encounter	
	emphasize			bet	

Voca

	repeat				development	
	relative				influence	
	frequency				lead	
	loss				factor	
	approach				decision	
	fade away		37		facial	
	similarly				recognition	
	collect				in terms of	
	figure out				identification	
	depending on				relate to	
	region				contain	
	insurance				instance	
	rely on				decrease	
36	adolescent				identify	
	decision-making				enroll	
	circuit				texture	
	disadvantage				particularly	
	mature				appearance	
	task				wrinkle	
	evaluate				highlight	
	consequence				weight	
	responsible				be used to V	
	prevent A from -ing		38		decline	
	modify				diversity	
	on the other hand				crop	

Voca

❶ voca   ❷ text   ❸ [/]   ❹ ____   ❺ quiz 1   ❻ quiz 2   ❼ quiz 3   ❽ quiz 4   ❾ quiz 5

	attempt			conservative	
	extreme			pant	
	produce			athletic	
	grain			superior	
	wheat			opposing	
	enormous			alter	
	thousands of			modernize	
	traditional			keep up with	
	variety			abandon	
	be replaced by			neglect	
	strategy			root	
	to begin with			effect	
	production			surface	
	population		40	noticeable	
	contribution			connection	
	at risk			apply	
	when it comes to			innovation	
	disaster			account for	
	depend on			trait	
	narrow			necessarily	
	selection			acquire	
	plant			peer	
	survive			relevant	
39	be known for			similarity	
	contrast			revise	

Voca

❶ voca	❷ text	❸ [/]	❹ ____	❺ quiz 1	❻ quiz 2	❼ quiz 3	❽ quiz 4	❾ quiz 5

	diverse			definitely	
41 - 42	force			arouse	
	movement			except	
	straight			isolation	
	constant			competitive	
	gravity			opposite	
	A as well as B			protective	
	resistance		43 - 45	stop by	
	accordingly			surrounded	
	curved			solution	
	path			request	
	represent			take care of	
	combination			stand up	
	elementary			realize	
	mention			no matter how	
	isolated				
	namely				
	joint				
	arrangement				
	attention				
	separately				
	significance				
	greatly				
	increase				
	tendency				

Voca

❶ voca	❷ text	❸ [/]	❹ ____	❺ quiz 1	❻ quiz 2	❼ quiz 3	❽ quiz 4	❾ quiz 5

18		아주 ~해서 ...하다			계속 ~하다
		진가를 알아보다, 이해하다, 감사하다			건강한, 건전한
		확신하는, 자신에 찬			~하겠다고 약속하다
		~에 반응[응답]하여			바치다, 헌신하다, 전념하다
		졸업하다; 대학원생, 졸업생			그렇지 않으면, ~와 다르게
		보조의; 조수			~하기 쉽다, ~할 가능성이 있다
		발달[개발]하다, (병에) 걸리다			진보[발전]하다, 전진하다; 진보, 발전
		~을 지원[신청]하다			그 결과
		편의, 편리(성)	21		목표, 목적; 객관적인
		~하기를 고대하다			재산, 부동산, 특성, 속성
19		그늘, 가리개; 그늘지게 하다			튀어 분리되다, ~에 대한 반응을 살피다
		설치하다, 마련하다, 시작하다			반영하다, 나타내다, 숙고하다
		전달하다, 전송하다; 앞으로			논쟁[논의]하다, 주장하다
		이국적인, 진기한, 외래의, 이국의			물리적인, 육체의
		~을 가리키다			거의, ~외에 모두
		철로, 선로; 추적하다, 탐지하다			존재하다, 실존하다
		가라앉다, 침몰하다; 싱크대			유지하다, 주장하다
20		불행하게도, 안타깝게도			교정하다; 정확한, 올바른
		책임; 해야 할 일			우주, 은하계, 세계
		성장, 발육, 발전			등록하다, 기재하다; 등록부, 명부
		계속 ~하다			해석하다, 통역하다, 설명하다
		(힘든 일을) 간신히 해내다	22		소설; 새로운, 참신한
		~로 끝나다			요구하다, 필요로 하다; 요구, 수요
		부족, 결핍; ~가 부족하다			세부 (항목); 자세히 말하다, 열거하다
		묘사하다, 기술하다, 설명하다			정리하다, 체계화[구조화]하다

Voca

❶ voca	❷ text	❸ [/]	❹ ____	❺ quiz 1	❻ quiz 2	❼ quiz 3	❽ quiz 4	❾ quiz 5
		~하기 위하여			전체의, 완전한; 전부, 전체			
		예의 바른, 공손한			위험; 위험을 무릅쓰다			
		허락, 허가	24		조만간, 머지않아			
		특정한, 개개의; 사항, 상세			묻다, 매장하다			
		발견하다, 알다, 깨닫다			신경, 긴장, 담력, 정신력			
		문제, 사안, 물질; 문제가 되다, 중요하다			줄이다, 낮추다, 감소하다			
		드러내다, 폭로하다			최초의, 초기의; 머리글자(의)			
		필수적인, 결정적인, 아주 중요한			대답, 응답			
		결과, 결론			자극 (stimulus의복수형)			
		긴장, 팽팽함			일어나다, 발생하다, 존재하다			
		분쟁, 충돌, 갈등; 충돌하다, 다투다			반면에, 동시에			
23		거의, 대략, 간신히, 면밀하게			신경 단위, 뉴런			
		겪다, 경험[통과]하다, 자세히 조사[검토]하다			향상시키다, 강화하다, 높이다			
		~에 도착하다			아마			
		나머지			진화하다, (서서히) 발전하다			
		A가 B하지 못하게 하다			조상, 선조			
		적절한, 적당한, 충분한			생존, 생존자; 생존을 위한			
		막다, 예방하다, 방지하다			~에 주의를 기울이다, 집중하다			
		해로운			반응, 반작용, 반발			
		혈류			환경, 주위(의 상황)			
		~에 영향을 미치다, ~인 척하다; 정서			거부[거절]하다, 낮추다, 쇠퇴하다			
		측면, 면, 양상, 관점			신경(계)의			
		빙산			위협, 협박			
		반영, 반사, 숙고, 반성			두드러지다, 눈에 띄다, 뛰어나다			
		질병, 질환			동등한, 상당하는; 등가물, 상당하는 것			

Voca

❶ voca	❷ text	❸ [/]	❹ ____	❺ quiz 1	❻ quiz 2	❼ quiz 3	❽ quiz 4	❾ quiz 5

		끄다, 잠그다, 흥미를 잃다, (길이) 갈라지다		받다, 받아들이다
25		세계적인, 전 세계의, 전체적인		자격증, 증명서; 자격증[면허증]을 교부하다
		투자		참가, 출품(작), 입구, 참가자
		화석 연료		참여, 참가
		넘다, 초과하다, 초월하다		등록 (서류), 기재
26		노예 제도, 노예의 신분	28	놀랄 만한, 굉장한
		성공적으로		도시의
		~에서 달아나다		탐구하다, 탐험하다
		달아나다, 벗어나다; 탈출, 도망		풀다, 해결하다
		돕다, 거들다		단서, 실마리
		노예		완성[완료]하다; 완전한
		펴다, 퍼뜨리다, 퍼지다; 확장, 유포, 보급		한정하다, 제한하다; 한계, 제한
		잘 알려진, 유명한		참가하다, 가입하다
		~을 포함하여	29	결심[결정]하다, 알아내다
		(타국에서 온) 이주민, 이민자		옮기다, 전하다; 이동, 환승
		자서전		가이드라인, 지침, 지표
		~뿐만 아니라, ~에 더하여		고려 (사항), 배려, 숙고
		후보자, 지원자		요건, 필요조건
		부사장, 부통령		명시하다, 자세히 말하다
		상태, 국가, 주; 진술하다		진단, 분석 ((복수형 diagnoses))
27		야외의, 실외의		~에 관해서, ~의 경우에는
		경쟁, 시합		가능성이 있는, 잠재적인; 가능성, 잠재력
		수행, 성과, 성적, 공연		엄한, 엄격한, 엄밀한, 정확한
		경기, 시합, 호적수; 경쟁시키다, 어울리다		조절, 규제, 규정
		참여자, 참가자		의심, 불확실성; 의심하다

Voca

❶ voca	❷ text	❸ [/]	❹ ____	❺ quiz 1	❻ quiz 2	❼ quiz 3	❽ quiz 4	❾ quiz 5
		목적, 의도; 의도하다			특징, 특성, 특색; 독특한, 특징적인			
		얻다, 구하다, 획득하다, 행해지다			조정하다, 적응시키다, 개작하다			
		과정, 절차; 처리하다, 가공하다			심리학자			
		일관성, 일치, 조화			인상적인, 감명 깊은			
		적어도, 최소한			뒤바꾸다, 반전시키다; 반대(의), 뒤(의)			
		~의 경우에는, ~에 대해서 말하자면			말 그대로, 문자 그대로			
		즉각적인, 직접의, 인접한			~을 뒤집다			
		~할 작정이다, 의도하다			~을 ...에 넣다			
30		기간, 용어, (-s) 조건, 관점; 말하다			~에 맞추다, 적응하다			
		인상, 감명, 흔적			보통, 일반적으로, 정상적으로			
		희생하다, 헌신하다; 헌신, 희생, 제물			똑바른, 수직의, 올바른, 정직한			
		소유(권), (-s) 소지품, 재산			집중하다, 농축하다; 농축액			
		자연스럽게, 본래			벗다, 이륙하다, 없애다			
		~에서 생기다, 유래하다			직면하다, 맞서다			
		거리, 간격, 차이			다행히, 운이 좋게(도)			
		감정의, 감정적인			인식, 인지, 지각			
		가정, 추정, 생각			수익, 귀환, 반환; 돌아오다			
		~을 제거하다[없애다]	32		단계, 시기, 국면			
		쓸모없는, 소용없는, 헛된			~을 찾다			
		극복하다, (남을) 이기다			~하는 것이 허용되다			
		명료함, 명확함			제공하다, 주다; 현재의, 출석한; 현재, 선물			
		시대, 시기			관련이 없는			
		없애다, 제거하다, 실격시키다			이익, 이점; 이롭게 하다			
		물건, 물질, 재료; 채우다, 채워 넣다			마찬가지로, 똑같이, 평등하게			
31		놀랄 만한, 주목할 만한, 훌륭한			지식이 있는, 정통한			

Voca

❶ voca	❷ text	❸ [/]	❹ ____	❺ quiz 1	❻ quiz 2	❼ quiz 3	❽ quiz 4	❾ quiz 5

		찾다, 수색하다; 찾기	34		포함하다, 포괄하다
		제안하다, 암시하다, 시사하다			설명하다, 해명하다
		접근, 이용; 접근하다, 이용하다			말하다, 나타내다, 표시하다
		향상[개선]시키다, 향상하다			조각하다, 새기다
		판단, 판결, 견해			끌다, 그리다, 비기다; 끌기, 제비(뽑기)
33		인류학자			지적하다, 언급하다
		~하는 경향이 있다			실제로, 사실
		집중하다, 초점을 맞추다; 중심, 초점			소유하다, ~의 마음을 사로잡다
		특징, 특집, 용모; 특집으로 하다, 특집으로 삼다			주제, 과목, 대상; 지배하다, 복종시키다
		확대하다			쇠퇴, 부패; 부패[부식]하다, 쇠퇴하다
		~에 반대하다; 목표, 대상, 물체			비상한, 비범한, 특파의, 임시의
		개인; 개인의, 개별적인, 독특한			형태, 모양, 양식; 형성하다, 만들다
		대우하다, 다루다, 치료하다; 대접			우주의, 보편적인, 광범위한
		종, 종류			추격, 추구; 뒤쫓다, 추구하다
		생태계			느끼다, 감지하다; 감각, 느낌, 분별
		관점, 시각, 전망, 경치, 원근법	35		통계학, (-s) 통계, 통계 자료
		추가적인, 추가의			예측, 예상, 예언
		도구, 연장			~에 의하면, ~에 따라
		차지하다, 시작하다, 계속하다			실험, 시험, 시도; 실험하다, 시도하다
		한 번에, 한꺼번에			~을 하다, 지휘하다, (전기 등을) 전도하다; 행동
		~에 주목하다			평균; 평균의; 평균이 ~가 되다
		다양한, 다채로운			~할 것으로 기대되다
		생태(학)의, 환경 친화적인			예를 들면
		포함[수반]하다, 필요로 하다, 관련시키다			접하다, 마주치다; 마주침, (뜻밖의) 만남
		강조하다, 두드러지게 하다			내기하다, 단언하다; 내기

Voca

		되풀이하다, 반복하다; 반복			발달, 발전, 성장
		상대적[비교적]인, 관련된; 친척, 동족			영향을 미치다; 영향(력)
		빈번함, 빈도, 진동수			인도하다, 이끌다, 안내하다, 지도하다
		손실, 손해, 상실, 패배			요인, 요소, 지수
		접근하다; 접근(법)			결정, 결심, 판결
		흐려지다, 사라지다	37		얼굴의, 안면의
		유사하게, 마찬가지로			인정, 표창, 인식
		모으다, 수집하다, 징수하다			~ 면에서, ~에 관하여
		산출[계산]하다, 알아내다			동일시, 공감
		~에 따라			~을 이해하다, ~와 관련이 있다
		지역, 지방			포함[함유]하다, 억누르다, 억제하다
		보험			사례, 경우
		~에 의존[의지]하다			감소; 감소하다
36		청소년, 젊은이; 청소년기의			알아보다, 확인하다, 동일시하다
		의사 결정			등록하다, 입학[입회]시키다
		순회 (노선), 순환, 회로			감촉, 질감, 결, 구조; ~을 짜서 만들다
		약점, 불리, 불이익; 불리하게 하다			특히, 상세히
		성숙한, 원숙한; 성숙해지다			외모, (겉)모습, 출현, 등장
		일, 과업; ~에 과중한 부담을 주다			주름; 주름이 지다, 찌푸리다
		평가하다, 감정하다			집중하다, 강조하다; 가장 중요한 부분
		결과, 영향(력), 중요성			무게, 체중
		책임있는			~하는 데 사용되다
		A가 ~하지 못하게 하다[막다]	38		하락[감소]하다, 거절하다; 감소, 하락
		수정하다, 바꾸다			다양(성)
		한편, 반면에			(농)작물, 수확(량)

❶ voca	❷ text	❸ [/]	❹ ____	❺ quiz 1	❻ quiz 2	❼ quiz 3	❽ quiz 4	❾ quiz 5
		시도; 시도하다			보존적인, 보수적인			
		극단의, 극단적인; 극단			숨을 헐떡이다; 헐떡임, (-s) 바지			
		생산[제조]하다, 초래하다; 농산물			운동 경기의			
		곡물, 낟알, 알갱이			우수한, 상위의, 뛰어난; 상사, 윗사람			
		밀, 소맥			상반된, 대립되는, 상대방의			
		엄청난, 거대한, 막대한			바꾸다, 변경하다, 고치다			
		수천의, 많은			현대화하다			
		전통적인, 고풍의			~을 따라잡다, 뒤처지지 않다, 알다			
		변화, 다양(성), 품종			버리다, 단념[포기]하다; 방종			
		~에 의해 대체되다			무시[방치]하다; 소홀, 무시			
		전략, 전술, 계획, 방법			뿌리, 근원; 뿌리를 내리다			
		우선, 첫째로			결과, 영향, 효과; 초래하다, 이루다			
		생산, 산출물, 연출, 제작, 상연			표면, 외관; 표면의; 겉으로 드러나다			
		인구, 개체 수	40		주목할 만한, 두드러진			
		(원인) 제공, 기여, 기고, 분담금			연결, 접속, 연관(성), 인맥, 관계			
		위험에 처한			지원[신청]하다, 적용하다, 바르다			
		~에 관한 한, ~라면			혁신, 쇄신			
		재앙, 재난, 재해			(~의 비율을) 차지하다, 설명하다			
		~에 의존하다, ~에 달려 있다			특성, 특색, 특징			
		좁은, 편협한, 가까스로의; 좁히다			반드시, 필연적으로			
		선택, 선별, 선발			얻다, 습득하다			
		식물, 공장; 심다, 이식하다, 설치하다			또래, 동료; 자세히 들여다보다			
		살아남다, 생존하다			관련 있는, 연관된, 적절한			
39		~로 알려져 있다			유사성, 닮음			
		차이, 대조; 대조하다, 대비시키다			수정하다, 고치다			

Voca

❶ voca	❷ text	❸ [/]	❹ _____	❺ quiz 1	❻ quiz 2	❼ quiz 3	❽ quiz 4	❾ quiz 5
		다양한, 여러 가지의				확실히, 틀림없이		
41 - 42		강요하다; 힘, 세력				불러일으키다, 자극하다, 깨우다		
		운동, 움직임, 행동				제외하고; 제외하다		
		똑바로, 일직선으로, 곧장, 솔직하게				고립, 격리, 분리		
		일정한,지속적인, 변함없는				경쟁력이 있는, 경쟁하는		
		중력, 만유인력, 심각성				반대(되는사람[것]); 반대의		
		B뿐만 아니라 A도				보호하는, 방어적인		
		저항(력), 반항, 반대	43 - 45			잠시 들르다, 잠깐 방문하다		
		그에 따라, 그래서				~로 둘러싸인		
		굽은, 곡선 모양의				해결(책), 용액		
		(작은) 길, 진로, 보도, 경로				요청, 요구; 요청[요구]하다		
		표현하다, 나타내다				~을 돌보다, 보살피다		
		조합, 결합(물)				일어서다,여전히 유효하다		
		초보의, 기본의, 초등학교의				깨닫다, 알아차리다, 인식하다, 실현하다		
		말하다, 언급하다; 언급				어떻든간에, 어떻게 하든, ~하더라도		
		외딴, 고립된, 격리된						
		즉, 다시 말해						
		공동의, 합동의; 관절, 연결 부위						
		배열, 배치						
		주의(력), 집중(력), 관심						
		제각각, 각자, 따로따로						
		중요성						
		크게, 몹시, 대단히, 위대하게						
		(수량이) 늘다, 증가하다; 증가						
		경향, 추세, 성향, 체질						

2023 고1 11월 모의고사

❶ voca ❷ text ❸ [/] ❹ _____ ❺ quiz 1 ❻ quiz 2 ❼ quiz 3 ❽ quiz 4 ❾ quiz 5

18 목적

❶ Dear Ms. MacAlpine,

친애하는 MacAlpine씨께,

❷ I was so excited to hear that your brand is opening a new shop on Bruns Street next month.

저는 당신의 브랜드가 다음 달에 Bruns 거리에 새 매장을 연다는 것을 듣고 매우 들떴습니다.

❸ I have always appreciated the way your brand helps women to feel more stylish and confident.

저는 당신의 브랜드가 여성들이 더 멋지고 자신감 있게 느끼도록 도와주는 방식을 항상 높이 평가해 왔습니다.

❹ I am writing in response to your ad in the Bruns Journal.

저는 Bruns Journal에 있는 당신의 광고에 대한 응답으로 편지를 쓰고 있습니다.

❺ I graduated from the Meline School of Fashion and have worked as a sales assistant at LoganMart for the last five years.

저는 Meline 패션 학교를 졸업했고 지난 5년간 LoganMart에서 판매 보조원으로 일해 왔습니다.

❻ During that time, I've developed strong customer service and sales skills, and now I would like to apply for the sales position in your clothing store.

그 기간 동안 저는 뛰어난 고객 서비스 및 판매 기술을 발달시켜 왔고, 이제 당신의 의류 매장의 판매직에 지원하고 싶습니다.

❼ I am available for an interview at your earliest convenience.

저는 당신이 편한 가장 빠른 시간에 인터뷰가 가능합니다.

❽ I look forward to hearing from you.

당신으로부터 대답을 듣게 되기를 기대합니다.

❾ Thank you for reading my letter.

저의 편지를 읽어 주셔서 감사드립니다.

❿ Yours sincerely, Grace Braddock

Grace Braddock 드림

19 심경

❶ I had never seen a beach with such white sand or water that was such a beautiful shade of blue.
나는 그렇게 하얀 모래나 그렇게 아름다운 푸른 색조의 바다를 가진 해변을 한 번도 본 적이 없었다.

❷ Jane and I set up a blanket on the sand while looking forward to our ten days of honeymooning on an exotic island.
이국적인 섬에서의 열흘간의 신혼여행을 기대하면서 Jane과 나는 모래 위에 담요를 깔았다.

❸ "Look!" Jane waved her hand to point at the beautiful scene before us — and her gold wedding ring went flying off her hand.
"저기 좀 봐!" Jane이 그녀의 손을 흔들어 우리 앞의 아름다운 풍경을 가리켰다. 그러자 그녀의 금으로 된 결혼반지가 그녀의 손에서 빠져 날아갔다.

❹ I tried to see where it went, but the sun hit my eyes and I lost track of it.
나는 그것이 날아간 곳을 보려고 노력했지만, 햇빛이 눈에 들어와 그것의 가던 방향을 놓쳤다.

❺ I didn't want to lose her wedding ring, so I started looking in the area where I thought it had landed.
나는 그녀의 결혼반지를 잃어버리고 싶지 않아서 내가 생각하기에 그것이 떨어졌을 장소를 들여다보기 시작했다.

❻ However, the sand was so fine and I realized that anything heavy, like gold, would quickly sink and might never be found again.
하지만 모래가 너무 고왔고 나는 금처럼 무거운 것은 빨리 가라앉아 다시는 발견되지 않을 수도 있겠다는 것을 깨달았다.

20 요지

❶ Unfortunately, many people don't take personal responsibility for their own growth.

안타깝게도 많은 사람들이 그들 자신의 성장에 대해 개인적인 책임을 지지 않는다.

❷ Instead, they simply run the race laid out for them.

대신, 그들은 단지 그들에게 놓인 경주를 한다.

❸ They do well enough in school to keep advancing.

그들은 학교에서 계속 발전할 만큼 제법 잘한다.

❹ Maybe they manage to get a good job at a well-run company.

아마도 그들은 잘 운영되는 회사에서 좋은 일자리를 얻는 것을 해낸다.

❺ But so many think and act as if their learning journey ends with college.

하지만 아주 많은 사람들이 마치 그들의 배움의 여정이 대학으로 끝나는 것처럼 생각하고 행동한다.

❻ They have checked all the boxes in the life that was laid out for them and now lack a road map describing the right ways to move forward and continue to grow.

그들은 그들에게 놓인 삶의 모든 사항을 체크했고 이제는 앞으로 나아가고 계속 성장할 수 있는 올바른 방법을 설명해 주는 로드 맵이 없다.

❼ In truth, that's when the journey really begins.

사실, 그때가 여정이 진정으로 시작되는 때이다.

❽ When school is finished, your growth becomes voluntary.

학교 교육이 끝나면, 여러분의 성장은 자발적이게 된다.

❾ Like healthy eating habits or a regular exercise program, you need to commit to it and devote thought, time, and energy to it.

건강한 식습관이나 규칙적인 운동 프로그램처럼 여러분은 그것에 전념하고 그것에 생각, 시간, 그리고 에너지를 쏟을 필요가 있다.

❿ Otherwise, it simply won't happen — and your life and career are likely to stop progressing as a result.

그렇지 않으면 그것은 그냥 일어나지 않을 것이고, 결과적으로 여러분의 삶과 경력이 진전을 멈출 가능성이 있다.

21 주장

❶ Many people take the commonsense view that color is an objective property of things, or of the light that bounces off them.

많은 사람들이 색은 사물 또는 사물로부터 튕겨 나오는 빛의 객관적인 속성이라는 상식적인 견해를 취한다.

❷ They say a tree's leaves are green because they reflect green light — a greenness that is just as real as the leaves.

그들은 나뭇잎이 녹색 빛(정확히 나뭇잎만큼 진짜인 녹색)을 반사하기 때문에 녹색이라고 말한다.

❸ Others argue that color doesn't inhabit the physical world at all but exists only in the eye or mind of the viewer.

다른 사람들은 색이 물리적인 세계에 전혀 존재하지 않고 보는 사람의 눈이나 정신 안에만 존재한다고 주장한다.

❹ They maintain that if a tree fell in a forest and no one was there to see it, its leaves would be colorless — and so would everything else.

그들은 만약 나무가 숲에서 쓰러지고 그것을 볼 사람이 아무도 거기에 없다면, 그것의 잎은 색이 없을 것이고, 다른 모든 것들도 그럴 것이라고 주장한다.

❺ They say there is no such thing as color; there are only the people who see it.

그들은 색 같은 '것'은 없고 그것을 보는 사람들만 있다고 말한다.

❻ Both positions are, in a way, correct.

두 가지 입장 모두 어떤 면에서는 옳다.

❼ Color is objective and subjective — "the place," as Paul Cézanne put it, "where our brain and the universe meet."

색은 객관적이고 '동시에' 주관적이며, Paul Cézanne이 말했듯이 '우리의 뇌와 우주가 만나는 곳'이다.

❽ Color is created when light from the world is registered by the eyes and interpreted by the brain.

색은 세상으로부터의 빛이 눈에 의해 등록되고 뇌에 의해 해석될 때 만들어진다.

22 의미

❶ When writing a novel, research for information needs to be done.
소설을 쓸 때 정보를 위한 조사가 행해질 필요가 있다.

❷ The thing is that some kinds of fiction demand a higher level of detail: crime fiction, for example, orscientific thrillers.
문제는 예를 들어 범죄 소설이나 과학 스릴러와 같은 어떤 종류의 소설은 더 높은 수준의 세부 사항을 요구한다는 것이다.

❸ The information is never hard to find; one website for authors even organizes trips to police stations, so that crime writers can get it right.
정보는 찾기에 결코 어렵지 않다. 작가들을 위한 한 웹사이트는 범죄물 작가들이 정보를 제대로 얻을 수 있도록 심지어 경찰서로의 탐방을 조직하기도 한다.

❹ Often, a polite letter will earn you permission to visit a particular location and record all the details that you need.
종종 정중한 편지는 여러분에게 특정한 장소를 방문하고 필요한 모든 세부 사항을 기록할 수 있는 허가를 얻어 줄 것이다.

❺ But remember that you will drive your readers to boredom if you think that you need to pack everything you discover into your work.
하지만 만약 여러분이 발견한 모든 것을 작품에 담아야 한다고 생각할 경우 여러분은 독자들을 지루하게 만들 것이라는 것을 기억하라.

❻ The details that matter are those that reveal the human experience.
중요한 세부 사항은 인간의 경험을 드러내는 것이다.

❼ The crucial thing is telling a story, finding the characters, the tension, and the conflict — not the train timetable or the building blueprint.
중요한 것은 기차 시간표나 건물 청사진이 아니라 인물, 긴장, 그리고 갈등을 찾아가며 이야기를 말하는 것이다.

23 주제

❶ Nearly everything has to go through your mouth to get to the rest of you, from food and air to bacteria and viruses.

음식과 공기에서부터 박테리아와 바이러스까지 거의 모든 것이 여러분의 나머지 부분에 도달하기 위해 여러분의 입을 거쳐야 한다.

❷ A healthy mouth can help your body get what it needs and prevent it from harm — with adequate space for air to travel to your lungs, and healthy teeth and gums that prevent harmful microorganisms from entering your bloodstream.

건강한 입은 공기가 폐로 이동할 수 있는 적당한 공간, 그리고 해로운 미생물이 혈류로 들어가는 것을 막는 건강한 치아와 잇몸으로 여러분의 몸이 필요한 것을 얻고, 피해로부터 몸을 지키도록 도와줄 수 있다.

❸ From the moment you are created, oral health affects every aspect of your life.

여러분이 생겨난 순간부터 구강 건강은 여러분의 삶의 모든 측면에 영향을 미친다.

❺ What happens in the mouth is usually just the tip of the iceberg and a reflection of what is happening in other parts of the body.

입안에서 일어나는 일은 대개 빙산의 일각일 뿐이며 신체의 다른 부분에서 일어나고 있는 일의 반영이다.

❻ Poor oral health can be a cause of a disease that affects the entire body.

나쁜 구강 건강은 전체 몸에 영향을 끼치는 질병의 원인일 수 있다.

❼ The microorganisms in an unhealthy mouth can enter the bloodstream and travel anywhere in the body, posing serious health risks.

건강하지 않은 입안의 미생물은 혈류로 들어가고 신체의 어느 곳이든 이동하여 심각한 건강상의 위험을 초래할 수 있다.

24 제목

❶ Kids tire of their toys, college students get sick of cafeteria food, and sooner or later most of us lose interest in our favorite TV shows.

아이들은 자기들의 장난감에 지루해하고, 대학생들은 카페테리아 음식에 싫증을 내고, 머지않아 우리 중 대부분은 우리가 가장 좋아하는 TV 쇼에 흥미를 잃는다.

❷ The bottom line is that we humans are easily bored.

요점은 우리 인간이 쉽게 지루해한다는 것이다.

❸ But why should this be true?

그런데 왜 이것이 사실이어야 할까?

❹ The answer lies buried deep in our nerve cells, which are designed to reduce their initial excited response to stimuli each time they occur.

답은 자극이 일어날 때마다 그것에 대한 초기의 흥분된 반응을 약화하도록 설계된 우리의 신경 세포 내에 깊이 숨어 있다.

❺ At the same time, these neurons enhance their responses to things that change — especially things that change quickly.

동시에 이 뉴런들은 변화하는 것들, 특히 빠르게 변화하는 것들에 대한 반응을 강화한다.

❻ We probably evolved this way because our ancestors got more survival value, for example, from attending to what was moving in a tree (such as a puma) than to the tree itself.

예를 들면 우리는 아마도 우리의 조상이 나무 그 자체보다 (퓨마처럼) 나무에서 움직이는 것에 주의를 기울이는 것으로부터 더 많은 생존 가치를 얻었기 때문에 이런 방식으로 진화했을 것이다.

❼ Boredom in reaction to an unchanging environment turns down the level of neural excitation so that new stimuli (like our ancestor's hypothetical puma threat) stand out more.

변하지 않는 환경에 대한 반응으로의 지루함은 신경 흥분의 수준을 낮춰 (우리 조상이 가정한 퓨마의 위협과 같은) 새로운 자극이 더 두드러지게 한다.

❽ It's the neural equivalent of turning off a front door light to see the fireflies.

이것은 반딧불이를 보기 위해 앞문의 불을 끄는 것의 신경적 대응물이다.

26 일치

❶ Frederick Douglass was born into slavery at a farm in Maryland.

Frederick Douglass는 Maryland의 한 농장에서 노예로 태어났다.

❷ His full name at birth was Frederick Augustus Washington Bailey.

태어났을 때 그의 성명은 Frederick Augustus Washington Bailey였다.

❸ He changed his name to Frederick Douglass after he successfully escaped from slavery in 1838.

그는 1838년에 노예 상태에서 성공적으로 탈출한 후 자신의 이름을 Frederick Douglass로 바꿨다.

❹ He became a leader of the Underground Railroad — a network of people, places, and routes that helped enslaved people escape to the north.

그는 노예가 된 사람들을 북쪽으로 탈출하도록 돕는 사람, 장소, 경로의 조직인 Underground Railroad의 리더가 되었다.

❺ He assisted other runaway slaves until they could safely get to other areas in the north.

그는 다른 도망친 노예들이 북쪽의 다른 지역에 안전하게 도착할 수 있을 때까지 그들을 도왔다.

❻ As a slave, he had taught himself to read and write and he spread that knowledge to other slaves as well.

노예로서 그는 읽고 쓰는 것을 독학했고, 그 지식을 다른 노예들에게도 전파했다.

❼ Once free, he became a well-known abolitionist and strong believer in equality for all people including Blacks, Native Americans, women, and recent immigrants.

자유로워지고 난 뒤 그는 유명한 노예제 폐지론자이자 흑인, 아메리카 원주민, 여성, 그리고 최근 이민자들을 포함한 모든 사람들을 위한 평등에 대한 강한 신봉자가 되었다.

❽ He wrote several autobiographies describing his experiences as a slave.

그는 노예로서의 자신의 경험을 묘사한 몇 권의 자서전을 썼다.

❾ In addition to all this, he became the first African-American candidate for vice president of the United States.

이 모든 것에 더하여 그는 미국의 첫 아프리카계 미국인 부통령 후보가 되었다.

29 어법

❶ Some countries have proposed tougher guidelines for determining brain death when transplantation — transferring organs to others — is under consideration.

일부 국가는 장기 이식, 즉 다른 사람에게 장기를 전달하는 것을 고려 중일 때 뇌사를 결정하는 것에 대한 더 엄격한 지침을 제안했다.

❷ In several European countries, there are legal requirements which specify that a whole team of doctors must agree over the diagnosis of death in the case of a potential donor.

몇몇 유럽 국가에는 잠재적 기증자의 경우 의사 팀 전체가 사망 진단에 동의해야 한다고 명시하는 법적 요건들이 있다.

❸ The reason for these strict regulations for diagnosing brain death in potential organ donors is, no doubt, to ease public fears of a premature diagnosis of brain death for the purpose of obtaining organs.

잠재적인 장기 기증자의 뇌사 진단에 대한 이러한 엄격한 규정들의 이유는 의심할 바 없이 장기 확보를 위한 너무 이른 뇌사 진단에 대한 대중의 두려움을 완화하기 위한 것이다.

❹ But it is questionable whether these requirements reduce public suspicions as much as they create them.

하지만 이러한 요건들이 대중의 의심을 만들어 내는 만큼 그것을 줄여 주는지는 의문이다.

❺ They certainly maintain mistaken beliefs that diagnosing brain death is an unreliable process lacking precision.

그것들은 뇌사 진단이 정확성이 결여된 신뢰하기 어려운 과정이라는 잘못된 믿음을 확실히 유지시킨다.

❻ As a matter of consistency, at least, criteria for diagnosing the deaths of organ donors should be exactly the same as for those for whom immediate burial or cremation is intended.

적어도 일관성의 이유로 장기 기증자의 사망 진단 기준은 즉각적인 매장 또는 화장이 예정된 사람들에 대한 그것과 정확히 동일해야 한다.

30 어휘

❶ The term minimalism gives a negative impression to some people who think that it is all about sacrificing valuable possessions.
미니멀리즘이라는 용어는 그것을 소중한 소유물을 희생하는 것에 관한 것으로만 생각하는 일부 사람들에게 부정적인 인상을 준다.

❷ This insecurity naturally stems from their attachment to their possessions.
이러한 불안은 자신의 소유물에 대한 애착에서 자연스럽게 비롯된다.

❸ It is difficult to distance oneself from something that has been around for quite some time.
꽤 오랫동안 곁에 있어 왔던 것으로부터 자신을 멀리 두는 것은 어렵다.

❹ Being an emotional animal, human beings give meaning to the things around them.
감정의 동물이기 때문에, 인간은 그들의 곁에 있는 물건에 의미를 부여한다.

❺ So, the question arising here is that if minimalism will hurt one's emotions, why become a minimalist?
그래서 여기서 생기는 질문은 미니멀리즘이 사람의 감정을 상하게 한다면 왜 미니멀리스트가 되느냐는 것이다.

❻ The answer is very simple; the assumption of the question is fundamentally wrong.
대답은 매우 간단하다. 그 질문의 가정은 근본적으로 틀리다.

❻ Minimalism does not hurt emotions.
미니멀리즘은 감정을 상하게 하지 않는다.

❼ You might feel a bit sad while getting rid of a useless item but sooner than later, this feeling will be overcome by the joy of clarity.
여러분은 쓸모없는 물건을 치우면서 조금 슬퍼할 수도 있지만 머지않아 이 느낌은 명료함의 기쁨으로 극복될 것이다.

❽ Minimalists never argue that you should leave every convenience of the modern era.
미니멀리스트는 여러분이 현대의 모든 편의를 버려야 한다고 주장하지 않는다.

❾ They are of the view that you only need to eliminate stuff that is unused or not going to be used in the near future.
그들은 여러분이 사용되지 않거나 가까운 미래에 사용되지 않을 물건을 없애기만 하면 된다는 견해를 가지고 있다.

31 빈칸

❶ A remarkable characteristic of the visual system is that it has the ability of adapting itself.
시각 체계의 두드러진 특징은 스스로 적응하는 능력이 있다는 것이다.

❷ Psychologist George M. Stratton made this clear in an impressive self-experiment.
심리학자 George M. Stratton은 인상적인 자가 실험에서 이것을 분명히 했다.

❸ Stratton wore reversing glasses for several days, which literally turned the world upside down for him.
Stratton은 며칠 동안 반전 안경을 착용했는데 그 안경은 말 그대로 그에게 세상을 뒤집어 놓았다.

❹ In the beginning, this caused him great difficulties: just putting food in his mouth with a fork was a challenge for him.
처음에 이것은 그에게 큰 어려움을 초래하였다. 포크로 음식을 입에 넣는 것조차 그에게는 도전이었다.

❺ With time, however, his visual system adjusted to the new stimuli from reality, and he was able to act normally in his environment again, even seeing it upright when he concentrated.
그러나 시간이 지나면서 그의 시각 체계는 현실의 새로운 자극에 적응했고, 그가 집중했을 때는 심지어 똑바로 보면서, 다시 자신의 환경에서 정상적으로 행동할 수 있었다.

❻ As he took off his reversing glasses, he was again confronted with problems: he used the wrong hand when he wanted to reach for something, for example.
반전 안경을 벗었을 때 그는 다시 문제에 직면했다. 예를 들어 그가 무언가를 잡기를 원할 때 그는 반대 손을 사용했다.

❼ Fortunately, Stratton could reverse the perception, and he did not have to wear reversing glasses for the rest of his life.
다행히 Stratton은 지각을 뒤집을 수 있었고 평생 반전 안경을 착용하지 않아도 되었다.

❽ For him, everything returned to normal after one day.
그에게 하루 만에 모든 것이 정상으로 돌아왔다.

32 빈칸

❶ Participants in a study were asked to answer questions like "Why does the moon have phases?"
한 연구의 참가자들이 '달은 왜 상을 가지고 있을까'와 같은 질문들에 답하도록 요청받았다.

❷ Half the participants were told to search for the answers on the internet, while the other half weren't allowed to do so.
참가자의 절반은 인터넷에서 답을 검색하라는 말을 들었고 나머지 절반은 그렇게 하도록 허용되지 않았다.

❸ Then, in the second part of the study, all of the participants were presented with a new set of questions, such as "Why does Swiss cheese have holes?"
그다음, 연구의 두 번째 단계에서 모든 참가자는 '스위스 치즈에는 왜 구멍이 있을까'와 같은 일련의 새로운 질문들을 제시받았다.

❹ These questions were unrelated to the ones asked during the first part of the study, so participants who used the internet had absolutely no advantage over those who hadn't.
이 질문들은 연구의 첫 번째 단계에서 질문받았던 것들과는 관련이 없어서 인터넷을 사용한 참가자들은 그러지 않은 참가자들보다 이점이 전혀 없었다.

❺ You would think that both sets of participants would be equally sure or unsure about how well they could answer the new questions.
여러분은 두 집단의 참가자들이 새로운 질문들에 얼마나 잘 대답할 수 있을지에 대해 동일한 정도로 확신하거나 확신하지 못할 것으로 생각할 것이다.

❻ But those who used the internet in the first part of the study rated themselves as more knowledgeable than those who hadn't, even about questions they hadn't searched online for.
그러나 연구의 첫 번째 단계에서 인터넷을 사용했던 참가자들은 자신이 온라인에서 검색하지 않았던 질문들에 대해서조차 그러지 않았던 참가자들보다 스스로가 더 많이 알고 있다고 평가했다.

❼ The study suggests that having access to unrelated information was enough to pump up their intellectual confidence.
이 연구는 관련 없는 정보에 접근하는 것이 그들의 지적 자신감을 부풀리기에 충분했다는 것을 시사한다.

33 빈칸

❶ Anthropologist Gregory Bateson suggests that we tend to understand the world by focusing in on particular features within it.

인류학자 Gregory Bateson은 우리가 세상 안의 특정한 특징에 초점을 맞춤으로써 세상을 이해하는 경향이 있다고 제안한다.

❷ Take platypuses.

오리너구리를 예로 들어보자.

❸ We might zoom in so closely to their fur that each hair appears different.

우리가 그들의 털을 매우 가까이 확대하면 각 가닥이 다르게 보인다.

❹ We might also zoom out to the extent where it appears as a single, uniform object.

우리는 또한 그것이 하나의 동일한 개체로 보이는 정도까지 축소할 수도 있다.

❺ We might take the platypus as an individual, or we might treat it as part of a larger unit such as a species or an ecosystem.

우리는 오리너구리를 개체로 취급할 수도 있고 종 또는 생태계와 같이 더 큰 단위의 일부로 취급할 수도 있다.

❻ It's possible to move between many of these perspectives, although we may need some additional tools and skills to zoom in on individual pieces of hair or zoom out to entire ecosystems.

비록 개별 머리카락을 확대하거나 전체 생태계로 축소하기 위해 몇 가지 추가 도구와 기술이 필요할지도 모르지만, 이러한 많은 관점 사이를 이동하는 것은 가능하다.

❼ Crucially, however, we can only take up one perspective at a time.

그러나 결정적으로 우리는 한 번에 하나의 관점만 취할 수 있다.

❽ We can pay attention to the varied behavior of individual animals, look at what unites them into a single species, or look at them as part of bigger ecological patterns.

우리는 개별 동물의 다양한 행동에 주의를 기울일 수 있고, 그들을 단일 종으로 통합하는 것을 살펴볼 수도 있고, 더 큰 생태학적 패턴의 일부로서 그들을 살펴볼 수도 있다.

❾ Every possible perspective involves emphasizing certain aspects and ignoring others.

가능한 모든 관점은 특정 측면을 강조하고 다른 측면을 외면하는 것을 포함한다.

34 빈칸

❶ Plato's realism includes all aspects of experience but is most easily explained by considering the nature of mathematical and geometrical objects such as circles.

플라톤의 실재론은 경험의 모든 측면을 포함하지만, 원과 같은 수학적이고 기하학적인 대상의 특성을 고려함으로써 가장 쉽게 설명된다.

❷ He asked the question, what is a circle?

그는 '원이란 무엇인가'라는 질문을 했다.

❸ You might indicate a particular example carved into stone or drawn in the sand.

여러분은 돌에 새겨져 있거나 모래에 그려진 특정한 예를 가리킬 수 있다.

❹ However, Plato would point out that, if you looked closely enough, you would see that neither it, no indeed any physical circle, was perfect.

그러나 플라톤은 여러분이 충분히 면밀히 관찰한다면, 여러분이 그 어느 것도, 진정 어떤 물리적인 원도 완벽하지 않다는 것을 알게 될 것이라고 지적할 것이다.

❺ They all possessed flaws, and all were subject to change and decayed with time.

그것들 모두는 결함을 가지고 있었고, 모두 변화의 영향을 받고 시간이 지남에 따라 쇠하였다.

❻ So how can we talk about perfect circles if we cannot actually see or touch them?

그렇다면, 우리가 완벽한 원을 실제로 보거나 만질 수 없다면, 그것에 대해 어떻게 이야기할 수 있을까?

❼ Plato's extraordinary answer was that the world we see is a poor reflection of a deeper unseen reality of Forms, or universals, where perfect cats chase perfect mice in perfect circles around perfect rocks.

플라톤의 비범한 대답은 우리가 보는 세상이 완벽한 고양이가 완벽한 암석 주변에서 완벽한 원을 그리며 완벽한 쥐를 쫓는 '형상' 또는 '보편자'라는 더 깊은 보이지 않는 실재의 불충분한 반영물이라는 것이다.

❽ Plato believed that the Forms or universals are the true reality that exists in an invisible but perfect world beyond our senses.

플라톤은 '형상' 또는 '보편자'가 보이지 않지만 우리의 감각을 넘어선 완벽한 세계에 존재하는 진정한 실재라고 믿었다.

35 무관

❶ In statistics, the law of large numbers describes a situation where having more data is better for making predictions.

통계학에서 대수의 법칙은 더 많은 데이터를 갖는 것이 예측하는 데 더 좋은 상황을 설명한다.

❷ According to it, the more often an experiment is conducted, the closer the average of the results can be expected to match the true state of the world.

그것에 따르면 실험이 더 자주 수행될수록 그 결과의 평균이 세상의 실제 상태에 더 맞춰지는 것으로 예상될 수 있다.

❸ For instance, on your first encounter with the game of roulette, you may have beginner's luck after betting on 7.

예를 들어 룰렛 게임을 처음 접했을 때 7에 베팅한 후 여러분은 초보자의 운이 있을 수 있다.

❹ But the more often you repeat this bet, the closer the relative frequency of wins and losses is expected to approach the true chance of winning, meaning that your luck will at some point fade away.

하지만 당신이 이 베팅을 더 자주 반복할수록 승패의 상대적인 빈도가 진짜 승률에 더 가까워질 것으로 예상되는데 이는 당신의 운이 어느 순간 사라진다는 것을 의미한다.

❺ Similarly, car insurers collect large amounts of data to figure out the chances that drivers will cause accidents, depending on their age, region, or car brand.

마찬가지로 자동차 보험사는 운전자가 그들의 연령, 지역 또는 자동차 브랜드에 따라 사고를 일으킬 확률을 파악하기 위해 많은 양의 데이터를 수집한다.

❻ Both casinos and insurance industries rely on the law of large numbers to balance individual losses.

카지노와 보험 산업 모두 개별 손실의 균형을 맞추기 위해 대수의 법칙에 의존한다.

36 순서

❶ The adolescent brain is not fully developed until its early twenties.
청소년기의 뇌는 20대 초반까지는 완전히 발달하지 않는다.

❷ This means the way the adolescents' decision-making circuits integrate and process information may put them at a disadvantage.
이것은 청소년의 의사 결정 회로가 정보를 통합하고 처리하는 방식이 그들을 불리하게 만들 수 있음을 의미한다.

❸ One of their brain regions that matures later is the prefrontal cortex, which is the control center, tasked with thinking ahead and evaluating consequences.
나중에 성숙하는 뇌 영역 중 하나는 통제 센터인 전전두엽 피질이며, 그것은 미리 생각하고 결과를 평가하는 임무를 맡고 있다.

❹ It is the area of the brain responsible for preventing you from sending off an initial angry text and modifying it with kinder words.
그것은 당신이 초기의 화가 난 문자를 보내는 것을 막고 그것을 더 친절한 단어로 수정하게 하는 역할을 하는 뇌의 영역이다.

❺ On the other hand, the limbic system matures earlier, playing a central role in processing emotional responses.
반면 대뇌변연계는 더 일찍 성숙하여 정서적 반응을 처리하는 데 중심적인 역할을 한다.

❻ Because of its earlier development, it is more likely to influence decision-making.
그것의 더 이른 발달로 인해 그것이 의사 결정에 영향을 미칠 가능성이 더 높다.

❼ Decision-making in the adolescent brain is led by emotional factors more than the perception of consequences.
청소년기의 뇌에서 의사 결정은 결과의 인식보다 감정적인 요인에 의해 이끌어진다.

❽ Due to these differences, there is an imbalance between feeling-based decision-making ruled by the more mature limbic system and logical-based decision-making by the not-yet-mature prefrontal cortex.
이러한 차이점 때문에 더 성숙한 대뇌변연계에 의해 지배되는 감정 기반 의사 결정과 아직 성숙하지 않은 전전두엽 피질에 의한 논리 기반 의사 결정 사이에는 불균형이 존재한다.

❾ This may explain why some teens are more likely to make bad decisions.
이것은 왜 일부 십대들이 그릇된 결정을 내릴 가능성이 더 높은지를 설명해 줄 수 있다.

37 순서

❶ Despite the remarkable progress in deep-learning based facial recognition approaches in recent years, in terms of identification performance, they still have limitations.

최근 몇 년 동안 딥 러닝 기반의 얼굴 인식 접근법의 눈에 띄는 발전에도 불구하고, 식별 성능 측면에서 여전히 그것은 한계를 가지고 있다.

❷ These limitations relate to the database used in the learning stage.

이러한 한계는 학습 단계에서 사용되는 데이터베이스와 관련이 있다.

❸ If the selected database does not contain enough instances, the result may be systematically affected.

선택된 데이터베이스가 충분한 사례를 포함하지 않으면 그 결과가 시스템적으로 영향을 받을 수 있다.

❹ For example, the performance of a facial biometric system may decrease if the person to be identified was enrolled over 10 years ago.

예를 들어 식별될 사람이 10년도 더 전에 등록된 경우 안면 생체 측정 시스템의 성능이 저하될 수 있다.

❺ The factor to consider is that this person may experience changes in the texture of the face, particularly with the appearance of wrinkles and sagging skin.

고려해야 할 요인은 이 사람이 특히 주름과 처진 피부가 나타나는 것을 동반한 얼굴의 질감 변화를 경험할 수 있다는 것이다.

❻ These changes may be highlighted by weight gain or loss.

이러한 변화는 체중 증가 또는 감소에 의해 두드러질 수 있다.

❼ To counteract this problem, researchers have developed models for face aging or digital de-aging.

이 문제에 대응하기 위해 연구자들은 얼굴 노화나 디지털 노화 완화의 모델을 개발했다.

❽ It is used to compensate for the differences in facial characteristics, which appear over a given time period.

그것은 주어진 기간 동안 나타나는 얼굴 특성의 차이를 보완하는 데 사용된다.

38 삽입

❶ The decline in the diversity of our food is an entirely human-made process.
우리 음식의 다양성의 감소는 전적으로 인간이 만든 과정이다.

❷ The biggest loss of crop diversity came in the decades that followed the Second World War.
농작물 다양성의 가장 큰 손실은 제2차 세계 대전 이후 수십 년 동안 나타났다.

❸ In an attempt to save millions from extreme hunger, crop scientists found ways to produce grains such as rice and wheat on an enormous scale.
수백만 명의 사람들을 극도의 배고픔에서 구하고자 하는 시도에서 작물 과학자들이 쌀과 밀과 같은 곡물을 엄청난 규모로 생산하는 방법을 발견했다.

❹ And thousands of traditional varieties were replaced by a small number of new super-productive ones.
그리고 수천 개의 전통적인 종들은 소수의 새로운 초(超)생산적인 종들로 대체되었다.

❺ The strategy worked spectacularly well, at least to begin with.
그 전략은 적어도 처음에는 굉장히 잘 작동했다.

❻ Because of it, grain production tripled, and between 1970 and 2020 the human population more than doubled.
그것 때문에 곡물 생산량은 세 배가 되었고 1970년과 2020년 사이에 인구는 두 배 이상 증가했다.

❼ Leaving the contribution of that strategy to one side, the danger of creating more uniform crops is that they are more at risk when it comes to disasters.
그 전략의 기여를 차치하고, 더 획일적인 작물을 만드는 것의 위험은 그것들이 재앙과 관련해 더 큰 위험에 처한다는 것이다.

❽ Specifically, a global food system that depends on just a narrow selection of plants has a greater chance of not being able to survive diseases, pests and climate extremes.
특히 농작물의 좁은 선택에만 의존하는 세계적인 식량 시스템은 질병, 해충 및 기후 위기로부터 생존하지 못할 더 높은 가능성을 가진다.

39 삽입

❶ Between 1940 and 2000, Cuba ruled the world baseball scene.

1940년과 2000년 사이에 쿠바는 세계 야구계를 지배했다.

❷ They won 25 of the first 28 World Cups and 3 of 5 Olympic Games.

그들은 첫 28회의 월드컵 중 25회와 5회의 올림픽 게임 중 3회를 이겼다.

❸ The Cubans were known for wearing uniforms covered in red from head to toe, a strong contrast to the more conservative North American style featuring grey or white pants.

쿠바인들은 머리부터 발끝까지 빨간색으로 뒤덮인 유니폼을 입는 것으로 알려져 있었는데, 이것은 회색이나 흰색 바지를 특징으로 하는 더 보수적인 북미 스타일과 강한 대조를 이룬다.

❹ Not only were their athletic talents superior, the Cubans appeared even stronger from just the colour of their uniforms.

쿠바인들의 운동 재능이 뛰어났을 뿐만 아니라 그들은 그들의 유니폼의 색깔만으로도 훨씬 더 강하게 보였다.

❺ A game would not even start and the opposing team would already be scared.

경기가 시작하지 않았는데도 상대 팀은 이미 겁에 질리곤 했다.

❻ A few years ago, Cuba altered that uniform style, modernizing it and perhaps conforming to other countries' style; interestingly, the national team has declined since that time.

몇 년 전 쿠바는 유니폼을 현대화하고 아마도 다른 나라의 스타일에 맞추면서 그 유니폼 스타일을 바꿨다. 흥미롭게도 국가 대표 팀은 그 시기부터 쇠퇴해 왔다.

❼ The country that ruled international baseball for decades has not been on top since that uniform change.

수십 년 동안 국제 야구를 지배했던 그 나라는 그 유니폼 교체 이후로 정상에 오른 적이 없었다.

❽ Traditions are important for a team; while a team brand or image can adjust to keep up with present times, if it abandons or neglects its roots, negative effects can surface.

전통은 팀에게 중요하다. 팀 브랜드나 이미지는 현시대를 따르기 위해 조정될 수 있지만 팀이 그들의 뿌리를 버리거나 무시하면 부정적인 영향이 표면화될 수 있다.

40 요약

❶ Many of the first models of cultural evolution drew noticeable connections between culture and genes by using concepts from theoretical population genetics and applying them to culture.

문화 진화의 많은 초기 모델들은 이론 집단 유전학의 개념을 사용함으로써 그리고 그것들을 문화에 적용함으로써 문화와 유전자 사이의 주목할 만한 접점을 이끌어 냈다.

❷ Cultural patterns of transmission, innovation, and selection are conceptually likened to genetic processes of transmission, mutation, and selection.

전파, 혁신, 선택의 문화적 방식은 전달, 돌연변이, 선택의 유전적 과정과 개념적으로 유사하다.

❸ However, these approaches had to be modified to account for the differences between genetic and cultural transmission.

그러나 이러한 접근법은 유전자의 전달과 문화 전파 사이의 차이점을 설명하기 위해 수정되어야만 했다.

❹ For example, we do not expect the cultural transmission to follow the rules of genetic transmission strictly.

예를 들어, 우리는 문화 전파가 유전자 전달의 규칙을 엄격하게 따를 것이라고 예상하지 않는다.

❺ If two biological parents have different forms of a cultural trait, their child is not necessarily equally likely to acquire the mother's or father's form of that trait.

만약 두 명의 생물학적인 부모가 서로 다른 문화적인 특성의 형태를 가진다면, 그들의 자녀는 반드시 엄마 혹은 아빠의 그 특성의 형태를 동일하게 획득하지 않을 수 있다.

❻ Further, a child can acquire cultural traits not only from its parents but also from nonparental adults and peers; thus, the frequency of a cultural trait in the population is relevant beyond just the probability that an individual's parents had that trait.

더욱이 아이는 문화적인 특성을 부모로부터 뿐만 아니라 부모가 아닌 성인이나 또래로부터도 얻을 수 있다. 따라서 집단의 문화적인 특성의 빈도는 단지 한 개인의 부모가 그 특성을 가졌을 확률을 넘어서 유의미하다.

❼ Early cultural evolution models used the similarity between culture and genes but had to be revised since cultural transmission allows for more diverse factors than genetic transmission.

초기의 문화 진화 모델들은 문화와 유전자 사이의 유사성을 사용했지만, 문화 전파가 유전자의 전달보다 더 다양한 요인을 허용하기 때문에 수정되어야만 했다.

41~42 제목, 어휘

❶ A ball thrown into the air is acted upon by the initial force given it, persisting as inertia of movement and tending to carry it in the same straight line, and by the constant pull of gravity downward, as well as by the resistance of the air.

공중으로 던져진 공은 초기에 그것에 주어진 힘에 의해 움직여지는데, 운동의 관성으로 지속하며 같은 직선으로 나아가려는 경향을 보이고, 공기의 저항뿐만 아니라 아래로 지속적으로 당기는 중력에 의해서도 움직여진다.

❷ It moves, accordingly, in a curved path.

그에 맞춰 공은 곡선의 경로로 움직인다.

❸ Now the path does not represent the working of any particular force; there is simply the combination of the three elementary forces mentioned; but in a real sense, there is something in the total action besides the isolated action of three forces, namely, their joint action.

이제 그 경로는 어떤 특정한 힘의 작동을 나타내지는 않는다. 언급된 세 가지 기본적인 힘의 결합이 존재할 뿐이다. 하지만 사실은 세 가지 힘의 고립된 작용 외에 전체적인 작용에 무언가가 있다. 이름하여 그들의 공동 작용이다.

❹ In the same way, when two or more human individuals are together, their mutual relationships and their arrangement into a group are things which would not be disclosed if we confined our attention to each individual separately.

같은 방식으로, 두 명 혹은 그 이상의 인간 개인이 같이 있을 때 그들의 상호 관계와 그들의 집단으로의 배치는 만약 우리가 관심을 개별적으로 각각의 개인에게 국한시킨다면 드러나지 않을 것들이다.

❺ The significance of group behavior is greatly increased in the case of human beings by the fact that some of the tendencies to action of the individual are related definitely to other persons, and could not be aroused except by other persons acting as stimuli.

개인 행동의 몇몇 경향은 명백하게 다른 사람들과 관련이 있고 자극으로 작동하는 다른 사람들 없이는 유발되지 않을 수 있다는 사실로 인해 그룹 행동의 중요성이 인간의 경우 크게 증가된다.

❻ An individual in complete isolation would not reveal their competitive tendencies, their tendencies towards the opposite sex, their protective tendencies towards children.

완전한 고립 속의 개인은 그들의 경쟁적인 성향, 이성에 대한 그들의 성향, 아이에 대한 그들의 보호적 성향을 드러내지 않을 것이다.

❼ This shows that the traits of human nature do not fully appear until the individual is brought into relationships with other individuals.

이것은 개인이 다른 개인과의 관계에 관여될 때까지는 인간 본성의 특성이 완전히 나타나지 않는다는 것을 보여 준다.

43~45 순서, 지칭, 세부 내용

❶ There once lived a man in a village who was not happy with his life.

옛날 어느 마을에 자신의 삶이 행복하지 않은 한 남자가 살았다.

❷ He was always troubled by one problem or another.

그는 항상 하나 혹은 또 다른 문제로 어려움을 겪었다.

❸ One day, a saint with his guards stopped by his village.

어느 날 한 성자가 그의 경호인들과 함께 그의 마을에 들렀다.

❹ Many people heard the news and started going to him with their problems.

많은 사람들이 그 소식을 듣고 그들의 문제를 가지고 그에게 가기 시작했다.

❺ The man also decided to visit the saint.

그 남자 역시 성자를 방문하기로 결정했다.

❻ Even after reaching the saint's place in the morning, he didn't get the opportunity to meet him till evening.

아침에 성자가 있는 곳에 도착하고 난 후에도 그(a man)는 저녁 때까지 그를 만날 기회를 얻지 못했다.

❼ When the man got to meet the saint, he confessed that he was very unhappy with life because problems always surrounded him, like workplace tension or worries about his health.

마침내 그가 성자를 만났을 때 그(a man)는 직장 내 긴장이나 건강에 대한 걱정과 같이 항상 문제가 자기를 둘러싸고 있어서 삶이 매우 불행하다고 고백했다.

❽ He said, "Please give me a solution so that all the problems in my life will end and I can live peacefully."

그(a man)는 "나의 삶의 모든 문제가 끝나고 제가 평화롭게 살 수 있도록 제발 해결책을 주세요."라고 말했다.

❾ The saint smiled and said that he would answer the request the next day.

성자는 미소 지으면서 그가 다음 날 그 요청에 답해 주겠다고 말했다.

❿ But the saint also asked if the man could do a small job for him.

그런데 성자는 또한 그 남자가 그를 위해 작은 일을 해 줄 수 있는지 물었다.

2023 고1 11월 모의고사　　　　　❶ 회차 :　　　　　점 / 204점

❶ voca　❷ text　❸ [/]　❹ ＿＿＿　❺ quiz 1　❻ quiz 2　❼ quiz 3　❽ quiz 4　❾ quiz 5

18

Dear Ms. MacAlpine,

I was so excited to hear **[that / what]**¹⁾ your brand is opening a new shop on Bruns Street next month. I **[have / had]**²⁾ always appreciated the way your brand helps women to feel more stylish and **[confident / confidently]**³⁾. I am writing in response to your ad in the Bruns Journal. I graduated from the Meline School of Fashion and have worked as a sales **[assistant / assistance]**⁴⁾ at LoganMart for the last five years. **[During / While]**⁵⁾ that time, I've developed strong customer service and sales skills, and now I would like to apply for the sales position in your clothing store. I am available for an interview at your earliest **[convenience / convenient]**⁶⁾. I look forward to **[hear / hearing]**⁷⁾ from you. Thank you for reading my letter.

Yours sincerely, Grace Braddock

친애하는 MacAlpine씨께,

저는 당신의 브랜드가 다음 달에 Bruns 거리에 새 매장을 연다는 것을 듣고 매우 들떴습니다. 저는 당신의 브랜드가 여성들이 더 멋지고 자신감 있게 느끼도록 도와주는 방식을 항상 높이 평가해 왔습니다. 저는 Bruns Journal에 있는 당신의 광고에 대한 응답으로 편지를 쓰고 있습니다. 저는 Meline 패션 학교를 졸업했고 지난 5년간 LoganMart에서 판매 보조원으로 일해 왔습니다. 그 기간 동안 저는 뛰어난 고객 서비스 및 판매 기술을 발달시켜 왔고, 이제 당신의 의류 매장의 판매직에 지원하고 싶습니다. 저는 당신이 편한 가장 빠른 시간에 인터뷰가 가능합니다. 당신으로부터 대답을 듣게 되기를 기대합니다. 저의 편지를 읽어 주셔서 감사드립니다.

Grace Braddock 드림

19

I had never seen a beach with such white sand or water **[that / what]**⁸⁾ was such a beautiful shade of blue. Jane and I set up a blanket on the sand **[during / while]**⁹⁾ looking forward to our ten days of honeymooning on an exotic island. "Look!" Jane waved her hand to point at the beautiful scene before us — and her gold wedding ring went **[fly / flying]**¹⁰⁾ off her hand. I tried **[seeing / to see]**¹¹⁾ where it went, but the sun hit my eyes and I lost track of it. I didn't want to lose her wedding ring, so I started looking in the area where I thought it **[had / have]**¹²⁾ landed. However, the sand was **[so / such]**¹³⁾ fine and I realized that anything heavy, like gold, would quickly sink and might never **[be found / found]**¹⁴⁾ again.

나는 그렇게 하얀 모래나 그렇게 아름다운 푸른 색조의 바다를 가진 해변을 한 번도 본 적이 없었다. 이국적인 섬에서의 열흘간의 신혼여행을 기대하면서 Jane과 나는 모래 위에 담요를 깔았다. "저기 좀 봐!" Jane이 그녀의 손을 흔들어 우리 앞의 아름다운 풍경을 가리켰다. 그러자 그녀의 금으로 된 결혼반지가 그녀의 손에서 빠져 날아갔다. 나는 그것이 날아간 곳을 보려고 노력했지만, 햇빛이 눈에 들어와 그것의 가던 방향을 놓쳤다. 나는 그녀의 결혼반지를 잃어버리고 싶지 않아서 내가 생각하기에 그것이 떨어졌을 장소를 들여다보기 시작했다. 하지만 모래가 너무 고왔고 나는 금처럼 무거운 것은 빨리 가라앉아 다시는 발견되지 않을 수도 있겠다는 것을 깨달았다.

20

The more people have to do unwanted things the more chances [**are** / **do**]15) that they create unpleasant environment for themselves and others. If you hate the thing you do but have to do it [**hence** / **nonetheless**]16) , you have choice between hating the thing and accepting [**that** / **what**]17) it needs to be done. Either way you will do it. [**Doing** / **Done**]18) it from place of hatred will develop hatred towards the self and others around you; doing it from the place of [**acceptance** / **assistance**]19) will create [**passion** / **compassion**]20) towards the self and allow for opportunities to find a [**more** / **less**]21) suitable way of accomplishing the task. If you decide to [**accept** / **avoid**]22) the fact [**that** / **which**]23) your task has to be done, start from recognising that your situation is a gift from life; this will help you [**to see** / **seeing**]24) it as a lesson in [**acceptance** / **resistance**]25) .

사람들은 원하지 않는 일을 더 해야 할수록, 그들 자신과 다른 사람에게 불편한 환경을 만들 가능성이 더 커진다. 만약 여러분이 자기가 하는 일을 싫어하지만, 그럼에도 불구하고 해야 한다면, 여러분은 그것을 싫어하는 것과 그것이 완료될 필요가 있다는 것을 받아들이는 것 중 하나를 선택할 수 있다. 어느 쪽이든 여러분은 그 일을 할 것이다. 증오의 영역에서 그것을 한다면 여러분 자신과 여러분 주변의 사람들을 향한 증오를 키울 것이고 수용의 영역에서 그것을 한다면 자신을 향한 연민을 일으키고 그 과업을 성취할 더 적합한 방법을 찾을 기회를 갖게 될 것이다. 여러분의 과업이 완료되어야 한다는 사실을 받아들이기로 한다면 여러분의 상황이 삶으로부터의 선물임을 인식하는 것으로부터 시작하라. 이는 여러분이 그것을 수용의 교훈으로 여기게 도울 것이다.

21

Everyone's heard the expression *don't let the perfect become the enemy of the good*. If you want to get [**over** / **into**]26) an obstacle so that your idea can become the solution-based policy you've long [**dreamed** / **dreamed of**]27), you can't have an all-or-nothing mentality. You have to be willing to [**altar** / **alter**]28) your idea and let others [**effect** / **influence**]29) its outcome. You have to be okay with the outcome [**be** / **being**]30) a little different, even a little [**less** / **more**]31) , than you wanted. Say you're pushing for a clean water [**act** / **action**]32) . Even if what [**emerges** / **submerges**]33) isn't as well-funded as you wished, or doesn't match how you originally [**conceived** / **deceived**]34) the bill, you'll have still succeeded in ensuring that kids in troubled areas have [**access** / **limit**]35) to clean water. That's what counts, [**that** / **which**]36) *they* will be safer because of your idea and your effort. Is it perfect? No. Is there more work to be done? Absolutely. But in almost every case, helping move the needle [**backward** / **forward**]37) is vastly better than not helping at all.

'완벽함이 좋음의 적이 되게 두지 말라'는 표현은 누구나 들어 본 적이 있다. 여러분이 장애물을 극복해 자기 아이디어가 자신이 오랫동안 꿈꿔 왔던 해결을 기반으로 한 방책이 될 수 있도록 하고 싶다면, 전부 아니면 전무라고 여기는 사고방식을 가져서는 안 된다. 여러분은 기꺼이 자기 아이디어를 바꾸고 다른 사람이 그것의 결과에 영향을 미치도록 해야 한다. 결과가 여러분이 원했던 것과 조금 다르거나, 심지어 원했던 것보다 조금 '못'하여도 괜찮다고 여겨야 한다. 여러분이 수질 오염 방지법을 추진하고 있다고 가정해 보자. 비록 나타난 것이 여러분이 원했던 만큼의 자금이 충분하게 지원되지 않았거나, 여러분이 처음에 이 법안을 고안한 방식과 일치하지 않더라도, 여러분은 힘든 지역의 아이들이 깨끗한 물에 접근할 수 있도록 하는 데 여전히 성공하는 것이다. 중요한 것은 바로 여러분의 아이디어와 노력 덕분에 '그들'이 더 안전하리라는 것이다. 완벽한가? 아니다. 더 해야 할 일이 있는가? 당연하다. 하지만 거의 모든 경우에, 바늘을 앞으로 이동시키는 것을 돕는 것이 전혀 돕지 않는 것보다 훨씬 더 낫다.

22

When writing a novel, research for information needs to be done. The thing is that some kinds of fiction [**demand** / **demanding**]**38)** a higher level of detail: crime fiction, for example, or scientific thrillers. The information is never hard [**finding** / **to find**]**39)**; one website for authors even [**organize** / **organizes**]**40)** trips to police stations, [**in that** / **so that**]**41)** crime writers can get it right. Often, a polite letter will earn you [**admission** / **permission**]**42)** to visit a particular location and record all the details that you need. But remember that you will drive your readers [**in** / **to**]**43)** boredom if you think [**that** / **what**]**44)** you need to pack everything you discover into your work. The details that matter are those that [**conceal** / **reveal**]**45)** the human experience. The crucial thing is telling a story, [**finding** / **to find**]**46)** the characters, the tension, and the conflict — not the train timetable or the building blueprint.

소설을 쓸 때 정보를 위한 조사가 행해질 필요가 있다. 문제는 예를 들어 범죄 소설이나 과학 스릴러와 같은 어떤 종류의 소설은 더 높은 수준의 세부 사항을 요구한다는 것이다. 정보는 찾기에 결코 어렵지 않다. 작가들을 위한 한 웹사이트는 범죄물 작가들이 정보를 제대로 얻을 수 있도록 심지어 경찰서로의 탐방을 조직하기도 한다. 종종 정중한 편지는 여러분에게 특정한 장소를 방문하고 필요한 모든 세부 사항을 기록할 수 있는 허가를 얻어 줄 것이다. 하지만 만약 여러분이 발견한 모든 것을 작품에 담아야 한다고 생각할 경우 여러분은 독자들을 지루하게 만들 것이라는 것을 기억하라. 중요한 세부 사항은 인간의 경험을 드러내는 것이다. 중요한 것은 기차 시간표나 건물 청사진이 아니라 인물, 긴장, 그리고 갈등을 찾아가며 이야기를 말하는 것이다.

23

Nearly everything has to go through your mouth to get to the rest of you, from food and air to bacteria and viruses. A healthy mouth can help your body [**get** / **getting**]**47)** what it needs and [**prevent** / **prevents**]**48)** it from harm — with adequate space for air to travel to your lungs, and healthy teeth and gums that prevent harmful microorganisms [**from entering** / **to enter**]**49)** your bloodstream. From the moment you [**are created,** / **created**]**50)**, [**aural** / **oral**]**51)** health affects every [**aspect** / **aspects**]**52)** of your life. What happens in the mouth is usually just the tip of the iceberg and a reflection of [**that** / **what**]**53)** is happening in other parts of the body. Poor oral health can be a cause of a disease that affects the entire body. The microorganisms in an unhealthy mouth can enter the bloodstream and [**travel** / **travels**]**54)** anywhere in the body, [**pose** / **posing**]**55)** serious health risks.

음식과 공기에서부터 박테리아와 바이러스까지 거의 모든 것이 여러분의 나머지 부분에 도달하기 위해 여러분의 입을 거쳐야 한다. 건강한 입은 공기가 폐로 이동할 수 있는 적당한 공간, 그리고 해로운 미생물이 혈류로 들어가는 것을 막는 건강한 치아와 잇몸으로 여러분의 몸이 필요한 것을 얻고, 피해로부터 몸을 지키도록 도와줄 수 있다. 여러분이 생겨난 순간부터 구강 건강은 여러분의 삶의 모든 측면에 영향을 미친다. 입안에서 일어나는 일은 대개 빙산의 일각일 뿐이며 신체의 다른 부분에서 일어나고 있는 일의 반영이다. 나쁜 구강 건강은 전체 몸에 영향을 끼치는 질병의 원인일 수 있다. 건강하지 않은 입안의 미생물은 혈류로 들어가고 신체의 어느 곳이든 이동하여 심각한 건강상의 위험을 초래할 수 있다.

24

Kids tire of their toys, college students get sick of cafeteria food, and sooner or later most of us [**lose /** **to lose**]⁵⁶⁾ interest in our favorite TV shows. The bottom line is [**that / what**]⁵⁷⁾ we humans are easily bored. But why should this be true? The answer [**lays / lies**]⁵⁸⁾ buried deep in our nerve cells, which [**are designed / designed**]⁵⁹⁾ to reduce their initial excited response to stimuli each time they occur. At the same time, these neurons [**diminish / enhance**]⁶⁰⁾ their responses to things that change — especially things that change quickly. We probably [**evolved / involved**]⁶¹⁾ this way [**because / because of**]⁶²⁾ our ancestors got more survival value, for example, from attending to [**what / which**]⁶³⁾ was moving in a tree (such as a puma) than to the tree itself. Boredom in reaction to an [**unchanged / unchanging**]⁶⁴⁾ environment [**turns / turned**]⁶⁵⁾ down the level of neural excitation [**in that / so that**]⁶⁶⁾ new stimuli (like our ancestor's hypothetical puma threat) stand out [**less / more**]⁶⁷⁾. It's the neural equivalent of turning off a front door light to see the fireflies.

아이들은 자기들의 장난감에 지루해하고, 대학생들은 카페테리아 음식에 싫증을 내고, 머지않아 우리 중 대부분은 우리가 가장 좋아하는 TV 쇼에 흥미를 잃는다. 요점은 우리 인간이 쉽게 지루해한다는 것이다. 그런데 왜 이것이 사실이어야 할까? 답은 자극이 일어날 때마다 그것에 대한 초기의 흥분된 반응을 약화하도록 설계된 우리의 신경 세포 내에 깊이 숨어 있다. 동시에 이 뉴런들은 변화하는 것들, 특히 빠르게 변화하는 것들에 대한 반응을 강화한다. 예를 들면 우리는 아마도 우리의 조상이 나무 그 자체보다 (퓨마처럼) 나무에서 움직이는 것에 주의를 기울이는 것으로부터 더 많은 생존 가치를 얻었기 때문에 이런 방식으로 진화했을 것이다. 변하지 않는 환경에 대한 반응으로의 지루함은 신경 흥분의 수준을 낮춰 (우리 조상이 가정한 퓨마의 위협과 같은) 새로운 자극이 더 두드러지게 한다. 이것은 반딧불이를 보기 위해 앞문의 불을 끄는 것의 신경적 대응물이다.

26

Frederick Douglass [**born / was born**]⁶⁸⁾ into slavery at a farm in Maryland. His full name at birth was Frederick Augustus Washington Bailey. He changed his name to Frederick Douglass after he [**successfully / successively**]⁶⁹⁾ escaped from slavery in 1838. He became a leader of the Underground Railroad — a network of people, places, and routes that helped [**enslaved / enslaving**]⁷⁰⁾ people escape to the north. He assisted [**other / the other**]⁷¹⁾ runaway slaves until they could safely get to other areas in the north. As a slave, he had taught [**him / himself**]⁷²⁾ to read and write and he spread that knowledge to other slaves as well. Once free, he became a well-known abolitionist and strong believer in equality for all people [**include / including**]⁷³⁾ Blacks, Native Americans, women, and recent [**emigrants / immigrants**]⁷⁴⁾. He wrote several [**autobiographies / autographs**]⁷⁵⁾ [**described / describing**]⁷⁶⁾ his experiences as a slave. In addition to all this, he became the first African-American candidate for vice president of the United States.

Frederick Douglass는 Maryland의 한 농장에서 노예로 태어났다. 태어났을 때 그의 성명은 Frederick Augustus Washington Bailey였다. 그는 1838년에 노예 상태에서 성공적으로 탈출한 후 자신의 이름을 Frederick Douglass로 바꿨다. 그는 노예가 된 사람들을 북쪽으로 탈출하도록 돕는 사람, 장소, 경로의 조직인 Underground Railroad의 리더가 되었다. 그는 다른 도망친 노예들이 북쪽의 다른 지역에 안전하게 도착할 수 있을 때까지 그들을 도왔다. 노예로서 그는 읽고 쓰는 것을 독학했고, 그 지식을 다른 노예들에게도 전파했다. 자유로워지고 난 뒤 그는 유명한 노예제 폐지론자이자 흑인, 아메리카 원주민, 여성, 그리고 최근 이민자들을 포함한 모든 사람들을 위한 평등에 대한 강한 신봉자가 되었다. 그는 노예로서의 자신의 경험을 묘사한 몇 권의 자서전을 썼다. 이 모든 것에 더하여 그는 미국의 첫 아프리카계 미국인 부통령 후보가 되었다.

29

Some countries [**had** / **have**]⁷⁷⁾ proposed tougher guidelines for determining brain death when transplantation — transferring organs to others — [**are** / **is**]⁷⁸⁾ under consideration. In several European countries, there are legal requirements which specify [**that** / **what**]⁷⁹⁾ a whole team of doctors must agree over the diagnosis of death in the case of a [**actual** / **potential**]⁸⁰⁾ donor. The reason for these strict regulations for diagnosing brain death in potential organ donors [**are** / **is**]⁸¹⁾, no doubt, to ease public fears of a [**mature** / **premature**]⁸²⁾ diagnosis of brain death for the purpose of obtaining organs. But it is [**questionable** / **unquestionable**]⁸³⁾ whether these requirements reduce public suspicions as much as they create [**them** / **themselves**]⁸⁴⁾. They certainly maintain [**mistaken** / **mistaking**]⁸⁵⁾ beliefs that [**diagnose** / **diagnosing**]⁸⁶⁾ brain death is an [**reliable** / **unreliable**]⁸⁷⁾ process lacking precision. As a matter of consistency, at least, criteria for diagnosing the deaths of organ donors should be exactly the same as for [**that** / **those**]⁸⁸⁾ for whom [**immediate** / **intermediate**]⁸⁹⁾ burial or cremation is intended.

일부 국가는 장기 이식, 즉 다른 사람에게 장기를 전달하는 것을 고려 중일 때 뇌사를 결정하는 것에 대한 더 엄격한 지침을 제안했다. 몇몇 유럽 국가에는 잠재적 기증자의 경우 의사 팀 전체가 사망 진단에 동의해야 한다고 명시하는 법적 요건들이 있다. 잠재적인 장기 기증자의 뇌사 진단에 대한 이러한 엄격한 규정들의 이유는 의심할 바 없이 장기 확보를 위한 너무 이른 뇌사 진단에 대한 대중의 두려움을 완화하기 위한 것이다. 하지만 이러한 요건들이 대중의 의심을 만들어 내는 만큼 그것을 줄여 주는지는 의문이다. 그것들은 뇌사 진단이 정확성이 결여된 신뢰하기 어려운 과정이라는 잘못된 믿음을 확실히 유지시킨다. 적어도 일관성의 이유로 장기 기증자의 사망 진단 기준은 즉각적인 매장 또는 화장이 예정된 사람들에 대한 그것과 정확히 동일해야 한다.

30

The term minimalism gives a negative impression to some people who think that it is all about [**sacrificing** / **treasuring**]⁹⁰⁾ valuable possessions. This insecurity naturally stems from their [**attachment** / **aversion**]⁹¹⁾ to their possessions. It is difficult to distance [**one** / **oneself**]⁹²⁾ from something that has been around for quite some time. Being an emotional animal, human beings give meaning to the things around them. So, the question arising here is that if minimalism will hurt one's emotions, why become a minimalist? The answer is very simple; the assumption of the question is [**fundamental** / **fundamentally**]⁹³⁾ wrong. Minimalism does not hurt emotions. You might feel a bit sad [**during** / **while**]⁹⁴⁾ getting rid of a useless item but sooner than later, this feeling will [**be overcome** / **overcome**]⁹⁵⁾ by the joy of clarity. Minimalists never argue that you should [**cherish** / **leave**]⁹⁶⁾ every convenience of the modern era. They are of the view that you only need to [**eliminate** / **embrace**]⁹⁷⁾ stuff that is unused or not going to [**be used** / **use**]⁹⁸⁾ in the near future.

미니멀리즘이라는 용어는 그것을 소중한 소유물을 희생하는 것에 관한 것으로만 생각하는 일부 사람들에게 부정적인 인상을 준다. 이러한 불안은 자신의 소유물에 대한 애착에서 자연스럽게 비롯된다. 꽤 오랫동안 곁에 있어 왔던 것으로부터 자신을 멀리 두는 것은 어렵다. 감정의 동물이기 때문에, 인간은 그들의 곁에 있는 물건에 의미를 부여한다. 그래서 여기서 생기는 질문은 미니멀리즘이 사람의 감정을 상하게 한다면 왜 미니멀리스트가 되느냐는 것이다. 대답은 매우 간단하다. 그 질문의 가정은 근본적으로 틀리다. 미니멀리즘은 감정을 상하게 하지 않는다. 여러분은 쓸모 없는 물건을 치우면서 조금 슬퍼할 수도 있지만 머지않아 이 느낌은 명료함의 기쁨으로 극복될 것이다. 미니멀리스트는 여러분이 현대의 모든 편의를 버려야 한다고 주장하지 않는다. 그들은 여러분이 사용되지 않거나 가까운 미래에 사용되지 않을 물건을 없애기만 하면 된다는 견해를 가지고 있다.

31

A remarkable characteristic of the visual system is that it has the ability of adapting [**it / itself**]⁹⁹⁾. Psychologist George M. Stratton made this clear in an [**expressive / impressive**]¹⁰⁰⁾ self-experiment. Stratton wore [**reversed / reversing**]¹⁰¹⁾ glasses for several days, which literally turned the world upside down for him. In the beginning, this caused him great difficulties: just putting food in his mouth with a fork was a challenge for him. With time, however, his visual system [**adjusted / resisted**]¹⁰²⁾ to the new stimuli from reality, and he was able to act [**normal / normally**]¹⁰³⁾ in his environment again, even seeing it upright when he concentrated. As he took off his reversing glasses, he was again [**confronted / confronting**]¹⁰⁴⁾ with problems: he used the wrong hand when he wanted to reach for something, for example. Fortunately, Stratton could [**converse / reverse**]¹⁰⁵⁾ the perception, and he did not have to wear reversing glasses for the rest of his life. For him, everything returned to normal after one day.

시각 체계의 두드러진 특징은 스스로 적응하는 능력이 있다는 것이다. 심리학자 George M. Stratton은 인상적인 자가 실험에서 이것을 분명히 했다. Stratton은 며칠 동안 반전 안경을 착용했는데 그 안경은 말 그대로 그에게 세상을 뒤집어 놓았다. 처음에 이것은 그에게 큰 어려움을 초래하였다. 포크로 음식을 입에 넣는 것조차 그에게는 도전이었다. 그러나 시간이 지나면서 그의 시각 체계는 현실의 새로운 자극에 적응했고, 그가 집중했을 때는 심지어 똑바로 보면서, 다시 자신의 환경에서 정상적으로 행동할 수 있었다. 반전 안경을 벗었을 때 그는 다시 문제에 직면했다. 예를 들어 그가 무언가를 잡기를 원할 때 그는 반대 손을 사용했다. 다행히 Stratton은 지각을 뒤집을 수 있었고 평생 반전 안경을 착용하지 않아도 되었다. 그에게 하루 만에 모든 것이 정상으로 돌아왔다.

32

Participants in a study [**asked / were asked**]¹⁰⁶⁾ to answer questions like "Why does the moon have phases?" Half the participants were told to search for the answers on the internet, while [**the other / other**]¹⁰⁷⁾ half weren't allowed to do so. Then, in the second part of the study, all of the participants **were presented**[**/ presented**]¹⁰⁸⁾ with a new set of questions, such as "Why does Swiss cheese have holes?" These questions were unrelated to the [**one / ones**]¹⁰⁹⁾ asked during the first part of the study, so participants who used the internet had absolutely no advantage [**on / over**]¹¹⁰⁾ those who hadn't. You would think that both sets of participants would be [**equal / equally**]¹¹¹⁾ sure or unsure about how well they could answer the new questions. But those who used the internet in the first part of the study rated [**them / themselves**]¹¹²⁾ as more knowledgeable than those who hadn't, even about questions they [**hadn't / haven't**]¹¹³⁾ searched online for. The study suggests that [**have / having**]¹¹⁴⁾ access to unrelated information was enough to pump up their intellectual confidence.

한 연구의 참가자들이 '달은 왜 상을 가지고 있을까'와 같은 질문들에 답하도록 요청받았다. 참가자의 절반은 인터넷에서 답을 검색하라는 말을 들었고 나머지 절반은 그렇게 하도록 허용되지 않았다. 그다음, 연구의 두 번째 단계에서 모든 참가자는 '스위스 치즈에는 왜 구멍이 있을까'와 같은 일련의 새로운 질문들을 제시받았다. 이 질문들은 연구의 첫 번째 단계에서 질문받았던 것들과는 관련이 없어서 인터넷을 사용한 참가자들은 그러지 않은 참가자들보다 이점이 전혀 없었다. 여러분은 두 집단의 참가자들이 새로운 질문들에 얼마나 잘 대답할 수 있을지에 대해 동일한 정도로 확신하거나 확신하지 못할 것으로 생각할 것이다. 그러나 연구의 첫 번째 단계에서 인터넷을 사용했던 참가자들은 자신이 온라인에서 검색하지 않았던 질문들에 대해서조차 그러지 않았던 참가자들보다 스스로가 더 많이 알고 있다고 평가했다. 이 연구는 관련 없는 정보에 접근하는 것이 그들의 지적 자신감을 부풀리기에 충분했다는 것을 시사한다.

33

[**Anthropologist** / **Archaeologist**]115) Gregory Bateson suggests that we tend to understand the world by focusing in on particular features within it. Take platypuses. We might zoom in so [**close** / **closely**]116) to their fur that each hair appears [**different** / **differently**]117). We might also zoom out to the [**intent** / **extent**]118) where it appears as a single, uniform object. We might take the platypus as an individual, or we might treat it as part of a larger unit such as a species or an ecosystem. It's possible to move between many of these perspectives, [**although** / **because**]119) we may need some additional tools and skills to zoom in on individual pieces of hair or zoom out to entire ecosystems. [**Crucial** / **Crucially**]120), however, we can only [**take over** / **take up**]121) one perspective at a time. We can pay attention to the [**varied** / **varying**]122) behavior of individual animals, look at what [**unite** / **unites**]123) them into a single species, or look at them as part of bigger ecological patterns. Every possible [**perspective** / **perspectives**]124) involves emphasizing certain aspects and ignoring others.

인류학자 Gregory Bateson은 우리가 세상 안의 특정한 특징에 초점을 맞춤으로써 세상을 이해하는 경향이 있다고 제안한다. 오리너구리를 예로 들어보자. 우리가 그들의 털을 매우 가까이 확대하면 각 가닥이 다르게 보인다. 우리는 또한 그것이 하나의 동일한 개체로 보이는 정도까지 축소할 수도 있다. 우리는 오리너구리를 개체로 취급할 수도 있고 종 또는 생태계와 같이 더 큰 단위의 일부로 취급할 수도 있다. 비록 개별 머리카락을 확대하거나 전체 생태계로 축소하기 위해 몇 가지 추가 도구와 기술이 필요할지도 모르지만, 이러한 많은 관점 사이를 이동하는 것은 가능하다. 그러나 결정적으로 우리는 한 번에 하나의 관점만 취할 수 있다. 우리는 개별 동물의 다양한 행동에 주의를 기울일 수 있고, 그들을 단일 종으로 통합하는 것을 살펴볼 수도 있고, 더 큰 생태학적 패턴의 일부로서 그들을 살펴볼 수도 있다. 가능한 모든 관점은 특정 측면을 강조하고 다른 측면을 외면하는 것을 포함한다.

34

Plato's realism [**includes** / **including**]125) all aspects of experience but is most easily explained by considering the nature of mathematical and geometrical objects such as circles. He asked the question, what is a circle? You might indicate a particular example [**carved** / **carving**]126) into stone or drawn in the sand. However, Plato would point out that, if you looked [**close** / **closely**]127) enough, you would see that neither it, nor indeed any physical circle, was perfect. They all [**possessed** / **possessing**]128) flaws, and all were subject to change and [**decayed** / **decaying**]129) with time. So how can we talk about perfect circles if we cannot actually see or touch them? Plato's extraordinary answer was that the world we see is a [**rich** / **poor**]130) reflection of a deeper unseen reality of Forms, or universals, where perfect cats chase perfect mice in perfect circles around perfect rocks. Plato believed that the Forms or universals are the true reality that exists in an [**invisible** / **visible**]131) but perfect world [**beyond** / **in**]132) our senses.

플라톤의 실재론은 경험의 모든 측면을 포함하지만, 원과 같은 수학적이고 기하학적인 대상의 특성을 고려함으로써 가장 쉽게 설명된다. 그는 '원이란 무엇인가'라는 질문을 했다. 여러분은 돌에 새겨져 있거나 모래에 그려진 특정한 예를 가리킬 수 있다. 그러나 플라톤은 여러분이 충분히 면밀히 관찰한다면, 여러분이 그 어느 것도, 진정 어떤 물리적인 원도 완벽하지 않다는 것을 알게 될 것이라고 지적할 것이다. 그것들 모두는 결함을 가지고 있었고, 모두 변화의 영향을 받고 시간이 지남에 따라 쇠하였다. 그렇다면, 우리가 완벽한 원을 실제로 보거나 만질 수 없다면, 그것에 대해 어떻게 이야기할 수 있을까? 플라톤의 비범한 대답은 우리가 보는 세상이 완벽한 고양이가 완벽한 암석 주변에서 완벽한 원을 그리며 완벽한 쥐를 쫓는 '형상' 또는 '보편자'라는 더 깊은 보이지 않는 실재의 불충분한 반영물이라는 것이다. 플라톤은 '형상' 또는 '보편자'가 보이지 않지만 우리의 감각을 넘어선 완벽한 세계에 존재하는 진정한 실재라고 믿었다.

35

In statistics, the law of large numbers [**describe / describes**]133) a situation [**where / which**]134) having more data is better for making predictions. According to it, the more often an experiment [**conducted / is conducted,**]135) the closer the average of the results can be expected to match the true state of the world. For instance, on your first encounter with the game of roulette, you may have beginner's luck after betting on 7. But the more often you repeat this bet, the closer the [**relative / relatively**]136) frequency of wins and losses [**are / is**]137) expected to approach the true chance of winning, [**meaning / means**]138) that your luck will at some point fade away. [**Conversely / Similarly**]139), car insurers collect large amounts of data to figure out the chances [**that / where**]140) drivers will cause accidents, depending on their age, region, or car brand. Both casinos and insurance industries rely on the law of large numbers [**balance / to balance**]141) individual losses.

통계학에서 대수의 법칙은 더 많은 데이터를 갖는 것이 예측하는 데 더 좋은 상황을 설명한다. 그것에 따르면 실험이 더 자주 수행될수록 그 결과의 평균이 세상의 실제 상태에 더 맞춰지는 것으로 예상될 수 있다. 예를 들어 룰렛 게임을 처음 접했을 때 7에 베팅한 후 여러분은 초보자의 운이 있을 수 있다. 하지만 당신이 이 베팅을 더 자주 반복할수록 승패의 상대적인 빈도가 진짜 승률에 더 가까워질 것으로 예상되는데 이는 당신의 운이 어느 순간 사라진다는 것을 의미한다. 마찬가지로 자동차 보험사는 운전자가 그들의 연령, 지역 또는 자동차 브랜드에 따라 사고를 일으킬 확률을 파악하기 위해 많은 양의 데이터를 수집한다. 카지노와 보험 산업 모두 개별 손실의 균형을 맞추기 위해 대수의 법칙에 의존한다.

36

The adolescent brain is not fully developed [**since / until**]142) its early twenties. This means the way the adolescents' decision-making circuits integrate and [**process / processing**]143) information may put them at [**a disadvantage / an advantage**]144). One of their brain regions that [**mature / matures**]145) later is the prefrontal cortex, which is the control center, [**tasked / tasking**]146) with thinking ahead and evaluating consequences. It is the area of the brain responsible for preventing you [**from / to**]147) sending off an initial angry text and modifying it with kinder words. On the other hand, the limbic system matures earlier, [**playing / plays**]148) a central role in processing emotional responses. Because of its earlier development, it is [**less / more**]149) likely to influence decision-making. Decision-making in the adolescent brain is led by emotional factors more than the perception of consequences. [**Because / Due**]150) to these differences, there is an imbalance between feeling-based decision-making ruled by the more mature limbic system and logical-based decision-making by the not-yet-mature prefrontal cortex. This may explain why some teens are [**less / more**]151) likely to make bad decisions.

청소년기의 뇌는 20대 초반까지는 완전히 발달하지 않는다. 이것은 청소년의 의사 결정 회로가 정보를 통합하고 처리하는 방식이 그들을 불리하게 만들 수 있음을 의미한다. 나중에 성숙하는 뇌 영역 중 하나는 통제 센터인 전전두엽 피질이며, 그것은 미리 생각하고 결과를 평가하는 임무를 맡고 있다. 그것은 당신이 초기의 화가 난 문자를 보내는 것을 막고 그것을 더 친절한 단어로 수정하게 하는 역할을 하는 뇌의 영역이다. 반면 대뇌변연계는 더 일찍 성숙하여 정서적 반응을 처리하는 데 중심적인 역할을 한다. 그것의 더 이른 발달로 인해 그것이 의사 결정에 영향을 미칠 가능성이 더 높다. 청소년기의 뇌에서 의사 결정은 결과의 인식보다 감정적인 요인에 의해 이끌어진다. 이러한 차이점 때문에 더 성숙한 대뇌변연계에 의해 지배되는 감정 기반 의사 결정과 아직 성숙하지 않은 전전두엽 피질에 의한 논리 기반 의사 결정 사이에는 불균형이 존재한다. 이것은 왜 일부 십 대들이 그릇된 결정을 내릴 가능성이 더 높은지를 설명해 줄 수 있다.

37

Despite the remarkable progress in deep-learning based facial recognition approaches in recent years, in terms of identification performance, they still have limitations. These limitations relate to the database [**used / using**]152) in the learning stage. If the [**selected / selecting**]153) database does not contain enough instances, the result may be systematically [**affected / affect**]154). For example, the performance of a facial biometric system may [**decrease / increase**]155) if the person to [**be identified / identify**]156) was enrolled over 10 years ago. The factor to consider is that this person may experience changes in the texture of the face, particularly with the appearance of wrinkles and [**sagging / sagged**]157) skin. These changes may [**be highlighted / highlight**]158) by weight gain or loss. To counteract this problem, researchers [**had / have**]159) developed models for face aging or digital de-aging. It [**is used / used**]160) to compensate for the differences in facial characteristics, which appear over a given time period.

최근 몇 년 동안 딥 러닝 기반의 얼굴 인식 접근법의 눈에 띄는 발전에도 불구하고, 식별 성능 측면에서 여전히 그것은 한계를 가지고 있다. 이러한 한계는 학습 단계에서 사용되는 데이터베이스와 관련이 있다. 선택된 데이터베이스가 충분한 사례를 포함하지 않으면 그 결과가 시스템적으로 영향을 받을 수 있다. 예를 들어 식별될 사람이 10년도 더 전에 등록된 경우 안면 생체 측정 시스템의 성능이 저하될 수 있다. 고려해야 할 요인은 이 사람이 특히 주름과 처진 피부가 나타나는 것을 동반한 얼굴의 질감 변화를 경험할 수 있다는 것이다. 이러한 변화는 체중 증가 또는 감소에 의해 두드러질 수 있다. 이 문제에 대응하기 위해 연구자들은 얼굴 노화나 디지털 노화 완화의 모델을 개발했다. 그것은 주어진 기간 동안 나타나는 얼굴 특성의 차이를 보완하는 데 사용된다.

38

The decline in the diversity of our food is an [**entire / entirely**]161) human-made process. The biggest loss of crop diversity came in the decades that [**followed / following**]162) the Second World War. In an attempt to save millions [**at / from**]163) extreme hunger, crop scientists found ways to produce grains such as rice and wheat on an enormous scale. And thousands of traditional varieties [**replaced / were replaced**]164) by a small number of new super-productive ones. The strategy worked spectacularly well, at least to begin with. [**Because / Because of**]165) it, grain production tripled, and between 1970 and 2020 the human population more than doubled. [**Leaving / Left**]166) the contribution of that strategy to one side, the danger of creating more uniform crops [**are / is**]167) that they are more [**at / in**]168) risk when it comes to disasters. Specifically, a global food system that depends on just a narrow selection of plants [**have / has**]169) a [**greater / smaller**]170) chance of not being able to survive diseases, pests and climate extremes.

우리 음식의 다양성의 감소는 전적으로 인간이 만든 과정이다. 농작물 다양성의 가장 큰 손실은 제2차 세계 대전 이후 수십 년 동안 나타났다. 수백만 명의 사람들을 극도의 배고픔에서 구하고자 하는 시도에서 작물 과학자들이 쌀과 밀과 같은 곡물을 엄청난 규모로 생산하는 방법을 발견했다. 그리고 수천 개의 전통적인 종들은 소수의 새로운 초(超)생산적인 종들로 대체되었다. 그 전략은 적어도 처음에는 굉장히 잘 작동했다. 그것 때문에 곡물 생산량은 세 배가 되었고 1970년과 2020년 사이에 인구는 두 배 이상 증가했다. 그 전략의 기여를 차치하고, 더 획일적인 작물을 만드는 것의 위험은 그것들이 재앙과 관련해 더 큰 위험에 처한다는 것이다. 특히 농작물의 좁은 선택에만 의존하는 세계적인 식량 시스템은 질병, 해충 및 기후 위기로부터 생존하지 못할 더 높은 가능성을 가진다.

39

Between 1940 and 2000, Cuba [**ruled / was ruled**]¹⁷¹⁾ the world baseball scene. They won 25 of the first 28 World Cups and 3 of 5 Olympic Games. The Cubans [**known / were known**]¹⁷²⁾ for wearing uniforms covered in red from head to toe, a strong contrast to the more [**conservative / progressive**]¹⁷³⁾ North American style featuring grey or white pants. Not only [**are / were**]¹⁷⁴⁾ their athletic talents [**inferior / superior**]¹⁷⁵⁾, the Cubans appeared even stronger from just the colour of their uniforms. A game would not even start and the [**oppose / opposing**]¹⁷⁶⁾ team would already be scared. A few years ago, Cuba [**altered / altering**]¹⁷⁷⁾ that uniform style, modernizing it and perhaps [**confirming / conforming**]¹⁷⁸⁾ to other countries' style; interestingly, the national team has declined since that time. The country that ruled international baseball for decades [**had / has**]¹⁷⁹⁾ not been on top since [**that / those**]¹⁸⁰⁾ uniform change. Traditions are important for a team; while a team brand or image can adjust to keep up with present times, if it [**abandon / abandons**]¹⁸¹⁾ or [**neglect / neglects**]¹⁸²⁾ its roots, negative effects can surface.

1940년과 2000년 사이에 쿠바는 세계 야구계를 지배했다. 그들은 첫 28회의 월드컵 중 25회와 5회의 올림픽 게임 중 3회를 이겼다. 쿠바인들은 머리부터 발끝까지 빨간색으로 뒤덮인 유니폼을 입는 것으로 알려져 있었는데, 이것은 회색이나 흰색 바지를 특징으로 하는 더 보수적인 북미 스타일과 강한 대조를 이룬다. 쿠바인들의 운동 재능이 뛰어났을 뿐만 아니라 그들은 그들의 유니폼의 색깔만으로도 훨씬 더 강하게 보였다. 경기가 시작하지 않았는데도 상대 팀은 이미 겁에 질리곤 했다. 몇 년 전 쿠바는 유니폼을 현대화하고 아마도 다른 나라의 스타일에 맞추면서 그 유니폼 스타일을 바꿨다. 흥미롭게도 국가 대표 팀은 그 시기부터 쇠퇴해 왔다. 수십 년 동안 국제 야구를 지배했던 그 나라는 그 유니폼 교체 이후로 정상에 오른 적이 없었다. 전통은 팀에게 중요하다. 팀 브랜드나 이미지는 현시대를 따르기 위해 조정될 수 있지만 팀이 그들의 뿌리를 버리거나 무시하면 부정적인 영향이 표면화될 수 있다.

40

Many of the first models of cultural evolution drew noticeable connections between culture and genes by using concepts [**at / from**]¹⁸³⁾ theoretical population genetics and [**apply / applying**]¹⁸⁴⁾ them to culture. Cultural patterns of transmission, innovation, and selection are conceptually likened to genetic processes of transmission, mutation, and selection. However, these approaches had to [**be modified / motified**]¹⁸⁵⁾ to account for the differences between genetic and cultural transmission. For example, we do not expect the cultural transmission [**follow / to follow**]¹⁸⁶⁾ the rules of genetic transmission strictly. If two biological parents have different forms of a cultural trait, their child is not necessarily equally likely to [**acquire / inquire**]¹⁸⁷⁾ the mother's or father's form of that trait. Further, a child can acquire cultural traits not only from [**its / their**]¹⁸⁸⁾ parents but also from nonparental adults and peers; thus, the frequency of a cultural trait in the population is [**irrelevant / relevant**]¹⁸⁹⁾ beyond just the probability that an individual's parents had that trait.

문화 진화의 많은 초기 모델들은 이론 집단 유전학의 개념을 사용함으로써 그리고 그것들을 문화에 적용함으로써 문화와 유전자 사이의 주목할 만한 접점을 이끌어 냈다. 전파, 혁신, 선택의 문화적 방식은 전달, 돌연변이, 선택의 유전적 과정과 개념적으로 유사하다. 그러나 이러한 접근법은 유전자의 전달과 문화 전파 사이의 차이점을 설명하기 위해 수정되어야만 했다. 예를 들어, 우리는 문화 전파가 유전자 전달의 규칙을 엄격하게 따를 것이라고 예상하지 않는다. 만약 두 명의 생물학적인 부모가 서로 다른 문화적인 특성의 형태를 가진다면, 그들의 자녀는 반드시 엄마 혹은 아빠의 그 특성의 형태를 동일하게 획득하지 않을 수 있다. 더욱이 아이는 문화적인 특성을 부모로부터 뿐만 아니라 부모가 아닌 성인이나 또래로부터도 얻을 수 있다. 따라서 집단의 문화적인 특성의 빈도는 단지 한 개인의 부모가 그 특성을 가졌을 확률을 넘어서 유의미하다.

41~42

A ball thrown into the air [**acts / is acted**]¹⁹⁰⁾ upon by the initial force given it, persisting as inertia of movement and tending to carry it in the same straight line, and by the constant pull of gravity downward, as well as by the resistance of the air. It moves, accordingly, in a curved path. Now the path does not represent the working of any particular force; there is simply the combination of the three elementary forces mentioned; but in a real sense, there is something in the total action besides the [**isolated / isolating**]¹⁹¹⁾ action of three forces, namely, their joint action. In the same way, when two or more human individuals are together, their [**mature / mutual**]¹⁹²⁾ relationships and their arrangement into a group are things which would not be revealed if we confined our attention to each individual separately. The significance of group behavior is greatly [**increased / increasing**]¹⁹³⁾ in the case of human beings by the fact that some of the tendencies to action of the individual [**are / is**]¹⁹⁴⁾ related definitely to other persons, and could not be aroused except by other persons acting as stimuli. An individual in [**complete / incomplete**]¹⁹⁵⁾ isolation would not reveal their competitive tendencies, their tendencies towards the opposite sex, their protective tendencies towards children. This shows that the traits of human nature do not fully appear until the individual is brought into relationships with [**other / the other**]¹⁹⁶⁾ individuals.

공중으로 던져진 공은 초기에 그것에 주어진 힘에 의해 움직여지는데, 운동의 관성으로 지속하며 같은 직선으로 나아가려는 경향을 보이고, 공기의 저항뿐만 아니라 아래로 지속적으로 당기는 중력에 의해서도 움직여진다. 그에 맞춰 공은 곡선의 경로로 움직인다. 이제 그 경로는 어떤 특정한 힘의 작동을 나타내지는 않는다. 언급된 세 가지 기본적인 힘의 결합이 존재할 뿐이다. 하지만 사실은 세 가지 힘의 고립된 작용 외에 전체적인 작용에 무언가가 있다. 이름하여 그들의 공동 작용이다. 같은 방식으로, 두 명 혹은 그 이상의 인간 개인이 같이 있을 때 그들의 상호 관계와 그들의 집단으로의 배치는 만약 우리가 관심을 개별적으로 각각의 개인에게 국한시킨다면 드러나지 않을 것이다. 개인 행동의 몇몇 경향은 명백하게 다른 사람들과 관련이 있고 자극으로 작동하는 다른 사람들 없이는 유발되지 않을 수 있다는 사실로 인해 그룹 행동의 중요성이 인간의 경우 크게 증가된다. 완전한 고립 속의 개인은 그들의 경쟁적인 성향, 이성에 대한 그들의 성향, 아이에 대한 그들의 보호적 성향을 드러내지 않을 것이다. 이것은 개인이 다른 개인과의 관계에 관여될 때까지는 인간 본성의 특성이 완전히 나타나지 않는다는 것을 보여 준다.

43~45

There once lived a man in a village who was not happy [**at / with**]197) his life. He was always troubled by one problem or [**another / the other**]198). One day, a saint with his guards stopped by his village. Many people heard the news and started going to him with their problems. The man also decided to visit the saint. Even after reaching the saint's place in the morning, he didn't get the opportunity to meet him till evening. When the man got to meet the saint, he confessed that he was very unhappy with life [**because / because of**]199) problems always [**surrounded / surrounding**]200) him, like workplace tension or worries about his health. He said, "Please give me a solution [**so that / that**]201) all the problems in my life will end and I can live peacefully." The saint smiled and said that he would answer the request the next day. But the saint also asked if the man could do a small job for him. He told the man to take care of a hundred camels in his group that night, [**said / saying**]202) "When all hundred camels sit down, you can go to sleep." The man agreed. The next morning when the saint met that man, he asked if the man had slept well. Tired and sad, the man replied that he couldn't sleep even for a moment. In fact, the man tried very hard but couldn't make all the camels sit at the same time because every time he made one camel sit, [**another / the other**]203) would stand up. The saint told him, "You realized that no matter how hard you try, you can't make all the camels sit down. If one problem is solved, for some reason, another will [**arise / rise**]204) like the camels did. So, humans should enjoy life despite these problems."

옛날 어느 마을에 자신의 삶이 행복하지 않은 한 남자가 살았다. 그는 항상 하나 혹은 또 다른 문제로 어려움을 겪었다. 어느 날 한 성자가 그의 경호인들과 함께 그의 마을에 들렀다. 많은 사람들이 그 소식을 듣고 그들의 문제를 가지고 그에게 가기 시작했다. 그 남자 역시 성자를 방문하기로 결정했다. 아침에 성자가 있는 곳에 도착하고 난 후에도 그는 저녁 때까지 그를 만날 기회를 얻지 못했다. 마침내 그가 성자를 만났을 때 그는 직장 내 긴장이나 건강에 대한 걱정과 같이 항상 문제가 자기를 둘러싸고 있어서 삶이 매우 불행하다고 고백했다. 그는 "나의 삶의 모든 문제가 끝나고 제가 평화롭게 살 수 있도록 제발 해결책을 주세요."라고 말했다. 성자는 미소 지으면서 그가 다음 날 그 요청에 답해 주겠다고 말했다. 그런데 성자는 또한 그 남자가 그를 위해 작은 일을 해 줄 수 있는지 물었다. 성자는 그 남자에게 "백 마리 낙타 모두가 자리에 앉으면 당신은 자러 가도 좋습니다."라고 말하면서 그날 밤에 그의 일행에 있는 백 마리 낙타를 돌봐 달라고 말했다. 그 남자는 동의했다. 다음 날 아침에 성자가 그 남자를 만났을 때 그는 남자가 잠을 잘 잤는지 물어보았다. 피곤해하고 슬퍼하면서 남자는 한순간도 잠을 자지 못했다고 대답했다. 사실 그 남자는 아주 열심히 노력했지만 그가 낙타 한 마리를 앉힐 때마다 다른 낙타 한 마리가 일어섰기 때문에 모든 낙타를 동시에 앉게 할 수 없었다. 그 성자는 그에게 "당신이 아무리 열심히 노력하더라도 모든 낙타를 앉게 만들 수는 없다는 것을 깨달았습니다. 만약 한 가지 문제가 해결되면 낙타가 그런 것처럼 어떤 이유로 또 다른 문제가 일어날 것입니다. 그래서 인간은 이러한 문제에도 불구하고 삶을 즐겨야 합니다."라고 말했다.

18

Dear Ms. MacAlpine,

I was so excited to hear [**that** / what]¹⁾ your brand is opening a new shop on Bruns Street next month. I [**have** / had]²⁾ always appreciated the way your brand helps women to feel more stylish and [**confident** / confidently]³⁾. I am writing in response to your ad in the Bruns Journal. I graduated from the Meline School of Fashion and have worked as a sales [**assistant** / assistance]⁴⁾ at LoganMart for the last five years. [**During** / While]⁵⁾ that time, I've developed strong customer service and sales skills, and now I would like to apply for the sales position in your clothing store. I am available for an interview at your earliest [**convenience** / convenient]⁶⁾. I look forward to [hear / **hearing**]⁷⁾ from you. Thank you for reading my letter.

Yours sincerely, Grace Braddock

19

I had never seen a beach with such white sand or water [that / **what**]⁸⁾ was such a beautiful shade of blue. Jane and I set up a blanket on the sand [during / **while**]⁹⁾ looking forward to our ten days of honeymooning on an exotic island. "Look!" Jane waved her hand to point at the beautiful scene before us — and her gold wedding ring went [fly / **flying**]¹⁰⁾ off her hand. I tried [seeing / **to see**]¹¹⁾ where it went, but the sun hit my eyes and I lost track of it. I didn't want to lose her wedding ring, so I started looking in the area where I thought it [**had** / have]¹²⁾ landed. However, the sand was [**so** / such]¹³⁾ fine and I realized that anything heavy, like gold, would quickly sink and might never [**be found** / found]¹⁴⁾ again.

20

The more people have to do unwanted things the more chances [**are** / do]¹⁵⁾ that they create unpleasant environment for themselves and others. If you hate the thing you do but have to do it [hence / **nonetheless**]¹⁶⁾ , you have choice between hating the thing and accepting [**that** / what]¹⁷⁾ it needs to be done. Either way you will do it. [**Doing** / Done]¹⁸⁾ it from place of hatred will develop hatred towards the self and others around you; doing it from the place of [**acceptance** / assistance]¹⁹⁾ will create [passion / **compassion**]²⁰⁾ towards the self and allow for opportunities to find a [**more** / less]²¹⁾ suitable way of accomplishing the task. If you decide to [**accept** / avoid]²²⁾ the fact [**that** / which]²³⁾ your task has to be done, start from recognising that your situation is a gift from life; this will help you [**to see** / seeing]²⁴⁾ it as a lesson in [**acceptance** / resistance]²⁵⁾ .

21

Everyone's heard the expression *don't let the perfect become the enemy of the good*. If you want to get [**over** / **into**]²⁶⁾ an obstacle so that your idea can become the solution-based policy you've long [**dreamed** / **dreamed of**]²⁷⁾, you can't have an all-or-nothing mentality. You have to be willing to [**altar** / **alter**]²⁸⁾ your idea and let others [**effect** / **influence**]²⁹⁾ its outcome. You have to be okay with the outcome [**be** / **being**]³⁰⁾ a little different, even a little [**less** / **more**]³¹⁾ , than you wanted. Say you're pushing for a clean water [**act** / **action**]³²⁾ . Even if what [**emerges** / **submerges**]³³⁾ isn't as well-funded as you wished, or doesn't match how you originally [**conceived** / **deceived**]³⁴⁾ the bill, you'll have still succeeded in ensuring that kids in troubled areas have [**access** / **limit**]³⁵⁾ to clean water. That's what counts, [**that** / **which**]³⁶⁾ *they* will be safer because of your idea and your effort. Is it perfect? No. Is there more work to be done? Absolutely. But in almost every case, helping move the needle [**backward** / **forward**]³⁷⁾ is vastly better than not helping at all.

22

When writing a novel, research for information needs to be done. The thing is that some kinds of fiction [**demand** / **demanding**]³⁸⁾ a higher level of detail: crime fiction, for example, or scientific thrillers. The information is never hard [**finding** / **to find**]³⁹⁾; one website for authors even [**organize** / **organizes**]⁴⁰⁾ trips to police stations, [**in that** / **so that**]⁴¹⁾ crime writers can get it right. Often, a polite letter will earn you [**admission** / **permission**]⁴²⁾ to visit a particular location and record all the details that you need. But remember that you will drive your readers [**in** / **to**]⁴³⁾ boredom if you think [**that** / **what**]⁴⁴⁾ you need to pack everything you discover into your work. The details that matter are those that [**conceal** / **reveal**]⁴⁵⁾ the human experience. The crucial thing is telling a story, [**finding** / **to find**]⁴⁶⁾ the characters, the tension, and the conflict — not the train timetable or the building blueprint.

23

Nearly everything has to go through your mouth to get to the rest of you, from food and air to bacteria and viruses. A healthy mouth can help your body [**get** / **getting**]⁴⁷⁾ what it needs and [**prevent** / **prevents**]⁴⁸⁾ it from harm — with adequate space for air to travel to your lungs, and healthy teeth and gums that prevent harmful microorganisms [**from entering** / **to enter**]⁴⁹⁾ your bloodstream. From the moment you [**are created,** / **created**]⁵⁰⁾, [**aural** / **oral**]⁵¹⁾ health affects every [**aspect** / **aspects**]⁵²⁾ of your life. What happens in the mouth is usually just the tip of the iceberg and a reflection of [**that** / **what**]⁵³⁾ is happening in other parts of the body. Poor oral health can be a cause of a disease that affects the entire body. The microorganisms in an unhealthy mouth can enter the bloodstream and [**travel** / **travels**]⁵⁴⁾ anywhere in the body, [**pose** / **posing**]⁵⁵⁾ serious health risks.

24

Kids tire of their toys, college students get sick of cafeteria food, and sooner or later most of us [lose / to lose]56) interest in our favorite TV shows. The bottom line is [that / what]57) we humans are easily bored. But why should this be true? The answer [lays / lies]58) buried deep in our nerve cells, which [are designed / designed]59) to reduce their initial excited response to stimuli each time they occur. At the same time, these neurons [diminish / enhance]60) their responses to things that change — especially things that change quickly. We probably [evolved / involved]61) this way [because / because of]62) our ancestors got more survival value, for example, from attending to [what / which]63) was moving in a tree (such as a puma) than to the tree itself. Boredom in reaction to an [unchanged / unchanging]64) environment [turns / turned]65) down the level of neural excitation [in that / so that]66) new stimuli (like our ancestor's hypothetical puma threat) stand out [less / more]67). It's the neural equivalent of turning off a front door light to see the fireflies.

26

Frederick Douglass [born / was born]68) into slavery at a farm in Maryland. His full name at birth was Frederick Augustus Washington Bailey. He changed his name to Frederick Douglass after he [successfully / successively]69) escaped from slavery in 1838. He became a leader of the Underground Railroad — a network of people, places, and routes that helped [enslaved / enslaving]70) people escape to the north. He assisted [other / the other]71) runaway slaves until they could safely get to other areas in the north. As a slave, he had taught [him / himself]72) to read and write and he spread that knowledge to other slaves as well. Once free, he became a well-known abolitionist and strong believer in equality for all people [include / including]73) Blacks, Native Americans, women, and recent [emigrants / immigrants]74). He wrote several [autobiographies / autographs]75) [described / describing]76) his experiences as a slave. In addition to all this, he became the first African-American candidate for vice president of the United States.

29

Some countries [had / have]77) proposed tougher guidelines for determining brain death when transplantation — transferring organs to others — [are / is]78) under consideration. In several European countries, there are legal requirements which specify [that / what]79) a whole team of doctors must agree over the diagnosis of death in the case of a [actual / potential]80) donor. The reason for these strict regulations for diagnosing brain death in potential organ donors [are / is]81), no doubt, to ease public fears of a [mature / premature]82) diagnosis of brain death for the purpose of obtaining organs. But it is [questionable / unquestionable]83) whether these requirements reduce public suspicions as much as they create [them / themselves]84). They certainly maintain [mistaken / mistaking]85) beliefs that [diagnose / diagnosing]86) brain death is an [reliable / unreliable]87) process lacking precision. As a matter of consistency, at least, criteria for diagnosing the deaths of organ donors should be exactly the same as for [that / those]88) for whom [immediate / intermediate]89) burial or cremation is intended.

30

The term minimalism gives a negative impression to some people who think that it is all about [**sacrificing / treasuring**]90) valuable possessions. This insecurity naturally stems from their [**attachment / aversion**]91) to their possessions. It is difficult to distance [**one / oneself**]92) from something that has been around for quite some time. Being an emotional animal, human beings give meaning to the things around them. So, the question arising here is that if minimalism will hurt one's emotions, why become a minimalist? The answer is very simple; the assumption of the question is [**fundamental / fundamentally**]93) wrong. Minimalism does not hurt emotions. You might feel a bit sad [**during / while**]94) getting rid of a useless item but sooner than later, this feeling will [**be overcome / overcome**]95) by the joy of clarity. Minimalists never argue that you should [**cherish / leave**]96) every convenience of the modern era. They are of the view that you only need to [**eliminate / embrace**]97) stuff that is unused or not going to [**be used / use**]98) in the near future.

31

A remarkable characteristic of the visual system is that it has the ability of adapting [**it / itself**]99). Psychologist George M. Stratton made this clear in an [**expressive / impressive**]100) self-experiment. Stratton wore [**reversed / reversing**]101) glasses for several days, which literally turned the world upside down for him. In the beginning, this caused him great difficulties: just putting food in his mouth with a fork was a challenge for him. With time, however, his visual system [**adjusted / resisted**]102) to the new stimuli from reality, and he was able to act [**normal / normally**]103) in his environment again, even seeing it upright when he concentrated. As he took off his reversing glasses, he was again [**confronted / confronting**]104) with problems: he used the wrong hand when he wanted to reach for something, for example. Fortunately, Stratton could [**converse / reverse**]105) the perception, and he did not have to wear reversing glasses for the rest of his life. For him, everything returned to normal after one day.

32

Participants in a study [**asked / were asked**]106) to answer questions like "Why does the moon have phases?" Half the participants were told to search for the answers on the internet, while [**the other / other**]107) half weren't allowed to do so. Then, in the second part of the study, all of the participants **were presented**[**/ presented**]108) with a new set of questions, such as "Why does Swiss cheese have holes?" These questions were unrelated to the [**one / ones**]109) asked during the first part of the study, so participants who used the internet had absolutely no advantage [**on / over**]110) those who hadn't. You would think that both sets of participants would be [**equal / equally**]111) sure or unsure about how well they could answer the new questions. But those who used the internet in the first part of the study rated [**them / themselves**]112) as more knowledgeable than those who hadn't, even about questions they [**hadn't / haven't**]113) searched online for. The study suggests that [**have / having**]114) access to unrelated information was enough to pump up their intellectual confidence.

33

[**Anthropologist** / **Archaeologist**]¹¹⁵⁾ Gregory Bateson suggests that we tend to understand the world by focusing in on particular features within it. Take platypuses. We might zoom in so [**close** / **closely**]¹¹⁶⁾ to their fur that each hair appears [**different** / **differently**]¹¹⁷⁾. We might also zoom out to the [**intent** / **extent**]¹¹⁸⁾ where it appears as a single, uniform object. We might take the platypus as an individual, or we might treat it as part of a larger unit such as a species or an ecosystem. It's possible to move between many of these perspectives, [**although** / **because**]¹¹⁹⁾ we may need some additional tools and skills to zoom in on individual pieces of hair or zoom out to entire ecosystems. [**Crucial** / **Crucially**]¹²⁰⁾, however, we can only [**take over** / **take up**]¹²¹⁾ one perspective at a time. We can pay attention to the [**varied** / **varying**]¹²²⁾ behavior of individual animals, look at what [**unite** / **unites**]¹²³⁾ them into a single species, or look at them as part of bigger ecological patterns. Every possible [**perspective** / **perspectives**]¹²⁴⁾ involves emphasizing certain aspects and ignoring others.

34

Plato's realism [**includes** / **including**]¹²⁵⁾ all aspects of experience but is most easily explained by considering the nature of mathematical and geometrical objects such as circles. He asked the question, what is a circle? You might indicate a particular example [**carved** / **carving**]¹²⁶⁾ into stone or drawn in the sand. However, Plato would point out that, if you looked [**close** / **closely**]¹²⁷⁾ enough, you would see that neither it, nor indeed any physical circle, was perfect. They all [**possessed** / **possessing**]¹²⁸⁾ flaws, and all were subject to change and [**decayed** / **decaying**]¹²⁹⁾ with time. So how can we talk about perfect circles if we cannot actually see or touch them? Plato's extraordinary answer was that the world we see is a [**rich** / **poor**]¹³⁰⁾ reflection of a deeper unseen reality of Forms, or universals, where perfect cats chase perfect mice in perfect circles around perfect rocks. Plato believed that the Forms or universals are the true reality that exists in an [**invisible** / **visible**]¹³¹⁾ but perfect world [**beyond** / **in**]¹³²⁾ our senses.

35

In statistics, the law of large numbers [**describe** / **describes**]¹³³⁾ a situation [**where** / **which**]¹³⁴⁾ having more data is better for making predictions. According to it, the more often an experiment [**conducted** / **is conducted,**]¹³⁵⁾ the closer the average of the results can be expected to match the true state of the world. For instance, on your first encounter with the game of roulette, you may have beginner's luck after betting on 7. But the more often you repeat this bet, the closer the [**relative** / **relatively**]¹³⁶⁾ frequency of wins and losses [**are** / **is**]¹³⁷⁾ expected to approach the true chance of winning, [**meaning** / **means**]¹³⁸⁾ that your luck will at some point fade away. [**Conversely** / **Similarly**]¹³⁹⁾, car insurers collect large amounts of data to figure out the chances [**that** / **where**]¹⁴⁰⁾ drivers will cause accidents, depending on their age, region, or car brand. Both casinos and insurance industries rely on the law of large numbers [**balance** / **to balance**]¹⁴¹⁾ individual losses.

36

The adolescent brain is not fully developed [**since / until**]142) its early twenties. This means the way the adolescents' decision-making circuits integrate and [**process / processing**]143) information may put them at [**a disadvantage / an advantage**]144). One of their brain regions that [**mature / matures**]145) later is the prefrontal cortex, which is the control center, [**tasked / tasking**]146) with thinking ahead and evaluating consequences. It is the area of the brain responsible for preventing you [**from / to**]147) sending off an initial angry text and modifying it with kinder words. On the other hand, the limbic system matures earlier, [**playing / plays**]148) a central role in processing emotional responses. Because of its earlier development, it is [**less / more**]149) likely to influence decision-making. Decision-making in the adolescent brain is led by emotional factors more than the perception of consequences. [**Because / Due**]150) to these differences, there is an imbalance between feeling-based decision-making ruled by the more mature limbic system and logical-based decision-making by the not-yet-mature prefrontal cortex. This may explain why some teens are [**less / more**]151) likely to make bad decisions.

37

Despite the remarkable progress in deep-learning based facial recognition approaches in recent years, in terms of identification performance, they still have limitations. These limitations relate to the database [**used / using**]152) in the learning stage. If the [**selected / selecting**]153) database does not contain enough instances, the result may be systematically [**affected / affect**]154). For example, the performance of a facial biometric system may [**decrease / increase**]155) if the person to [**be identified / identify**]156) was enrolled over 10 years ago. The factor to consider is that this person may experience changes in the texture of the face, particularly with the appearance of wrinkles and [**sagging / sagged**]157) skin. These changes may [**be highlighted / highlight**]158) by weight gain or loss. To counteract this problem, researchers [**had / have**]159) developed models for face aging or digital de-aging. It [**is used / used**]160) to compensate for the differences in facial characteristics, which appear over a given time period.

38

The decline in the diversity of our food is an [**entire / entirely**]161) human-made process. The biggest loss of crop diversity came in the decades that [**followed / following**]162) the Second World War. In an attempt to save millions [**at / from**]163) extreme hunger, crop scientists found ways to produce grains such as rice and wheat on an enormous scale. And thousands of traditional varieties [**replaced / were replaced**]164) by a small number of new super-productive ones. The strategy worked spectacularly well, at least to begin with. [**Because / Because of**]165) it, grain production tripled, and between 1970 and 2020 the human population more than doubled. [**Leaving / Left**]166) the contribution of that strategy to one side, the danger of creating more uniform crops [**are / is**]167) that they are more [**at / in**]168) risk when it comes to disasters. Specifically, a global food system that depends on just a narrow selection of plants [**have / has**]169) a [**greater / smaller**]170) chance of not being able to survive diseases, pests and climate extremes.

39

Between 1940 and 2000, Cuba **[ruled / was ruled]**[171] the world baseball scene. They won 25 of the first 28 World Cups and 3 of 5 Olympic Games. The Cubans **[known / were known]**[172] for wearing uniforms covered in red from head to toe, a strong contrast to the more **[conservative / progressive]**[173] North American style featuring grey or white pants. Not only **[are / were]**[174] their athletic talents **[inferior / superior]**[175], the Cubans appeared even stronger from just the colour of their uniforms. A game would not even start and the **[oppose / opposing]**[176] team would already be scared. A few years ago, Cuba **[altered / altering]**[177] that uniform style, modernizing it and perhaps **[confirming / conforming]**[178] to other countries' style; interestingly, the national team has declined since that time. The country that ruled international baseball for decades **[had / has]**[179] not been on top since **[that / those]**[180] uniform change. Traditions are important for a team; while a team brand or image can adjust to keep up with present times, if it **[abandon / abandons]**[181] or **[neglect / neglects]**[182] its roots, negative effects can surface.

40

Many of the first models of cultural evolution drew noticeable connections between culture and genes by using concepts **[at / from]**[183] theoretical population genetics and **[apply / applying]**[184] them to culture. Cultural patterns of transmission, innovation, and selection are conceptually likened to genetic processes of transmission, mutation, and selection. However, these approaches had to **[be modified / motified]**[185] to account for the differences between genetic and cultural transmission. For example, we do not expect the cultural transmission **[follow / to follow]**[186] the rules of genetic transmission strictly. If two biological parents have different forms of a cultural trait, their child is not necessarily equally likely to **[acquire / inquire]**[187] the mother's or father's form of that trait. Further, a child can acquire cultural traits not only from **[its / their]**[188] parents but also from nonparental adults and peers; thus, the frequency of a cultural trait in the population is **[irrelevant / relevant]**[189] beyond just the probability that an individual's parents had that trait.

41~42

A ball thrown into the air [**acts** / **is acted**]¹⁹⁰⁾ upon by the initial force given it, persisting as inertia of movement and tending to carry it in the same straight line, and by the constant pull of gravity downward, as well as by the resistance of the air. It moves, accordingly, in a curved path. Now the path does not represent the working of any particular force; there is simply the combination of the three elementary forces mentioned; but in a real sense, there is something in the total action besides the [**isolated** / **isolating**]¹⁹¹⁾ action of three forces, namely, their joint action. In the same way, when two or more human individuals are together, their [**mature** / **mutual**]¹⁹²⁾ relationships and their arrangement into a group are things which would not be revealed if we confined our attention to each individual separately. The significance of group behavior is greatly [**increased** / **increasing**]¹⁹³⁾ in the case of human beings by the fact that some of the tendencies to action of the individual [**are** / **is**]¹⁹⁴⁾ related definitely to other persons, and could not be aroused except by other persons acting as stimuli. An individual in [**complete** / **incomplete**]¹⁹⁵⁾ isolation would not reveal their competitive tendencies, their tendencies towards the opposite sex, their protective tendencies towards children. This shows that the traits of human nature do not fully appear until the individual is brought into relationships with [**other** / **the other**]¹⁹⁶⁾ individuals.

43~45

There once lived a man in a village who was not happy [**at** / **with**]¹⁹⁷⁾ his life. He was always troubled by one problem or [**another** / **the other**]¹⁹⁸⁾. One day, a saint with his guards stopped by his village. Many people heard the news and started going to him with their problems. The man also decided to visit the saint. Even after reaching the saint's place in the morning, he didn't get the opportunity to meet him till evening. When the man got to meet the saint, he confessed that he was very unhappy with life [**because** / **because of**]¹⁹⁹⁾ problems always [**surrounded** / **surrounding**]²⁰⁰⁾ him, like workplace tension or worries about his health. He said, "Please give me a solution [**so that** / **that**]²⁰¹⁾ all the problems in my life will end and I can live peacefully." The saint smiled and said that he would answer the request the next day. But the saint also asked if the man could do a small job for him. He told the man to take care of a hundred camels in his group that night, [**said** / **saying**]²⁰²⁾ "When all hundred camels sit down, you can go to sleep." The man agreed. The next morning when the saint met that man, he asked if the man had slept well. Tired and sad, the man replied that he couldn't sleep even for a moment. In fact, the man tried very hard but couldn't make all the camels sit at the same time because every time he made one camel sit, [**another** / **the other**]²⁰³⁾ would stand up. The saint told him, "You realized that no matter how hard you try, you can't make all the camels sit down. If one problem is solved, for some reason, another will [**arise** / **rise**]²⁰⁴⁾ like the camels did. So, humans should enjoy life despite these problems."

2023 고1 11월 모의고사   **1** 회차 :   점 / 315점

1 voca | **2** text | **3** [/] | **4** _____ | **5** quiz 1 | **6** quiz 2 | **7** quiz 3 | **8** quiz 4 | **9** quiz 5

18

I was so excited to hear **t**_____1) your brand is opening a new shop on Bruns Street next month. I **h**_____2) always **a**_____3) the way your brand helps women to feel more stylish and confident. I am writing **i**_____4) **r**_____5) **t**_____6) your ad in the Bruns Journal. I graduated from the Meline School of Fashion and have worked as a sales assistant at LoganMart for the **l**_____7) five years. **D**_____8) that time, I've developed strong customer service and sales skills, and now I would like to apply for the sales position in your clothing store. I am **a**_____9) for an interview at your earliest convenience. I look forward to hearing from you. Thank you for reading my letter.

저는 당신의 브랜드가 다음 달에 Bruns 거리에 새 매장을 연다는 것을 듣고 매우 들떴습니다. 저는 당신의 브랜드가 여성들이 더 멋지고 자신감 있게 느끼도록 도와주는 방식을 항상 높이 평가해 왔습니다. 저는 Bruns Journal에 있는 당신의 광고에 대한 응답으로 편지를 쓰고 있습니다. 저는 Meline 패션 학교를 졸업했고 지난 5년간 LoganMart에서 판매 보조원으로 일해 왔습니다. 그 기간 동안 저는 뛰어난 고객 서비스 및 판매 기술을 발달시켜 왔고, 이제 당신의 의류 매장의 판매직에 지원하고 싶습니다. 저는 당신이 편한 가장 빠른 시간에 인터뷰가 가능합니다. 당신으로부터 대답을 듣게 되기를 기대합니다. 저의 편지를 읽어 주셔서 감사드립니다.

19

I **h**_____10) never **s**_____11) a beach with such white sand or water that was such a beautiful shade of blue. Jane and I set up a blanket on the sand **w**_____12) looking forward to our ten days of honeymooning on an **e**_____13) island. "Look!" Jane waved her hand to point at the beautiful scene before us — and her gold wedding ring went flying off her hand. I tried to see where it went, but the sun hit my eyes and I **l**_____14) **t**_____15) **o**_____16) it. I didn't want to lose her wedding ring, so I started looking in the area where I thought it **h**_____17) **l**_____18). However, the sand was so **f**_____19) and I realized that anything heavy, like gold, would quickly sink and might never **b**_____20) **f**_____21) again.

나는 그렇게 하얀 모래나 그렇게 아름다운 푸른 색조의 바다를 가진 해변을 한 번도 본 적이 없었다. 이국적인 섬에서의 열흘간의 신혼여행을 기대하면서 Jane과 나는 모래 위에 담요를 깔았다. "저기 좀 봐!" Jane이 그녀의 손을 흔들어 우리 앞의 아름다운 풍경을 가리켰다. 그러자 그녀의 금으로 된 결혼반지가 그녀의 손에서 빠져 날아갔다. 나는 그것이 날아간 곳을 보려고 노력했지만, 햇빛이 눈에 들어와 그것의 가던 방향을 놓쳤다. 나는 그녀의 결혼반지를 잃어버리고 싶지 않아서 내가 생각하기에 그것이 떨어졌을 장소를 들여다보기 시작했다. 하지만 모래가 너무 고왔고 나는 금처럼 무거운 것은 빨리 가라앉아 다시는 발견되지 않을 수도 있겠다는 것을 깨달았다.

20

Unfortunately, many people don't take **p**_____ 22) responsibility for their own growth. **I**_____ _23), they simply run the race **l**_____ 24) **o**_____ 25) for them. They do well enough in school to **k**_____ 26) **a**_____ 27). Maybe they **m**_____ 28) **t**_____ 29) get a good job at a well-run company. But so many think and act **a**_____ 30) **i**_____ 31) their learning journey **e**_____ 32) with college. They **h**_____ 33) **c**_____ 34) all the boxes in the life that was laid out for them and now **l**_____ 35) a road map **d**_____ 36) the right ways to move forward and continue to grow. In truth, that's when the journey really begins. When school is finished, your growth becomes **v**_____ 37). Like healthy eating habits or a regular exercise program, you need to commit to it and **d**_____ 38) thought, time, and energy to it. **O**_____ 39), it simply won't happen — and your life and career are likely to stop progressing as a result.

안타깝게도 많은 사람들이 그들 자신의 성장에 대해 개인적인 책임을 지지 않는다. 대신, 그들은 단지 그들에게 놓인 경주를 한다. 그들은 학교에서 계속 발전할 만큼 제법 잘한다. 아마도 그들은 잘 운영되는 회사에서 좋은 일자리를 얻는 것을 해낸다. 하지만 아주 많은 사람들이 마치 그들의 배움의 여정이 대학으로 끝나는 것처럼 생각하고 행동한다. 그들은 그들에게 놓인 삶의 모든 사항을 체크했고 이제는 앞으로 나아가고 계속 성장할 수 있는 올바른 방법을 설명해 주는 로드 맵이 없다. 사실, 그때가 여정이 진정으로 시작되는 때이다. 학교 교육이 끝나면, 여러분의 성장은 자발적이게 된다. 건강한 식습관이나 규칙적인 운동 프로그램처럼 여러분은 그것에 전념하고 그것에 생각, 시간, 그리고 에너지를 쏟을 필요가 있다. 그렇지 않으면 그것은 그냥 일어나지 않을 것이고, 결과적으로 여러분의 삶과 경력이 진전을 멈출 가능성이 있다.

21

Many people take the commonsense view that color is an **o**_____ 40) property of things, or of the light that bounces off them. They say a tree's leaves are green because they **r**_____ 41) green light — a greenness that is just **a**_____ 42) real **a**_____ 43) the leaves. **O**_____ 44) argue that color doesn't **i**_____ 45) the physical world at all but exists only in the eye or mind of the viewer. They maintain that **i**_____ 46) a tree **f**_____ 47) in a forest and no one was there to see it, its leaves would be **c**_____ 48)— and so would everything else. They say there is no such thing as color; there are only the people who see it. Both **p**_____ 49) are, in a way, correct. Color is **o**_____ 50) and **s**_____ 51)— "the place," as Paul Cézanne **p**_____ 52) it, "where our brain and the universe meet." Color is created when light from the world is **r**_____ 53) by the eyes and **i**_____ 54) by the brain.

많은 사람들이 색은 사물 또는 사물로부터 튕겨 나오는 빛의 객관적인 속성이라는 상식적인 견해를 취한다. 그들은 나뭇잎이 녹색 빛(정확히 나뭇잎만큼 진짜인 녹색)을 반사하기 때문에 녹색이라고 말한다. 다른 사람들은 색이 물리적인 세계에 전혀 존재하지 않고 보는 사람의 눈이나 정신 안에만 존재한다고 주장한다. 그들은 만약 나무가 숲에서 쓰러지고 그것을 볼 사람이 아무도 거기에 없다면, 그것의 잎은 색이 없을 것이고, 다른 모든 것들도 그럴 것이라고 주장한다. 그들은 색 같은 '것'은 없고 그것을 보는 사람들만 있다고 말한다. 두 가지 입장 모두 어떤 면에서는 옳다. 색은 객관적이고 '동시에' 주관적이며, Paul Cézanne이 말했듯이 '우리의 뇌와 우주가 만나는 곳'이다. 색은 세상으로부터의 빛이 눈에 의해 등록되고 뇌에 의해 해석될 때 만들어진다.

22

When writing a novel, research for information needs to be done. The thing is that some kinds of fiction d_____55) a higher level of detail: crime fiction, for example, or scientific thrillers. The information is never hard t_____56) f_____57); one website for authors e_____58) organizes trips to police stations, s_____59) t_____60) crime writers can get it right. Often, a polite letter will earn you p_____61) to visit a particular location and r_____62) all the details that you need. But remember that you will d_____63) your readers to boredom if you think t_____64) you need to pack everything you discover into your work. The details that m_____65) are t_____66) that reveal the human experience. The c_____67) thing is telling a story, finding the characters, the tension, and the conflict — not the train timetable or the building blueprint.

소설을 쓸 때 정보를 위한 조사가 행해질 필요가 있다. 문제는 예를 들어 범죄 소설이나 과학 스릴러와 같은 어떤 종류의 소설은 더 높은 수준의 세부 사항을 요구한다는 것이다. 정보는 찾기에 결코 어렵지 않다. 작가들을 위한 한 웹사이트는 범죄물 작가들이 정보를 제대로 얻을 수 있도록 심지어 경찰서로의 탐방을 조직하기도 한다. 종종 정중한 편지는 여러분에게 특정한 장소를 방문하고 필요한 모든 세부 사항을 기록할 수 있는 허가를 얻어 줄 것이다. 하지만 만약 여러분이 발견한 모든 것을 작품에 담아야 한다고 생각할 경우 여러분은 독자들을 지루하게 만들 것이라는 것을 기억하라. 중요한 세부 사항은 인간의 경험을 드러내는 것이다. 중요한 것은 기차 시간표나 건물 청사진이 아니라 인물, 긴장, 그리고 갈등을 찾아가며 이야기를 말하는 것이다.

23

Nearly e_____68) has to go through your mouth to get to t_____69) r_____70) of you, from food and air to bacteria and viruses. A healthy mouth can help your body get w_____71) it needs and p_____72) it f_____73) harm — with adequate space for air to travel to your lungs, and healthy teeth and gums that prevent harmful microorganisms from e_____74) your bloodstream. From the moment you are created, oral health affects e_____75) aspect of your life. W_____76) happens in the mouth is usually just the tip of the iceberg and a reflection of what is happening in o_____77) parts of the body. Poor oral health can be a cause of a disease that a_____78) the entire body. The microorganisms in an unhealthy mouth can enter the bloodstream and travel anywhere in the body, p_____79) serious health risks.

음식과 공기에서부터 박테리아와 바이러스까지 거의 모든 것이 여러분의 나머지 부분에 도달하기 위해 여러분의 입을 거쳐야 한다. 건강한 입은 공기가 폐로 이동할 수 있는 적당한 공간, 그리고 해로운 미생물이 혈류로 들어가는 것을 막는 건강한 치아와 잇몸으로 여러분의 몸이 필요한 것을 얻고, 피해로부터 몸을 지키도록 도와줄 수 있다. 여러분이 생겨난 순간부터 구강 건강은 여러분의 삶의 모든 측면에 영향을 미친다. 입안에서 일어나는 일은 대개 빙산의 일각일 뿐이며 신체의 다른 부분에서 일어나고 있는 일의 반영이다. 나쁜 구강 건강은 전체 몸에 영향을 끼치는 질병의 원인일 수 있다. 건강하지 않은 입안의 미생물은 혈류로 들어가고 신체의 어느 곳이든 이동하여 심각한 건강상의 위험을 초래할 수 있다.

24

Kids tire of their toys, college students get sick of cafeteria food, and s_____80) o_____81) l_____82) most of us lose interest in our favorite TV shows. The b_____83) l_____84) is that we humans are e_____85) bored. But why should this be true? The answer l_____86) buried deep in our nerve cells, which are designed to reduce their initial excited response to stimuli each time they occur. At the same time, these neurons enhance t_____87) responses to things that change — especially things t_____88) change quickly. We probably evolved this way b_____89) our ancestors got more survival value, for example, f_____90) attending to what was moving in a tree (such as a puma) than to the tree itself. Boredom in reaction to an u_____91) environment turns down the level of neural excitation s_____92) t_____93) new stimuli (like our ancestor's hypothetical puma threat) stand out more. It's the n_____94) equivalent of turning off a front door light to see the fireflies.

아이들은 자기들의 장난감에 지루해하고, 대학생들은 카페테리아 음식에 싫증을 내고, 머지않아 우리 중 대부분은 우리가 가장 좋아하는 TV 쇼에 흥미를 잃는다. 요점은 우리 인간이 쉽게 지루해한다는 것이다. 그런데 왜 이것이 사실이어야 할까? 답은 자극이 일어날 때마다 그것에 대한 초기의 흥분된 반응을 약화하도록 설계된 우리의 신경 세포 내에 깊이 숨어 있다. 동시에 이 뉴런들은 변화하는 것들, 특히 빠르게 변화하는 것들에 대한 반응을 강화한다. 예를 들면 우리는 아마도 우리의 조상이 나무 그 자체보다 (퓨마처럼) 나무에서 움직이는 것에 주의를 기울이는 것으로부터 더 많은 생존 가치를 얻었기 때문에 이런 방식으로 진화했을 것이다. 변하지 않는 환경에 대한 반응으로의 지루함은 신경 흥분의 수준을 낮춰 (우리 조상이 가정한 퓨마의 위협과 같은) 새로운 자극이 더 두드러지게 한다. 이것은 반딧불이를 보기 위해 앞문의 불을 끄는 것의 신경적 대응물이다.

26

Frederick Douglass w_____95) b_____96) i_____97) slavery at a farm in Maryland. His full name at birth was Frederick Augustus Washington Bailey. He changed his name to Frederick Douglass after he s_____98) escaped from slavery in 1838. He became a leader of the Underground Railroad — a network of people, places, and routes that helped e_____99) people e_____100) to the north. He assisted o_____101) runaway slaves until they could safely get to other areas in the north. A_____102) a slave, he had t_____103) h_____104) to read and write and he spread t_____105) knowledge to other slaves as well. O_____106) free, he became a well-known abolitionist and strong believer in e_____107) for all people including Blacks, Native Americans, women, and recent immigrants. He wrote several autobiographies d_____108) his experiences as a slave. In addition to all this, he became the first African-American c_____109) for vice president of the United States.

Frederick Douglass는 Maryland의 한 농장에서 노예로 태어났다. 태어났을 때 그의 성명은 Frederick Augustus Washington Bailey였다. 그는 1838년에 노예 상태에서 성공적으로 탈출한 후 자신의 이름을 Frederick Douglass로 바꿨다. 그는 노예가 된 사람들을 북쪽으로 탈출하도록 돕는 사람, 장소, 경로의 조직인 Underground Railroad의 리더가 되었다. 그는 다른 도망친 노예들이 북쪽의 다른 지역에 안전하게 도착할 수 있을 때까지 그들을 도왔다. 노예로서 그는 읽고 쓰는 것을 독학했고, 그 지식을 다른 노예들에게도 전파했다. 자유로워지고 난 뒤 그는 유명한 노예제 폐지론자이자 흑인, 아메리카 원주민, 여성, 그리고 최근 이민자들을 포함한 모든 사람들을 위한 평등에 대한 강한 신봉자가 되었다. 그는 노예로서의 자신의 경험을 묘사한 몇 권의 자서전을 썼다. 이 모든 것에 더하여 그는 미국의 첫 아프리카계 미국인 부통령 후보가 되었다.

29

Some countries h_____ 110) p_____ 111) tougher guidelines for determining brain death when transplantation—transferring organs to o_____ 112)—is under consideration. In several European countries, there are l_____ 113) requirements which specify that a whole team of doctors must agree over the diagnosis of death in the case of a p_____ 114) donor. The reason for t_____ 115) strict regulations for diagnosing brain death in potential organ donors is, no doubt, to e_____ 116) public fears of a p_____ 117) diagnosis of brain death for the purpose of obtaining organs. But it is q_____ 118) whether these requirements reduce public suspicions a_____ 119) much a_____ 120) they create them. They certainly maintain mistaken beliefs t_____ 121) diagnosing brain death is an unreliable process lacking precision. As a matter of consistency, at least, c_____ 122) for diagnosing the deaths of organ donors should be exactly the same as for those for w_____ 123) immediate burial or cremation is intended.

일부 국가는 장기 이식, 즉 다른 사람에게 장기를 전달하는 것을 고려 중일 때 뇌사를 결정하는 것에 대한 더 엄격한 지침을 제안했다. 몇몇 유럽 국가에는 잠재적 기증자의 경우 의사 팀 전체가 사망 진단에 동의해야 한다고 명시하는 법적 요건들이 있다. 잠재적인 장기 기증자의 뇌사 진단에 대한 이러한 엄격한 규정들의 이유는 의심할 바 없이 장기 확보를 위한 너무 이른 뇌사 진단에 대한 대중의 두려움을 완화하기 위한 것이다. 하지만 이러한 요건들이 대중의 의심을 만들어 내는 만큼 그것을 줄여 주는지는 의문이다. 그것들은 뇌사 진단이 정확성이 결여된 신뢰하기 어려운 과정이라는 잘못된 믿음을 확실히 유지시킨다. 적어도 일관성의 이유로 장기 기증자의 사망 진단 기준은 즉각적인 매장 또는 화장이 예정된 사람들에 대한 그것과 정확히 동일해야 한다.

30

The term minimalism gives a negative i_____ 124) to some people who think that it is all about s_____ 125) valuable possessions. This insecurity naturally s_____ 126) f_____ 127) their attachment to their possessions. It is difficult to d_____ 128) oneself from something t_____ 129) has been around for quite some time. Being an e_____ 130) animal, human beings give meaning to the things around them. So, the question a_____ 131) here is that if minimalism will hurt one's emotions, why b_____ 132) a minimalist? The answer is very s_____ 133); the assumption of the question is fundamentally wrong. Minimalism does not h_____ 134) emotions. You might feel a bit sad while getting rid of a useless item but sooner than later, this feeling will be o_____ 135) by the joy of clarity. Minimalists never argue that you should leave e_____ 136) convenience of the modern era. They are of the view that you only need to e_____ 137) stuff that is unused or not going to be used in the near future.

미니멀리즘이라는 용어는 그것을 소중한 소유물을 희생하는 것에 관한 것으로만 생각하는 일부 사람들에게 부정적인 인상을 준다. 이러한 불안은 자신의 소유물에 대한 애착에서 자연스럽게 비롯된다. 꽤 오랫동안 곁에 있어 왔던 것으로부터 자신을 멀리 두는 것은 어렵다. 감정의 동물이기 때문에, 인간은 그들의 곁에 있는 물건에 의미를 부여한다. 그래서 여기서 생기는 질문은 미니멀리즘이 사람의 감정을 상하게 한다면 왜 미니멀리스트가 되느냐는 것이다. 대답은 매우 간단하다. 그 질문의 가정은 근본적으로 틀리다. 미니멀리즘은 감정을 상하게 하지 않는다. 여러분은 쓸모 없는 물건을 치우면서 조금 슬퍼할 수도 있지만 머지않아 이 느낌은 명료함의 기쁨으로 극복될 것이다. 미니멀리스트는 여러분이 현대의 모든 편의를 버려야 한다고 주장하지 않는다. 그들은 여러분이 사용되지 않거나 가까운 미래에 사용되지 않을 물건을 없애기만 하면 된다는 견해를 가지고 있다.

31

A remarkable characteristic of the v_____138) system is that it has the ability of a_____139) itself. Psychologist George M. Stratton made this clear in an i_____140) self-experiment. Stratton wore r_____141) glasses for several days, which l_____142) turned the world upside down for him. In the b_____143), this caused him great difficulties: just putting food in his mouth with a fork was a c_____144) for him. With time, however, his visual system a_____145) to the new stimuli from reality, and he was able to act n_____146) in his environment again, even seeing it upright when he concentrated. As he took off his reversing glasses, he was again c_____147) w_____ _148) problems: he used the wrong hand when he wanted to r_____149) for something, for example. Fortunately, Stratton could reverse the perception, and he did not have to wear reversing glasses for t_____150) r_____151) of his life. For him, everything r_____152) to normal after one day.

시각 체계의 두드러진 특징은 스스로 적응하는 능력이 있다는 것이다. 심리학자 George M. Stratton은 인상적인 자가 실험에서 이것을 분명히 했다. Stratton은 며칠 동안 반전 안경을 착용했는데 그 안경은 말 그대로 그에게 세상을 뒤집어 놓았다. 처음에 이것은 그에게 큰 어려움을 초래하였다. 포크로 음식을 입에 넣는 것조차 그에게는 도전이었다. 그러나 시간이 지나면서 그의 시각 체계는 현실의 새로운 자극에 적응했고, 그가 집중했을 때는 심지어 똑바로 보면서, 다시 자신의 환경에서 정상적으로 행동할 수 있었다. 반전 안경을 벗었을 때 그는 다시 문제에 직면했다. 예를 들어 그가 무언가를 잡기를 원할 때 그는 반대 손을 사용했다. 다행히 Stratton은 지각을 뒤집을 수 있었고 평생 반전 안경을 착용하지 않아도 되었다. 그에게 하루 만에 모든 것이 정상으로 돌아왔다.

32

P_____153) in a study were asked to answer questions like "Why does the moon have phases?" H_____154) the participants were told to search for the answers on the internet, w_____155) t_____156) o_____157) half weren't allowed to do so. Then, in the second part of the study, a_____158) of the participants were p_____159) with a new set of questions, such as "Why does Swiss cheese have holes?" These questions were unrelated to the ones asked d_____160) the first part of the study, so participants who used the internet had absolutely no a_____161) over those who hadn't. You would think that both sets of participants would be e_____162) sure or unsure about how well they could answer the new questions. But t_____163) who used the internet in the first part of the study rated t_____164) as more knowledgeable than those who hadn't, even about questions they hadn't searched online for. The study suggests that h_____165) a_____ _166) t_____167) unrelated information was enough to pump up their i_____168) confidence.

한 연구의 참가자들이 '달은 왜 상을 가지고 있을까'와 같은 질문들에 답하도록 요청받았다. 참가자의 절반은 인터넷에서 답을 검색하라는 말을 들었고 나머지 절반은 그렇게 하도록 허용되지 않았다. 그다음, 연구의 두 번째 단계에서 모든 참가자는 '스위스 치즈에는 왜 구멍이 있을까'와 같은 일련의 새로운 질문들을 제시받았다. 이 질문들은 연구의 첫 번째 단계에서 질문받았던 것들과는 관련이 없어서 인터넷을 사용한 참가자들은 그러지 않은 참가자들보다 이점이 전혀 없었다. 여러분은 두 집단의 참가자들이 새로운 질문들에 얼마나 잘 대답할 수 있을지에 대해 동일한 정도로 확신하거나 확신하지 못할 것으로 생각할 것이다. 그러나 연구의 첫 번째 단계에서 인터넷을 사용했던 참가자들은 자신이 온라인에서 검색하지 않았던 질문들에 대해서조차 그러지 않았던 참가자들보다 스스로가 더 많이 알고 있다고 평가했다. 이 연구는 관련 없는 정보에 접근하는 것이 그들의 지적 자신감을 부풀리기에 충분했다는 것을 시사한다.

33

Anthropologist Gregory Bateson suggests that we **t**_____169) **t**_____170) understand the world by focusing in on particular features within it. **T**_____171) platypuses. We might zoom in **s**_____172) closely to their fur **t**_____173) each hair **a**_____174) different. We might also zoom out to the extent **w**_____175) it appears as a single, uniform object. We might take the platypus as an **i**_____176), or we might treat it as part of a larger unit such as a species or an ecosystem. It's possible to move between many of these perspectives, **a**_____177) we may need some **a**_____178) tools and skills to zoom in on individual pieces of hair or zoom out to **e**_____179) ecosystems. Crucially, however, we can only **t**_____180) **u**_____181) one perspective at a time. We can pay attention to the varied behavior of individual animals, look at **w**_____182) unites them into a single species, or look at them as part of bigger ecological patterns. Every possible perspective involves **e**_____183) certain aspects and **i**_____184) others.

인류학자 Gregory Bateson은 우리가 세상 안의 특정한 특징에 초점을 맞춤으로써 세상을 이해하는 경향이 있다고 제안한다. 오리너구리를 예로 들어보자. 우리가 그들의 털을 매우 가까이 확대하면 각 가닥이 다르게 보인다. 우리는 또한 그것이 하나의 동일한 개체로 보이는 정도까지 축소할 수도 있다. 우리는 오리너구리를 개체로 취급할 수도 있고 종 또는 생태계와 같이 더 큰 단위의 일부로 취급할 수도 있다. 비록 개별 머리카락을 확대하거나 전체 생태계로 축소하기 위해 몇 가지 추가 도구와 기술이 필요할지도 모르지만, 이러한 많은 관점 사이를 이동하는 것은 가능하다. 그러나 결정적으로 우리는 한 번에 하나의 관점만 취할 수 있다. 우리는 개별 동물의 다양한 행동에 주의를 기울일 수 있고, 그들을 단일 종으로 통합하는 것을 살펴볼 수도 있고, 더 큰 생태학적 패턴의 일부로서 그들을 살펴볼 수도 있다. 가능한 모든 관점은 특정 측면을 강조하고 다른 측면을 외면하는 것을 포함한다.

34

Plato's realism includes all aspects of experience **b**_____185) is most easily explained by considering the nature of mathematical and geometrical objects such as circles. He asked the question, **w**_____186) is a circle? You might **i**_____187) a particular example carved into stone or drawn in the sand. However, Plato would **p**_____188) **o**_____189) that, if you looked closely enough, you would see that **n**_____190) it, **n**_____191) indeed any physical circle, was perfect. They all possessed flaws, and all **w**_____192) **s**_____193) **t**_____194) change and decayed with time. So how can we talk about perfect circles if we cannot actually see or touch them? Plato's **e**_____195) answer was that the world we see is a poor **r**_____196) of a deeper unseen reality of Forms, or universals, **w**_____197) perfect cats chase perfect mice in perfect circles around perfect rocks. Plato believed **t**_____198) the Forms or universals are the true reality that exists in an invisible but perfect world beyond our senses.

플라톤의 실재론은 경험의 모든 측면을 포함하지만, 원과 같은 수학적이고 기하학적인 대상의 특성을 고려함으로써 가장 쉽게 설명된다. 그는 '원이란 무엇인가'라는 질문을 했다. 여러분은 돌에 새겨져 있거나 모래에 그려진 특정한 예를 가리킬 수 있다. 그러나 플라톤은 여러분이 충분히 면밀히 관찰한다면, 여러분이 그 어느 것도, 진정 어떤 물리적인 원도 완벽하지 않다는 것을 알게 될 것이라고 지적할 것이다. 그것들 모두는 결함을 가지고 있었고, 모두 변화의 영향을 받고 시간이 지남에 따라 쇠하였다. 그렇다면, 우리가 완벽한 원을 실제로 보거나 만질 수 없다면, 그것에 대해 어떻게 이야기할 수 있을까? 플라톤의 비범한 대답은 우리가 보는 세상이 완벽한 고양이가 완벽한 암석 주변에서 완벽한 원을 그리며 완벽한 쥐를 쫓는 '형상' 또는 '보편자'라는 더 깊은 보이지 않는 실재의 불충분한 반영물이라는 것이다. 플라톤은 '형상' 또는 '보편자'가 보이지 않지만 우리의 감각을 넘어선 완벽한 세계에 존재하는 진정한 실재라고 믿었다.

35

In statistics, the law of large numbers describes a situation w_____ 199) having more data is better for making predictions. A_____ 200) t_____ 201) it, the more often an experiment is conducted, the closer the average of the results can be expected to match the true state of the world. For instance, on your first e_____ 202) with the game of roulette, you may have beginner's luck after betting on 7. But t_____ 203) m_____ 204) often you repeat this bet, t_____ 205) c_____ 206) the relative frequency of wins and losses is expected to approach the true c_____ 207) of winning, meaning that your luck will at some point f_____ 208) a_____ 209). S_____ 210), car insurers collect large amounts of data to figure out the chances that drivers will cause accidents, d_____ 211) on their age, region, or car brand. Both casinos and insurance industries r_____ 212) o_____ 213) the law of large numbers to balance individual losses.

통계학에서 대수의 법칙은 더 많은 데이터를 갖는 것이 예측하는 데 더 좋은 상황을 설명한다. 그것에 따르면 실험이 더 자주 수행될수록 그 결과의 평균이 세상의 실제 상태에 더 맞춰지는 것으로 예상될 수 있다. 예를 들어 룰렛 게임을 처음 접했을 때 7에 베팅한 후 여러분은 초보자의 운이 있을 수 있다. 하지만 당신이 이 베팅을 더 자주 반복할수록 승패의 상대적인 빈도가 진짜 승률에 더 가까워질 것으로 예상되는데 이는 당신의 운이 어느 순간 사라진다는 것을 의미한다. 마찬가지로 자동차 보험사는 운전자가 그들의 연령, 지역 또는 자동차 브랜드에 따라 사고를 일으킬 확률을 파악하기 위해 많은 양의 데이터를 수집한다. 카지노와 보험 산업 모두 개별 손실의 균형을 맞추기 위해 대수의 법칙에 의존한다.

36

The a_____ 214) brain is not fully developed until its early twenties. This means the way the adolescents' decision-making circuits i_____ 215) and process information may put them at a d_____ 216). One of their brain regions that m_____ 217) later is the prefrontal cortex, w_____ 218) is the control center, tasked with thinking ahead and evaluating consequences. It is the area of the brain r_____ 219) f_____ 220) preventing you from sending off an initial angry text and modifying it with kinder words. On the other hand, the limbic system matures e_____ 221), playing a central role in processing emotional responses. B_____ 222) o_____ 223) its earlier development, it is more likely to influence decision-making. Decision-making in the adolescent brain is l_____ 224) by emotional factors more than the perception of consequences. Due to these differences, there is an imbalance b_____ 225) feeling-based decision-making ruled by the more mature limbic system a_____ 226) logical-based decision-making by the not-yet-mature prefrontal cortex. This may explain why some teens are m_____ 227) likely to make bad decisions.

청소년기의 뇌는 20대 초반까지는 완전히 발달하지 않는다. 이것은 청소년의 의사 결정 회로가 정보를 통합하고 처리하는 방식이 그들을 불리하게 만들 수 있음을 의미한다. 나중에 성숙하는 뇌 영역 중 하나는 통제 센터인 전전두엽 피질이며, 그것은 미리 생각하고 결과를 평가하는 임무를 맡고 있다. 그것은 당신이 초기의 화가 난 문자를 보내는 것을 막고 그것을 더 친절한 단어로 수정하게 하는 역할을 하는 뇌의 영역이다. 반면 대뇌변연계는 더 일찍 성숙하여 정서적 반응을 처리하는 데 중심적인 역할을 한다. 그것의 더 이른 발달로 인해 그것이 의사 결정에 영향을 미칠 가능성이 더 높다. 청소년기의 뇌에서 의사 결정은 결과의 인식보다 감정적인 요인에 의해 이끌어진다. 이러한 차이점 때문에 더 성숙한 대뇌변연계에 의해 지배되는 감정 기반 의사 결정과 아직 성숙하지 않은 전전두엽 피질에 의한 논리 기반 의사 결정 사이에는 불균형이 존재한다. 이것은 왜 일부 십 대들이 그릇된 결정을 내릴 가능성이 더 높은지를 설명해 줄 수 있다.

37

D_____228) the remarkable progress in deep-learning based facial recognition approaches in recent years, in terms of identification performance, they s_____229) have limitations. These limitations relate to the database u_____230) in the learning stage. If the selected database does not c_____231) enough instances, the result may be systematically a_____232). F_____233) e_____234), the performance of a facial biometric system may decrease if the person to be i_____235) was e_____236) over 10 years ago. The factor to consider is that this person may experience c_____237) in the texture of the face, particularly with the appearance of wrinkles and sagging skin. These changes may be h_____238) by weight gain or loss. To c_____239) this problem, researchers have developed models for face aging or digital de-aging. It is used to c_____240) f_____241) the differences in facial characteristics, which appear over a given time period.

최근 몇 년 동안 딥 러닝 기반의 얼굴 인식 접근법의 눈에 띄는 발전에도 불구하고, 식별 성능 측면에서 여전히 그것은 한계를 가지고 있다. 이러한 한계는 학습 단계에서 사용되는 데이터베이스와 관련이 있다. 선택된 데이터베이스가 충분한 사례를 포함하지 않으면 그 결과가 시스템적으로 영향을 받을 수 있다. 예를 들어 식별될 사람이 10년도 더 전에 등록된 경우 안면 생체 측정 시스템의 성능이 저하될 수 있다. 고려해야 할 요인은 이 사람이 특히 주름과 처진 피부가 나타나는 것을 동반한 얼굴의 질감 변화를 경험할 수 있다는 것이다. 이러한 변화는 체중 증가 또는 감소에 의해 두드러질 수 있다. 이 문제에 대응하기 위해 연구자들은 얼굴 노화나 디지털 노화 완화의 모델을 개발했다. 그것은 주어진 기간 동안 나타나는 얼굴 특성의 차이를 보완하는 데 사용된다.

38

The decline in the d_____242) of our food is an entirely human-made process. The biggest loss of crop diversity came in the decades t_____243) followed the Second World War. In an attempt to save millions from e_____244) hunger, crop scientists found ways to produce grains such as rice and wheat on an enormous s_____245). And thousands of t_____246) varieties were replaced by a small number of new super-productive ones. The s_____247) worked spectacularly well, a_____248) l_____249) to begin with. Because of it, grain production tripled, and between 1970 and 2020 the human population more than doubled. Leaving the c_____250) of that strategy to one side, the danger of creating more u_____251) crops is that they are more at risk when it comes to disasters. S_____252), a global food system that depends on just a n_____253) selection of plants has a g_____254) chance of not being able to survive diseases, pests and climate extremes.

우리 음식의 다양성의 감소는 전적으로 인간이 만든 과정이다. 농작물 다양성의 가장 큰 손실은 제2차 세계 대전 이후 수십 년 동안 나타났다. 수백만 명의 사람들을 극도의 배고픔에서 구하고자 하는 시도에서 작물 과학자들이 쌀과 밀과 같은 곡물을 엄청난 규모로 생산하는 방법을 발견했다. 그리고 수천 개의 전통적인 종들은 소수의 새로운 초(超)생산적인 종들로 대체되었다. 그 전략은 적어도 처음에는 굉장히 잘 작동했다. 그것 때문에 곡물 생산량은 세 배가 되었고 1970년과 2020년 사이에 인구는 두 배 이상 증가했다. 그 전략의 기여를 차치하고, 더 획일적인 작물을 만드는 것의 위험은 그것들이 재앙과 관련해 더 큰 위험에 처한다는 것이다. 특히 농작물의 좁은 선택에만 의존하는 세계적인 식량 시스템은 질병, 해충 및 기후 위기로부터 생존하지 못할 더 높은 가능성을 가진다.

39

Between 1940 and 2000, Cuba r_____255) the world baseball scene. They won 25 of the first 28 World Cups and 3 of 5 Olympic Games. The Cubans were known for wearing uniforms covered in red from head to toe, a strong c_____256) to the more c_____257) North American style featuring grey or white pants. N_____258) o_____259) were their athletic talents superior, the Cubans appeared e_____260) stronger from just the colour of their uniforms. A game would not even start and the o_____261) team would already be scared. A_____262) f_____263) years ago, Cuba altered that uniform style, modernizing it and perhaps conforming to other countries' style; interestingly, the national team has d_____264) since that time. The country that ruled international baseball for decades has not been on top s_____265) that uniform change. Traditions are important for a team; w_____266) a team brand or image can adjust to keep up with present times, if it a_____267) or n_____268) its roots, negative effects can surface.

1940년과 2000년 사이에 쿠바는 세계 야구계를 지배했다. 그들은 첫 28회의 월드컵 중 25회와 5회의 올림픽 게임 중 3회를 이겼다. 쿠바인들은 머리부터 발끝까지 빨간색으로 뒤덮인 유니폼을 입는 것으로 알려져 있었는데, 이것은 회색이나 흰색 바지를 특징으로 하는 더 보수적인 북미 스타일과 강한 대조를 이룬다. 쿠바인들의 운동 재능이 뛰어났을 뿐만 아니라 그들은 그들의 유니폼의 색깔만으로도 훨씬 더 강하게 보였다. 경기가 시작하지 않았는데도 상대 팀은 이미 겁에 질리곤 했다. 몇 년 전 쿠바는 유니폼을 현대화하고 아마도 다른 나라의 스타일에 맞추면서 그 유니폼 스타일을 바꿨다. 흥미롭게도 국가 대표 팀은 그 시기부터 쇠퇴해 왔다. 수십 년 동안 국제 야구를 지배했던 그 나라는 그 유니폼 교체 이후로 정상에 오른 적이 없었다. 전통은 팀에게 중요하다. 팀 브랜드나 이미지는 현시대를 따르기 위해 조정될 수 있지만 팀이 그들의 뿌리를 버리거나 무시하면 부정적인 영향이 표면화될 수 있다.

40

Many of the first models of cultural evolution d_____269) noticeable connections between culture and genes by using concepts from theoretical population genetics and a_____270) them to culture. Cultural patterns of transmission, innovation, and selection are c_____271) likened to genetic processes of transmission, mutation, and selection. However, t_____272) approaches had to be modified to a_____273) f_____274) the differences between genetic and cultural transmission. For example, we do not expect the cultural transmission to follow the rules of genetic transmission s_____275). If two biological parents have different forms of a cultural trait, their child is n_____276) n_____277) equally likely to acquire the mother's or father's form of that trait. Further, a child can acquire cultural traits not only from its parents but also from n_____278) adults and peers; thus, the frequency of a cultural trait in the population is r_____279) beyond just the p_____280) that an individual's parents had that trait.

문화 진화의 많은 초기 모델들은 이론 집단 유전학의 개념을 사용함으로써 그리고 그것들을 문화에 적용함으로써 문화와 유전자 사이의 주목할 만한 접점을 이끌어 냈다. 전파, 혁신, 선택의 문화적 방식은 전달, 돌연변이, 선택의 유전적 과정과 개념적으로 유사하다. 그러나 이러한 접근법은 유전자의 전달과 문화 전파 사이의 차이점을 설명하기 위해 수정되어야만 했다. 예를 들어, 우리는 문화 전파가 유전자 전달의 규칙을 엄격하게 따를 것이라고 예상하지 않는다. 만약 두 명의 생물학적인 부모가 서로 다른 문화적인 특성의 형태를 가진다면, 그들의 자녀는 반드시 엄마 혹은 아빠의 그 특성의 형태를 동일하게 획득하지 않을 수 있다. 더욱이 아이는 문화적인 특성을 부모로부터 뿐만 아니라 부모가 아닌 성인이나 또래로부터도 얻을 수 있다. 따라서 집단의 문화적인 특성의 빈도는 단지 한 개인의 부모가 그 특성을 가졌을 확률을 넘어서 유의미하다.

41~42

A ball thrown into the air is acted upon by the i_____281) force given it, persisting as inertia of movement and tending to carry it in the same straight line, and by the c_____282) pull of gravity downward, as well as by the r_____283) of the air. It moves, accordingly, in a c_____284) path. Now the path does not r_____285) the working of any particular force; there is simply the combination of the three e_____286) forces mentioned; but in a real sense, there is something in the total action b_____287) the isolated action of three forces, namely, their joint action. In the same way, w_____288) two or more human individuals are together, their m_____289) relationships and their arrangement into a group are things which would not be revealed if we confined our attention to e_____290) individual separately. The significance of group behavior is greatly increased in the case of human beings by the fact t_____291) some of the tendencies to action of the individual are related definitely to o_____292) persons, and could not be aroused except by other persons a_____293) as stimuli. An individual in complete i_____294) would not reveal their competitive tendencies, their tendencies towards the opposite sex, their p_____295) tendencies towards children. This shows that the traits of human nature do not fully appear until the individual is b_____296) i_____297) relationships with other individuals.

공중으로 던져진 공은 초기에 그것에 주어진 힘에 의해 움직여지는데, 운동의 관성으로 지속하며 같은 직선으로 나아가려는 경향을 보이고, 공기의 저항뿐만 아니라 아래로 지속적으로 당기는 중력에 의해서도 움직여진다. 그에 맞춰 공은 곡선의 경로로 움직인다. 이제 그 경로는 어떤 특정한 힘의 작동을 나타내지는 않는다. 언급된 세 가지 기본적인 힘의 결합이 존재할 뿐이다. 하지만 사실은 세 가지 힘의 고립된 작용 외에 전체적인 작용에 무언가가 있다. 이름하여 그들의 공동 작용이다. 같은 방식으로, 두 명 혹은 그 이상의 인간 개인이 같이 있을 때 그들의 상호 관계와 그들의 집단으로의 배치는 만약 우리가 관심을 개별적으로 각각의 개인에게 국한시킨다면 드러나지 않을 것이다. 개인 행동의 몇몇 경향은 명백하게 다른 사람들과 관련이 있고 자극으로 작동하는 다른 사람들 없이는 유발되지 않을 수 있다는 사실로 인해 그룹 행동의 중요성이 인간의 경우 크게 증가된다. 완전한 고립 속의 개인은 그들의 경쟁적인 성향, 이성에 대한 그들의 성향, 아이에 대한 그들의 보호적 성향을 드러내지 않을 것이다. 이것은 개인이 다른 개인과의 관계에 관여될 때까지는 인간 본성의 특성이 완전히 나타나지 않는다는 것을 보여 준다.

43~45

There once lived a man in a village who was not happy with his life. He was always troubled by one problem or a_____298). One day, a saint with his guards s_____299) b_____300) his village. Many people heard the news and started going to him w_____301) their problems. The man also decided to visit the saint. Even after reaching the saint's place in the morning, he didn't get the o_____302) to meet him till evening. When the man got to meet the saint, he c_____303) that he was very unhappy with life because problems always s_____304) him, l_____305) workplace tension or worries about his health. He said, "Please give me a s_____306) so that all the problems in my life will end and I can live peacefully." The saint smiled and said that he would answer the request the next day. But the saint also asked if the man c_____307) do a small job for him. He told the man to take care of a hundred camels in his group that night, s_____308) "When all hundred camels sit down, you can go to sleep." The man agreed. The next morning when the saint met that man, he asked if the man h_____309) s_____310) well. Tired and sad, the man replied that he couldn't sleep even for a moment. In fact, the man tried very hard but couldn't make all the camels sit at the same time because e_____311) time he m_____312) one camel sit, a_____313) would stand up. The saint told him, "You realized that no matter how hard you try, you can't make all the camels sit down. If one problem is solved, for some reason, a_____314) will arise like the camels did. So, humans should enjoy life d_____315) these problems."

옛날 어느 마을에 자신의 삶이 행복하지 않은 한 남자가 살았다. 그는 항상 하나 혹은 또 다른 문제로 어려움을 겪었다. 어느 날 한 성자가 그의 경호인들과 함께 그의 마을에 들렀다. 많은 사람들이 그 소식을 듣고 그들의 문제를 가지고 그에게 가기 시작했다. 그 남자 역시 성자를 방문하기로 결정했다. 아침에 성자가 있는 곳에 도착하고 난 후에도 그는 저녁 때까지 그를 만날 기회를 얻지 못했다. 마침내 그가 성자를 만났을 때 그는 직장 내 긴장이나 건강에 대한 걱정과 같이 항상 문제가 자기를 둘러싸고 있어서 삶이 매우 불행하다고 고백했다. 그는 "나의 삶의 모든 문제가 끝나고 제가 평화롭게 살 수 있도록 제발 해결책을 주세요."라고 말했다. 성자는 미소 지으면서 그가 다음 날 그 요청에 답해 주겠다고 말했다. 그런데 성자는 또한 그 남자가 그를 위해 작은 일을 해 줄 수 있는지 물었다. 성자는 그 남자에게 "백 마리 낙타 모두가 자리에 앉으면 당신은 자러 가도 좋습니다."라고 말하면서 그날 밤에 그의 일행에 있는 백 마리 낙타를 돌봐 달라고 말했다. 그 남자는 동의했다. 다음 날 아침에 성자가 그 남자를 만났을 때 그는 남자가 잠을 잘 잤는지 물어보았다. 피곤해하고 슬퍼하면서 남자는 한순간도 잠을 자지 못했다고 대답했다. 사실 그 남자는 아주 열심히 노력했지만 그가 낙타 한 마리를 앉힐 때마다 다른 낙타 한 마리가 일어섰기 때문에 모든 낙타를 동시에 앉게 할 수 없었다. 그 성자는 그에게 "당신이 아무리 열심히 노력하더라도 모든 낙타를 앉게 만들 수는 없다는 것을 깨달았습니다. 만약 한 가지 문제가 해결되면 낙타가 그런 것처럼 어떤 이유로 또 다른 문제가 일어날 것입니다. 그래서 인간은 이러한 문제에도 불구하고 삶을 즐겨야 합니다."라고 말했다.

2023 고1 11월 모의고사   ❷ 회차   :   점 / 315점

18

I was so excited to hear t_____ 1) your brand is opening a new shop on Bruns Street next month. I h_____ 2) always a_____ 3) the way your brand helps women to feel more stylish and confident. I am writing i_____ 4) r_____ 5) t_____ 6) your ad in the Bruns Journal. I graduated from the Meline School of Fashion and have worked as a sales assistant at LoganMart for the l_____ 7) five years. D_____ 8) that time, I've developed strong customer service and sales skills, and now I would like to apply for the sales position in your clothing store. I am a_____ 9) for an interview at your earliest convenience. I look forward to hearing from you. Thank you for reading my letter.

19

I h_____ 10) never s_____ 11) a beach with such white sand or water that was such a beautiful shade of blue. Jane and I set up a blanket on the sand w_____ 12) looking forward to our ten days of honeymooning on an e_____ 13) island. "Look!" Jane waved her hand to point at the beautiful scene before us — and her gold wedding ring went flying off her hand. I tried to see where it went, but the sun hit my eyes and I l_____ 14) t_____ 15) o_____ 16) it. I didn't want to lose her wedding ring, so I started looking in the area where I thought it h_____ 17) l_____ 18). However, the sand was so f_____ 19) and I realized that anything heavy, like gold, would quickly sink and might never b_____ 20) f_____ 21) again.

20

Unfortunately, many people don't take p_____ 22) responsibility for their own growth. I_____ _23), they simply run the race l_____ 24) o_____ 25) for them. They do well enough in school to k_____ 26) a_____ 27). Maybe they m_____ 28) t_____ 29) get a good job at a well-run company. But so many think and act a_____ 30) i_____ 31) their learning journey e_____ 32) with college. They h_____ 33) c_____ 34) all the boxes in the life that was laid out for them and now l_____ 35) a road map d_____ 36) the right ways to move forward and continue to grow. In truth, that's when the journey really begins. When school is finished, your growth becomes v_____ 37). Like healthy eating habits or a regular exercise program, you need to commit to it and d_____ 38) thought, time, and energy to it. O_____ 39), it simply won't happen — and your life and career are likely to stop progressing as a result.

21

Many people take the commonsense view that color is an o_____40) property of things, or of the light that bounces off them. They say a tree's leaves are green because they r_____41) green light — a greenness that is just a_____42) real a_____43) the leaves. O_____44) argue that color doesn't i_____45) the physical world at all but exists only in the eye or mind of the viewer. They maintain that i_____46) a tree f_____47) in a forest and no one was there to see it, its leaves would be c_____48)— and so would everything else. They say there is no such thing as color; there are only the people who see it. Both p_____49) are, in a way, correct. Color is o_____50) and s_____51)— "the place," as Paul Cézanne p_____52) it, "where our brain and the universe meet." Color is created when light from the world is r_____53) by the eyes and i_____54) by the brain.

22

When writing a novel, research for information needs to be done. The thing is that some kinds of fiction d_____55) a higher level of detail: crime fiction, for example, or scientific thrillers. The information is never hard t_____56) f_____57); one website for authors e_____58) organizes trips to police stations, s_____59) t_____60) crime writers can get it right. Often, a polite letter will earn you p_____61) to visit a particular location and r_____62) all the details that you need. But remember that you will d_____63) your readers to boredom if you think t_____64) you need to pack everything you discover into your work. The details that m_____65) are t_____ _66) that reveal the human experience. The c_____67) thing is telling a story, finding the characters, the tension, and the conflict — not the train timetable or the building blueprint.

23

Nearly e_____68) has to go through your mouth to get to t_____69) r_____70) of you, from food and air to bacteria and viruses. A healthy mouth can help your body get w_____71) it needs and p_____72) it f_____73) harm — with adequate space for air to travel to your lungs, and healthy teeth and gums that prevent harmful microorganisms from e_____74) your bloodstream. From the moment you are created, oral health affects e_____75) aspect of your life. W_____76) happens in the mouth is usually just the tip of the iceberg and a reflection of what is happening in o_____77) parts of the body. Poor oral health can be a cause of a disease that a_____78) the entire body. The microorganisms in an unhealthy mouth can enter the bloodstream and travel anywhere in the body, p_____79) serious health risks.

24

Kids tire of their toys, college students get sick of cafeteria food, and s_____80) o_____81) l_____82) most of us lose interest in our favorite TV shows. The b_____83) l_____84) is that we humans are e_____85) bored. But why should this be true? The answer l_____86) buried deep in our nerve cells, which are designed to reduce their initial excited response to stimuli each time they occur. At the same time, these neurons enhance t_____87) responses to things that change — especially things t_____88) change quickly. We probably evolved this way b_____89) our ancestors got more survival value, for example, f_____90) attending to what was moving in a tree (such as a puma) than to the tree itself. Boredom in reaction to an u_____91) environment turns down the level of neural excitation s_____92) t_____93) new stimuli (like our ancestor's hypothetical puma threat) stand out more. It's the n_____94) equivalent of turning off a front door light to see the fireflies.

26

Frederick Douglass w_____95) b_____96) i_____97) slavery at a farm in Maryland. His full name at birth was Frederick Augustus Washington Bailey. He changed his name to Frederick Douglass after he s_____98) escaped from slavery in 1838. He became a leader of the Underground Railroad — a network of people, places, and routes that helped e_____99) people e_____100) to the north. He assisted o_____101) runaway slaves until they could safely get to other areas in the north. A_____102) a slave, he had t_____103) h_____104) to read and write and he spread t_____105) knowledge to other slaves as well. O_____106) free, he became a well-known abolitionist and strong believer in e_____107) for all people including Blacks, Native Americans, women, and recent immigrants. He wrote several autobiographies d_____108) his experiences as a slave. In addition to all this, he became the first African-American c_____109) for vice president of the United States.

29

Some countries h_____110) p_____111) tougher guidelines for determining brain death when transplantation — transferring organs to o_____112) — is under consideration. In several European countries, there are l_____113) requirements which specify that a whole team of doctors must agree over the diagnosis of death in the case of a p_____114) donor. The reason for t_____115) strict regulations for diagnosing brain death in potential organ donors is, no doubt, to e_____116) public fears of a p_____117) diagnosis of brain death for the purpose of obtaining organs. But it is q_____118) whether these requirements reduce public suspicions a_____119) much a_____120) they create them. They certainly maintain mistaken beliefs t_____121) diagnosing brain death is an unreliable process lacking precision. As a matter of consistency, at least, c_____122) for diagnosing the deaths of organ donors should be exactly the same as for those for w_____123) immediate burial or cremation is intended.

30

The term minimalism gives a negative **i**_____124) to some people who think that it is all about **s**_____125) valuable possessions. This insecurity naturally **s**_____126) **f**_____127) their attachment to their possessions. It is difficult to **d**_____128) oneself from something **t**_____129) has been around for quite some time. Being an **e**_____130) animal, human beings give meaning to the things around them. So, the question **a**_____131) here is that if minimalism will hurt one's emotions, why **b**_____132) a minimalist? The answer is very **s**_____133); the assumption of the question is fundamentally wrong. Minimalism does not **h**_____134) emotions. You might feel a bit sad while getting rid of a useless item but sooner than later, this feeling will be **o**_____135) by the joy of clarity. Minimalists never argue that you should leave **e**_____136) convenience of the modern era. They are of the view that you only need to **e**_____137) stuff that is unused or not going to be used in the near future.

31

A remarkable characteristic of the **v**_____138) system is that it has the ability of **a**_____139) itself. Psychologist George M. Stratton made this clear in an **i**_____140) self-experiment. Stratton wore **r**_____141) glasses for several days, which **l**_____142) turned the world upside down for him. In the **b**_____143), this caused him great difficulties: just putting food in his mouth with a fork was a **c**_____144) for him. With time, however, his visual system **a**_____145) to the new stimuli from reality, and he was able to act **n**_____146) in his environment again, even seeing it upright when he concentrated. As he took off his reversing glasses, he was again **c**_____147) **w**_____148) problems: he used the wrong hand when he wanted to **r**_____149) for something, for example. Fortunately, Stratton could reverse the perception, and he did not have to wear reversing glasses for **t**_____150) **r**_____151) of his life. For him, everything **r**_____152) to normal after one day.

32

P_____153) in a study were asked to answer questions like "Why does the moon have phases?" **H**_____154) the participants were told to search for the answers on the internet, **w**_____155) **t**_____156) **o**_____157) half weren't allowed to do so. Then, in the second part of the study, **a**_____158) of the participants were **p**_____159) with a new set of questions, such as "Why does Swiss cheese have holes?" These questions were unrelated to the ones asked **d**_____160) the first part of the study, so participants who used the internet had absolutely no **a**_____161) over those who hadn't. You would think that both sets of participants would be **e**_____162) sure or unsure about how well they could answer the new questions. But **t**_____163) who used the internet in the first part of the study rated **t**_____164) as more knowledgeable than those who hadn't, even about questions they hadn't searched online for. The study suggests that **h**_____165) **a**_____166) **t**_____167) unrelated information was enough to pump up their **i**_____168) confidence.

33

Anthropologist Gregory Bateson suggests that we t_____169) t_____170) understand the world by focusing in on particular features within it. T_____171) platypuses. We might zoom in s_____172) closely to their fur t_____173) each hair a_____174) different. We might also zoom out to the extent w_____175) it appears as a single, uniform object. We might take the platypus as an i_____176), or we might treat it as part of a larger unit such as a species or an ecosystem. It's possible to move between many of these perspectives, a_____177) we may need some a_____178) tools and skills to zoom in on individual pieces of hair or zoom out to e_____179) ecosystems. Crucially, however, we can only t_____180) u_____181) one perspective at a time. We can pay attention to the varied behavior of individual animals, look at w_____182) unites them into a single species, or look at them as part of bigger ecological patterns. Every possible perspective involves e_____183) certain aspects and i_____184) others.

34

Plato's realism includes all aspects of experience b_____185) is most easily explained by considering the nature of mathematical and geometrical objects such as circles. He asked the question, w_____186) is a circle? You might i_____187) a particular example carved into stone or drawn in the sand. However, Plato would p_____188) o_____189) that, if you looked closely enough, you would see that n_____190) it, n_____191) indeed any physical circle, was perfect. They all possessed flaws, and all w_____192) s_____193) t_____194) change and decayed with time. So how can we talk about perfect circles if we cannot actually see or touch them? Plato's e_____195) answer was that the world we see is a poor r_____196) of a deeper unseen reality of Forms, or universals, w_____197) perfect cats chase perfect mice in perfect circles around perfect rocks. Plato believed t_____198) the Forms or universals are the true reality that exists in an invisible but perfect world beyond our senses.

35

In statistics, the law of large numbers describes a situation w_____199) having more data is better for making predictions. A_____200) t_____201) it, the more often an experiment is conducted, the closer the average of the results can be expected to match the true state of the world. For instance, on your first e_____202) with the game of roulette, you may have beginner's luck after betting on 7. But t_____203) m_____204) often you repeat this bet, t_____205) c_____206) the relative frequency of wins and losses is expected to approach the true c_____207) of winning, meaning that your luck will at some point f_____208) a_____209). S_____210), car insurers collect large amounts of data to figure out the chances that drivers will cause accidents, d_____211) on their age, region, or car brand. Both casinos and insurance industries r_____212) o_____213) the law of large numbers to balance individual losses.

36

The **a**_____214) brain is not fully developed until its early twenties. This means the way the adolescents' decision-making circuits **i**_____215) and process information may put them at a **d**_____216). One of their brain regions that **m**_____217) later is the prefrontal cortex, **w**_____218) is the control center, tasked with thinking ahead and evaluating consequences. It is the area of the brain **r**_____219) **f**_____220) preventing you from sending off an initial angry text and modifying it with kinder words. On the other hand, the limbic system matures **e**_____221), playing a central role in processing emotional responses. **B**_____222) **o**_____223) its earlier development, it is more likely to influence decision-making. Decision-making in the adolescent brain is **l**_____224) by emotional factors more than the perception of consequences. Due to these differences, there is an imbalance **b**_____225) feeling-based decision-making ruled by the more mature limbic system **a**_____226) logical-based decision-making by the not-yet-mature prefrontal cortex. This may explain why some teens are **m**_____227) likely to make bad decisions.

37

D_____228) the remarkable progress in deep-learning based facial recognition approaches in recent years, in terms of identification performance, they **s**_____229) have limitations. These limitations relate to the database **u**_____230) in the learning stage. If the selected database does not **c**_____231) enough instances, the result may be systematically **a**_____232). **F**_____233) **e**_____234), the performance of a facial biometric system may decrease if the person to be **i**_____235) was **e**_____236) over 10 years ago. The factor to consider is that this person may experience **c**_____237) in the texture of the face, particularly with the appearance of wrinkles and sagging skin. These changes may be **h**_____238) by weight gain or loss. To **c**_____239) this problem, researchers have developed models for face aging or digital de-aging. It is used to **c**_____240) **f**_____241) the differences in facial characteristics, which appear over a given time period.

38

The decline in the **d**_____242) of our food is an entirely human-made process. The biggest loss of crop diversity came in the decades **t**_____243) followed the Second World War. In an attempt to save millions from **e**_____244) hunger, crop scientists found ways to produce grains such as rice and wheat on an enormous **s**_____245). And thousands of **t**_____246) varieties were replaced by a small number of new super-productive ones. The **s**_____247) worked spectacularly well, **a**_____248) **l**_____249) to begin with. Because of it, grain production tripled, and between 1970 and 2020 the human population more than doubled. Leaving the **c**_____250) of that strategy to one side, the danger of creating more **u**_____251) crops is that they are more at risk when it comes to disasters. **S**_____252), a global food system that depends on just a **n**_____253) selection of plants has a **g**_____254) chance of not being able to survive diseases, pests and climate extremes.

39

Between 1940 and 2000, Cuba r_____255) the world baseball scene. They won 25 of the first 28 World Cups and 3 of 5 Olympic Games. The Cubans were known for wearing uniforms covered in red from head to toe, a strong c_____256) to the more c_____257) North American style featuring grey or white pants. N_____258) o_____259) were their athletic talents superior, the Cubans appeared e_____260) stronger from just the colour of their uniforms. A game would not even start and the o_____261) team would already be scared. A_____262) f_____263) years ago, Cuba altered that uniform style, modernizing it and perhaps conforming to other countries' style; interestingly, the national team has d_____264) since that time. The country that ruled international baseball for decades has not been on top s_____265) that uniform change. Traditions are important for a team; w_____266) a team brand or image can adjust to keep up with present times, if it a_____267) or n_____268) its roots, negative effects can surface.

40

Many of the first models of cultural evolution d_____269) noticeable connections between culture and genes by using concepts from theoretical population genetics and a_____270) them to culture. Cultural patterns of transmission, innovation, and selection are c_____271) likened to genetic processes of transmission, mutation, and selection. However, t_____272) approaches had to be modified to a_____273) f_____274) the differences between genetic and cultural transmission. For example, we do not expect the cultural transmission to follow the rules of genetic transmission s_____275). If two biological parents have different forms of a cultural trait, their child is n_____276) n_____277) equally likely to acquire the mother's or father's form of that trait. Further, a child can acquire cultural traits not only from its parents but also from n_____278) adults and peers; thus, the frequency of a cultural trait in the population is r_____279) beyond just the p_____280) that an individual's parents had that trait.

41~42

A ball thrown into the air is acted upon by the i_____281) force given it, persisting as inertia of movement and tending to carry it in the same straight line, and by the c_____282) pull of gravity downward, as well as by the r_____283) of the air. It moves, accordingly, in a c_____284) path. Now the path does not r_____285) the working of any particular force; there is simply the combination of the three e_____286) forces mentioned; but in a real sense, there is something in the total action b_____287) the isolated action of three forces, namely, their joint action. In the same way, w_____288) two or more human individuals are together, their m_____289) relationships and their arrangement into a group are things which would not be revealed if we confined our attention to e_____290) individual separately. The significance of group behavior is greatly increased in the case of human beings by the fact t_____291) some of the tendencies to action of the individual are related definitely to o_____292) persons, and could not be aroused except by other persons a_____293) as stimuli. An individual in complete i_____294) would not reveal their competitive tendencies, their tendencies towards the opposite sex, their p_____295) tendencies towards children. This shows that the traits of human nature do not fully appear until the individual is b_____296) i_____297) relationships with other individuals.

43~45

There once lived a man in a village who was not happy with his life. He was always troubled by one problem or a_____298). One day, a saint with his guards s_____299) b_____300) his village. Many people heard the news and started going to him w_____301) their problems. The man also decided to visit the saint. Even after reaching the saint's place in the morning, he didn't get the o_____302) to meet him till evening. When the man got to meet the saint, he c_____303) that he was very unhappy with life because problems always s_____304) him, l_____305) workplace tension or worries about his health. He said, "Please give me a s_____306) so that all the problems in my life will end and I can live peacefully." The saint smiled and said that he would answer the request the next day. But the saint also asked if the man c_____307) do a small job for him. He told the man to take care of a hundred camels in his group that night, s_____308) "When all hundred camels sit down, you can go to sleep." The man agreed. The next morning when the saint met that man, he asked if the man h_____309) s_____310) well. Tired and sad, the man replied that he couldn't sleep even for a moment. In fact, the man tried very hard but couldn't make all the camels sit at the same time because e_____311) time he m_____312) one camel sit, a_____313) would stand up. The saint told him, "You realized that no matter how hard you try, you can't make all the camels sit down. If one problem is solved, for some reason, a_____314) will arise like the camels did. So, humans should enjoy life d_____315) these problems."

2023 고1 11월 모의고사

❶ voca ❷ text ❸ [/] ❹ _____ ❺ quiz 1 ❻ quiz 2 ❼ quiz 3 ❽ quiz 4 ❾ quiz 5

☑ **다음 글을 읽고 물음에 답하시오.** (18)

During that time, I've developed strong customer service and sales skills, and now I would like to apply for the sales position in your clothing store.

Dear Ms. MacAlpine,I was so excited to hear that your brand is opening a new shop on Bruns Street next month. (①) I have always appreciated the way your brand helps women to feel more stylish and confident. I am writing in response to your ad in the Bruns Journal. (②) I graduated from the Meline School of Fashion and have worked as a sales assistant at LoganMart for the last five years. (③) I am available for an interview at your earliest convenience. (④) I look forward to hearing from you.(⑤) Thank you for reading my letter. Yours sincerely, Grace Braddock

1. 1)글의 흐름으로 보아, 주어진 문장이 들어가기에 <u>가장 적절한</u> 곳은?

☑ **다음 글을 읽고 물음에 답하시오.** (19)

I tried to see where it went, but the sun hit my eyes and I lost track of it.

I had never seen a beach with such white sand or water that was such a beautiful shade of blue. (①) Jane and I set up a blanket on the sand while looking forward to our ten days of honeymooning on an exotic island. (②) "Look"! Jane waved her hand to point at the beautiful scene before us—and her gold wedding ring went flying off her hand. (③) I didn't want to lose her wedding ring, so I started looking in the area where I thought it had landed. (④) However, the sand was so fine and I realized a truth. (⑤) Anything heavy, like gold, would quickly sink and might never be found again.

2. 2)글의 흐름으로 보아, 주어진 문장이 들어가기에 <u>가장 적절한</u> 곳은?

☑ **다음 글을 읽고 물음에 답하시오.** (19)

However, the sand was so fine and I realized a truth.

I had never seen a beach with such white sand or water that was such a beautiful shade of blue. (①) Jane and I set up a blanket on the sand while looking forward to our ten days of honeymooning on an exotic island. (②) "Look"! Jane waved her hand to point at the beautiful scene before us—and her gold wedding ring went flying off her hand. (③) I tried to see where it went, but the sun hit my eyes and I lost track of it. (④) I didn't want to lose her wedding ring, so I started looking in the area where I thought it had landed. (⑤) Anything heavy, like gold, would quickly sink and might never be found again.

3. 3)글의 흐름으로 보아, 주어진 문장이 들어가기에 <u>가장 적절한</u> 곳은?

☑ **다음 글을 읽고 물음에 답하시오.** (20)

Instead, they simply run the race laid out for them.

Unfortunately, many people don't take personal responsibility for their own growth. (①) They do well enough in school to keep advancing. Maybe they manage to get a good job at a well-run company. (②) But so many think and act as if their learning journey ends with college. (③) They have checked all the boxes in the life that was laid out for them and now lack a road map describing the right ways to move forward and continue to grow. In truth, that's when the journey really begins. When school is finished, your growth becomes voluntary. (④) Like healthy eating habits or a regular exercise program, you need to commit to it and devote thought, time, and energy to it. (⑤) Otherwise, it simply won't happen—and your life and career are likely to stop progressing as a result.

4. 4)글의 흐름으로 보아, 주어진 문장이 들어가기에 <u>가장 적절한</u> 곳은?

☑ **다음 글을 읽고 물음에 답하시오.** (20)

> Otherwise, it simply won't happen—and your life and career are likely to stop progressing as a result.

Unfortunately, many people don't take personal responsibility for their own growth. Instead, they simply run the race laid out for them. (①) They do well enough in school to keep advancing. Maybe they manage to get a good job at a well-run company. (②) But so many think and act as if their learning journey ends with college. (③) They have checked all the boxes in the life that was laid out for them and now lack a road map describing the right ways to move forward and continue to grow. (④) In truth, that's when the journey really begins. When school is finished, your growth becomes voluntary. (⑤) Like healthy eating habits or a regular exercise program, you need to commit to it and devote thought, time, and energy to it.

5. 5)글의 흐름으로 보아, 주어진 문장이 들어가기에 <u>가장 적절한</u> 곳은?

☑ **다음 글을 읽고 물음에 답하시오.** (20)

> But so many think and act as if their learning journey ends with college.

Unfortunately, many people don't take personal responsibility for their own growth. Instead, they simply run the race laid out for them. (①) They do well enough in school to keep advancing. Maybe they manage to get a good job at a well-run company. (②) They have checked all the boxes in the life that was laid out for them and now lack a road map describing the right ways to move forward and continue to grow. (③) In truth, that's when the journey really begins. When school is finished, your growth becomes voluntary. (④) Like healthy eating habits or a regular exercise program, you need to commit to it and devote thought, time, and energy to it. (⑤) Otherwise, it simply won't happen—and your life and career are likely to stop progressing as a result.

6. 6)글의 흐름으로 보아, 주어진 문장이 들어가기에 <u>가장 적절한</u> 곳은?

☑ **다음 글을 읽고 물음에 답하시오.** (21)

> Both positions are, in a way, correct.

Many people take the commonsense view that color is an objective property of things, or of the light that bounces off them. (①) They say a tree's leaves are green because they reflect green light—a greenness that is just as real as the leaves. (②) Others argue that color doesn't inhabit the physical world at all but exists only in the eye or mind of the viewer. (③) They maintain that if a tree fell in a forest and no one was there to see it, its leaves would be colorless—and so would everything else. (④) They say there is no such thing as color; there are only the people who see it. (⑤) Color is objective and subjective—"the place", as Paul Cézanne put it, "where our brain and the universe meet". Color is created when light from the world is registered by the eyes and interpreted by the brain.

7. 7)글의 흐름으로 보아, 주어진 문장이 들어가기에 <u>가장 적절한</u> 곳은?

☑ **다음 글을 읽고 물음에 답하시오.** (22)

> But remember that you will drive your readers to boredom if you think that you need to pack everything you discover into your work.

When writing a novel, research for information needs to be done. (①) The thing is that some kinds of fiction demand a higher level of detail: crime fiction, for example, or scientific thrillers. (②) The information is never hard to find; one website for authors even organizes trips to police stations, so that crime writers can get it right. (③) Often, a polite letter will earn you permission to visit a particular location and record all the details that you need. (④) The details that matter are those that reveal the human experience. (⑤) The crucial thing is telling a story, finding the characters, the tension, and the conflict—not the train timetable or the building blueprint.

8. 8)글의 흐름으로 보아, 주어진 문장이 들어가기에 <u>가장 적절한</u> 곳은?

☑ **다음 글을 읽고 물음에 답하시오.** (23)

> What happens in the mouth is usually just the tip of the iceberg and a reflection of what is happening in other parts of the body.

Nearly everything has to go through your mouth to get to the rest of you, from food and air to bacteria and viruses. (①) A healthy mouth can help your body get what it needs and prevent it from harm. (②) The mouth provides you with adequate space for air to travel to your lungs, and healthy teeth and gums that prevent harmful microorganisms from entering your bloodstream. (③) From the moment you are created, oral health affects every aspect of your life. (④) Poor oral health can be a cause of a disease that affects the entire body. (⑤) The microorganisms in an unhealthy mouth can enter the bloodstream and travel anywhere in the body, posing serious health risks.

9. 9)글의 흐름으로 보아, 주어진 문장이 들어가기에 <u>가장 적절한</u> 곳은?

☑ **다음 글을 읽고 물음에 답하시오.** (24)

> But why should this be true?

Kids tire of their toys, college students get sick of cafeteria food, and sooner or later most of us lose interest in our favorite TV shows. The bottom line is that we humans are easily bored. (①) The answer lies buried deep in our nerve cells, which are designed to reduce their initial excited response to stimuli each time they occur. (②) At the same time, these neurons enhance their responses to things that change— especially things that change quickly. (③) We probably evolved this way because our ancestors got more survival value, for example, from attending to what was moving in a tree (such as a puma) than to the tree itself. (④) Boredom in reaction to an unchanging environment turns down the level of neural excitation so that new stimuli (like our ancestor's hypothetical puma threat) stand out more. (⑤) It's the neural equivalent of turning off a front door light to see the fireflies.

10. 10)글의 흐름으로 보아, 주어진 문장이 들어가기에 <u>가장 적절한</u> 곳은?

☑ **다음 글을 읽고 물음에 답하시오.** (24)

> At the same time, these neurons enhance their responses to things that change—especially things that change quickly.

Kids tire of their toys, college students get sick of cafeteria food, and sooner or later most of us lose interest in our favorite TV shows. The bottom line is that we humans are easily bored. (①) But why should this be true? (②) The answer lies buried deep in our nerve cells, which are designed to reduce their initial excited response to stimuli each time they occur. (③) We probably evolved this way because our ancestors got more survival value, for example, from attending to what was moving in a tree (such as a puma) than to the tree itself. (④) Boredom in reaction to an unchanging environment turns down the level of neural excitation so that new stimuli (like our ancestor's hypothetical puma threat) stand out more. (⑤) It's the neural equivalent of turning off a front door light to see the fireflies.

11. 11)글의 흐름으로 보아, 주어진 문장이 들어가기에 <u>가장 적절한</u> 곳은?

☑ 다음 글을 읽고 물음에 답하시오. (25)

> The investment gap between clean energy and fossil fuels in 2020 was larger than that in 2019.

The above graph shows global energy investment in clean energy and in fossil fuels between 2018 and 2022. (①) Since 2018 global energy investment in clean energy continued to rise, reaching its highest level in 2022. (②) Investment in fossil fuels was highest in 2018 and lowest in 2020. (③) In 2021, investment in clean energy exceeded 1,200 billion dollars, while investment in fossil fuels did not. (④) In 2022, the global investment in clean energy was less than double that of fossil fuels.(⑤)

12. 12)글의 흐름으로 보아, 주어진 문장이 들어가기에 <u>가장 적절한</u> 곳은?

☑ 다음 글을 읽고 물음에 답하시오. (26)

> He assisted other runaway slaves until they could safely get to other areas in the north.

Frederick Douglass was born into slavery at a farm in Maryland. His full name at birth was Frederick Augustus Washington Bailey. He changed his name to Frederick Douglass after he successfully escaped from slavery in 1838. (①) He became a leader of the Underground Railroad—a network of people, places, and routes that helped enslaved people escape to the north. (②) As a slave, he had taught himself to read and write and he spread that knowledge to other slaves as well. (③) Once free, he became a well-known abolitionist and strong believer in equality for all people including Blacks, Native Americans, women, and recent immigrants. (④) He wrote several autobiographies describing his experiences as a slave. (⑤) In addition to all this, he became the first African-American candidate for vice president of the United States.

13. 13)글의 흐름으로 보아, 주어진 문장이 들어가기에 <u>가장 적절한</u> 곳은?

☑ 다음 글을 읽고 물음에 답하시오. (26)

> In addition to all this, he became the first African-American candidate for vice president of the United States.

Frederick Douglass was born into slavery at a farm in Maryland. His full name at birth was Frederick Augustus Washington Bailey. He changed his name to Frederick Douglass after he successfully escaped from slavery in 1838. (①) He became a leader of the Underground Railroad—a network of people, places, and routes that helped enslaved people escape to the north. (②) He assisted other runaway slaves until they could safely get to other areas in the north. (③) As a slave, he had taught himself to read and write and he spread that knowledge to other slaves as well. (④) Once free, he became a well-known abolitionist and strong believer in equality for all people including Blacks, Native Americans, women, and recent immigrants. (⑤) He wrote several autobiographies describing his experiences as a slave.

14. 14)글의 흐름으로 보아, 주어진 문장이 들어가기에 <u>가장 적절한</u> 곳은?

☑ 다음 글을 읽고 물음에 답하시오. (29)

The reason for these strict regulations for diagnosing brain death in potential organ donors is, no doubt, to ease public fears of a premature diagnosis of brain death for the purpose of obtaining organs.

Some countries have proposed tougher guidelines for determining brain death when transplantation—transferring organs to others—is under consideration. (①) In several European countries, there are legal requirements which specify that a whole team of doctors must agree over the diagnosis of death in the case of a potential donor. (②) But it is questionable whether these requirements reduce public suspicions as much as they create them. (③) They certainly maintain mistaken beliefs that diagnosing brain death is an unreliable process lacking precision. (④) As a matter of consistency, at least, criteria for diagnosing the deaths of organ donors should be exactly the same as for those for whom immediate burial or cremation is intended.(⑤)

15. 15)글의 흐름으로 보아, 주어진 문장이 들어가기에 가장 적절한 곳은?

☑ 다음 글을 읽고 물음에 답하시오. (29)

But it is questionable whether these requirements reduce public suspicions as much as they create them.

Some countries have proposed tougher guidelines for determining brain death when transplantation—transferring organs to others—is under consideration. (①) In several European countries, there are legal requirements which specify that a whole team of doctors must agree over the diagnosis of death in the case of a potential donor. (②) The reason for these strict regulations for diagnosing brain death in potential organ donors is, no doubt, to ease public fears of a premature diagnosis of brain death for the purpose of obtaining organs. (③) They certainly maintain mistaken beliefs that diagnosing brain death is an unreliable process lacking precision. (④) As a matter of consistency, at least, criteria for diagnosing the deaths of organ donors should be exactly the same as for those for whom immediate burial or cremation is intended.(⑤)

16. 16)글의 흐름으로 보아, 주어진 문장이 들어가기에 가장 적절한 곳은?

☑ 다음 글을 읽고 물음에 답하시오. (30)

They are of the view that you only need to eliminate stuff that is unused or not going to be used in the near future.

The term minimalism gives a negative impression to some people who think that it is all about sacrificing valuable possessions. This insecurity naturally stems from their attachment to their possessions. It is difficult to distance oneself from something that has been around for quite some time. (①) Being an emotional animal, human beings give meaning to the things around them. (②) So, the question arising here is that if minimalism will hurt one's emotions, why become a minimalist? (③) The answer is very simple; the assumption of the question is fundamentally wrong. Minimalism does not hurt emotions. (④) You might feel a bit sad while getting rid of a useless item but sooner than later, this feeling will be overcome by the joy of clarity. (⑤) Minimalists never argue that you should leave every convenience of the modern era.

17. 17)글의 흐름으로 보아, 주어진 문장이 들어가기에 가장 적절한 곳은?

☑ **다음 글을 읽고 물음에 답하시오.** (31)

With time, however, his visual system adjusted to the new stimuli from reality, and he was able to act normally in his environment again, even seeing it upright when he concentrated.

A remarkable characteristic of the visual system is that it has the ability of adapting itself. Psychologist George M. Stratton made this clear in an impressive self-experiment. (①) Stratton wore reversing glasses for several days, which literally turned the world upside down for him. (②) In the beginning, this caused him great difficulties: just putting food in his mouth with a fork was a challenge for him. (③) As he took off his reversing glasses, he was again confronted with problems: he used the wrong hand when he wanted to reach for something, for example. (④) Fortunately, Stratton could reverse the perception, and he did not have to wear reversing glasses for the rest of his life. (⑤) For him, everything returned to normal after one day.

18. 18)글의 흐름으로 보아, 주어진 문장이 들어가기에 가장 적절한 곳은?

☑ **다음 글을 읽고 물음에 답하시오.** (31)

As he took off his reversing glasses, he was again confronted with problems: he used the wrong hand when he wanted to reach for something, for example.

A remarkable characteristic of the visual system is that it has the ability of adapting itself. Psychologist George M. Stratton made this clear in an impressive self-experiment. (①) Stratton wore reversing glasses for several days, which literally turned the world upside down for him. (②) In the beginning, this caused him great difficulties: just putting food in his mouth with a fork was a challenge for him. (③) With time, however,

his visual system adjusted to the new stimuli from reality, and he was able to act normally in his environment again, even seeing it upright when he concentrated. (④) Fortunately, Stratton could reverse the perception, and he did not have to wear reversing glasses for the rest of his life. (⑤) For him, everything returned to normal after one day.

19. 19)글의 흐름으로 보아, 주어진 문장이 들어가기에 가장 적절한 곳은?

☑ **다음 글을 읽고 물음에 답하시오.** (32)

These questions were unrelated to the ones asked during the first part of the study, so participants who used the internet had absolutely no advantage over those who hadn't.

Participants in a study were asked to answer questions like "Why does the moon have phases"? (①) Half the participants were told to search for the answers on the internet, while the other half weren't allowed to do so. (②) Then, in the second part of the study, all of the participants were presented with a new set of questions, such as "Why does Swiss cheese have holes"? (③) You would think that both sets of participants would be equally sure or unsure about how well they could answer the new questions. (④) But those who used the internet in the first part of the study rated themselves as more knowledgeable than those who hadn't, even about questions they hadn't searched online for. (⑤) The study suggests that having access to unrelated information was enough to pump up their intellectual confidence.

20. 20)글의 흐름으로 보아, 주어진 문장이 들어가기에 가장 적절한 곳은?

☑ **다음 글을 읽고 물음에 답하시오.** (32)

But those who used the internet in the first part of the study rated themselves as more knowledgeable than those who hadn't, even about questions they hadn't searched online for.

Participants in a study were asked to answer questions like "Why does the moon have phases"? (①) Half the participants were told to search for the answers on the internet, while the other half weren't allowed to do so. (②) Then, in the second part of the study, all of the participants were presented with a new set of questions, such as "Why does Swiss cheese have holes"? (③) These questions were unrelated to the ones asked during the first part of the study, so participants who used the internet had absolutely no advantage over those who hadn't. (④) You would think that both sets of participants would be equally sure or unsure about how well they could answer the new questions. (⑤) The study suggests that having access to unrelated information was enough to pump up their intellectual confidence.

21. 21)글의 흐름으로 보아, 주어진 문장이 들어가기에 <u>가장</u> <u>적절한</u> 곳은?

☑ **다음 글을 읽고 물음에 답하시오.** (33)

It's possible to move between many of these perspectives, although we may need some additional tools and skills to zoom in on individual pieces of hair or zoom out to entire ecosystems.

Anthropologist Gregory Bateson suggests that we tend to understand the world by focusing in on particular features within it. Take platypuses. We might zoom in so closely to their fur that each hair appears different. (①) We might also zoom out to the extent where it appears as a single, uniform object. (②) We might take the platypus as an individual, or we might treat it as part of a larger unit such as a species or an ecosystem. (③) Crucially, however, we can only take up one perspective at a time. (④) We can pay attention to the varied behavior of individual animals, look at what unites them into a single species, or look at them as part of bigger ecological patterns. (⑤) Every possible perspective involves emphasizing certain aspects and ignoring others.

22. 22)글의 흐름으로 보아, 주어진 문장이 들어가기에 <u>가장</u> <u>적절한</u> 곳은?

☑ **다음 글을 읽고 물음에 답하시오.** (33)

Crucially, however, we can only take up one perspective at a time.

Anthropologist Gregory Bateson suggests that we tend to understand the world by focusing in on particular features within it. Take platypuses. We might zoom in so closely to their fur that each hair appears different. (①) We might also zoom out to the extent where it appears as a single, uniform object. (②) We might take the platypus as an individual, or we might treat it as part of a larger unit such as a species or an ecosystem. (③) It's possible to move between many of these perspectives, although we may need some additional tools and skills to zoom in on individual pieces of hair or zoom out to entire ecosystems. (④) We can pay attention to the varied behavior of individual animals, look at what unites them into a single species, or look at them as part of bigger ecological patterns. (⑤) Every possible perspective involves emphasizing certain aspects and ignoring others.

23. 23)글의 흐름으로 보아, 주어진 문장이 들어가기에 <u>가장</u> <u>적절한</u> 곳은?

☑ 다음 글을 읽고 물음에 답하시오. (34)

However, Plato would point out that, if you looked closely enough, you would see that neither it, nor indeed any physical circle, was perfect.

Plato's realism includes all aspects of experience but is most easily explained by considering the nature of mathematical and geometrical objects such as circles. He asked the question, what is a circle? (①) You might indicate a particular example carved into stone or drawn in the sand. (②) They all possessed flaws, and all were subject to change and decayed with time. (③) So how can we talk about perfect circles if we cannot actually see or touch them? (④) Plato's extraordinary answer was that the world we see is a poor reflection of a deeper unseen reality of Forms, or universals, where perfect cats chase perfect mice in perfect circles around perfect rocks. (⑤) Plato believed that the Forms or universals are the true reality that exists in an invisible but perfect world beyond our senses.

24. 24)글의 흐름으로 보아, 주어진 문장이 들어가기에 가장 적절한 곳은?

☑ 다음 글을 읽고 물음에 답하시오. (34)

They all possessed flaws, and all were subject to change and decayed with time.

Plato's realism includes all aspects of experience but is most easily explained by considering the nature of mathematical and geometrical objects such as circles. He asked the question, what is a circle? (①) You might indicate a particular example carved into stone or drawn in the sand. (②) However, Plato would point out that, if you looked closely enough, you would see that neither it, nor indeed any physical circle, was perfect. (③) So how can we talk about perfect circles if we cannot actually see or touch them? (④) Plato's extraordinary answer was that the world we see is a poor reflection of a

deeper unseen reality of Forms, or universals, where perfect cats chase perfect mice in perfect circles around perfect rocks. (⑤) Plato believed that the Forms or universals are the true reality that exists in an invisible but perfect world beyond our senses.

25. 25)글의 흐름으로 보아, 주어진 문장이 들어가기에 가장 적절한 곳은?

☑ 다음 글을 읽고 물음에 답하시오. (35)

But the more often you repeat this bet, the closer the relative frequency of wins and losses is expected to approach the true chance of winning, meaning that your luck will at some point fade away.

In statistics, the law of large numbers describes a situation where having more data is better for making predictions. (①) According to it, the more often an experiment is conducted, the closer the average of the results can be expected to match the true state of the world. (②) For instance, on your first encounter with the game of roulette, you may have beginner's luck after betting on 7. (③) Similarly, car insurers collect large amounts of data to figure out the chances that drivers will cause accidents, depending on their age, region, or car brand. (④) Both casinos and insurance industries rely on the law of large numbers to balance individual losses.(⑤)

26. 26)글의 흐름으로 보아, 주어진 문장이 들어가기에 가장 적절한 곳은?

☑ **다음 글을 읽고 물음에 답하시오.** (35)

> Similarly, car insurers collect large amounts of data to figure out the chances that drivers will cause accidents, depending on their age, region, or car brand.

In statistics, the law of large numbers describes a situation where having more data is better for making predictions. (①) According to it, the more often an experiment is conducted, the closer the average of the results can be expected to match the true state of the world. (②) For instance, on your first encounter with the game of roulette, you may have beginner's luck after betting on 7. (③) But the more often you repeat this bet, the closer the relative frequency of wins and losses is expected to approach the true chance of winning, meaning that your luck will at some point fade away. (④) Both casinos and insurance industries rely on the law of large numbers to balance individual losses.(⑤)

27. 27)글의 흐름으로 보아, 주어진 문장이 들어가기에 <u>가장 적절한</u> 곳은?

☑ **다음 글을 읽고 물음에 답하시오.** (35)

> Both casinos and insurance industries rely on the law of large numbers to balance individual losses.

In statistics, the law of large numbers describes a situation where having more data is better for making predictions. (①) According to it, the more often an experiment is conducted, the closer the average of the results can be expected to match the true state of the world. (②) For instance, on your first encounter with the game of roulette, you may have beginner's luck after betting on 7. (③) But the more often you repeat this bet, the closer the relative frequency of wins and losses is expected to approach the true chance of winning, meaning that your luck will at some point fade

away. (④) Similarly, car insurers collect large amounts of data to figure out the chances that drivers will cause accidents, depending on their age, region, or car brand. (⑤)

28. 28)글의 흐름으로 보아, 주어진 문장이 들어가기에 <u>가장 적절한</u> 곳은?

☑ **다음 글을 읽고 물음에 답하시오.** (36)

> On the other hand, the limbic system matures earlier, playing a central role in processing emotional responses.

The adolescent brain is not fully developed until its early twenties. This means the way the adolescents' decision-making circuits integrate and process information may put them at a disadvantage. One of their brain regions that matures later is the prefrontal cortex, which is the control center, tasked with thinking ahead and evaluating consequences. (①) It is the area of the brain responsible for preventing you from sending off an initial angry text and modifying it with kinder words. (②) Because of its earlier development, it is more likely to influence decision-making. (③) Decision-making in the adolescent brain is led by emotional factors more than the perception of consequences. (④) Due to these differences, there is an imbalance between feeling-based decision-making ruled by the more mature limbic system and logical-based decision-making by the not-yet-mature prefrontal cortex. (⑤) This may explain why some teens are more likely to make bad decisions.

29. 29)글의 흐름으로 보아, 주어진 문장이 들어가기에 <u>가장 적절한</u> 곳은?

☑ 다음 글을 읽고 물음에 답하시오. (36)

Due to these differences, there is an imbalance between feeling-based decision-making ruled by the more mature limbic system and logical-based decision-making by the not-yet-mature prefrontal cortex.

The adolescent brain is not fully developed until its early twenties. This means the way the adolescents' decision-making circuits integrate and process information may put them at a disadvantage. One of their brain regions that matures later is the prefrontal cortex, which is the control center, tasked with thinking ahead and evaluating consequences. (①) It is the area of the brain responsible for preventing you from sending off an initial angry text and modifying it with kinder words. (②) On the other hand, the limbic system matures earlier, playing a central role in processing emotional responses. (③) Because of its earlier development, it is more likely to influence decision-making. (④) Decision-making in the adolescent brain is led by emotional factors more than the perception of consequences. (⑤) This may explain why some teens are more likely to make bad decisions.

30. 30)글의 흐름으로 보아, 주어진 문장이 들어가기에 가장 적절한 곳은?

☑ 다음 글을 읽고 물음에 답하시오. (37)

These changes may be highlighted by weight gain or loss.

Despite the remarkable progress in deep-learning based facial recognition approaches in recent years, in terms of identification performance, they still have limitations. These limitations relate to the database used in the learning stage. (①) If the selected database does not contain enough instances, the result may be systematically affected. (②) For example, the

performance of a facial biometric system may decrease if the person to be identified was enrolled over 10 years ago. (③) The factor to consider is that this person may experience changes in the texture of the face, particularly with the appearance of wrinkles and sagging skin. (④) To counteract this problem, researchers have developed models for face aging or digital de-aging. (⑤) It is used to compensate for the differences in facial characteristics, which appear over a given time period.

31. 31)글의 흐름으로 보아, 주어진 문장이 들어가기에 가장 적절한 곳은?

☑ 다음 글을 읽고 물음에 답하시오. (37)

To counteract this problem, researchers have developed models for face aging or digital de-aging.

Despite the remarkable progress in deep-learning based facial recognition approaches in recent years, in terms of identification performance, they still have limitations. These limitations relate to the database used in the learning stage. (①) If the selected database does not contain enough instances, the result may be systematically affected. (②) For example, the performance of a facial biometric system may decrease if the person to be identified was enrolled over 10 years ago. (③) The factor to consider is that this person may experience changes in the texture of the face, particularly with the appearance of wrinkles and sagging skin. (④) These changes may be highlighted by weight gain or loss. (⑤) It is used to compensate for the differences in facial characteristics, which appear over a given time period.

32. 32)글의 흐름으로 보아, 주어진 문장이 들어가기에 가장 적절한 곳은?

☑ **다음 글을 읽고 물음에 답하시오.** (38)

> The strategy worked spectacularly well, at least to begin with.

The decline in the diversity of our food is an entirely human-made process. The biggest loss of crop diversity came in the decades that followed the Second World War. (①) In an attempt to save millions from extreme hunger, crop scientists found ways to produce grains such as rice and wheat on an enormous scale. (②) And thousands of traditional varieties were replaced by a small number of new super-productive ones. (③) Because of it, grain production tripled, and between 1970 and 2020 the human population more than doubled. (④) Leaving the contribution of that strategy to one side, the danger of creating more uniform crops is that they are more at risk when it comes to disasters. (⑤) Specifically, a global food system that depends on just a narrow selection of plants has a greater chance of not being able to survive diseases, pests and climate extremes.

33. 33)글의 흐름으로 보아, 주어진 문장이 들어가기에 <u>가장 적절한</u> 곳은?

☑ **다음 글을 읽고 물음에 답하시오.** (38)

> Leaving the contribution of that strategy to one side, the danger of creating more uniform crops is that they are more at risk when it comes to disasters.

The decline in the diversity of our food is an entirely human-made process. The biggest loss of crop diversity came in the decades that followed the Second World War. (①) In an attempt to save millions from extreme hunger, crop scientists found ways to produce grains such as rice and wheat on an enormous scale. (②) And thousands of traditional varieties were replaced by a small number of new super-productive ones. (③) The strategy worked spectacularly well, at least to begin with. (④) Because of it, grain production tripled, and between 1970 and 2020 the human population more than doubled. (⑤) Specifically, a global food system that depends on just a narrow selection of plants has a greater chance of not being able to survive diseases, pests and climate extremes.

34. 34)글의 흐름으로 보아, 주어진 문장이 들어가기에 <u>가장 적절한</u> 곳은?

☑ **다음 글을 읽고 물음에 답하시오.** (39)

> Not only were their athletic talents superior, the Cubans appeared even stronger from just the colour of their uniforms.

Between 1940 and 2000, Cuba ruled the world baseball scene. They won 25 of the first 28 World Cups and 3 of 5 Olympic Games. (①) The Cubans were known for wearing uniforms covered in red from head to toe, a strong contrast to the more conservative North American style featuring grey or white pants. (②) A game would not even start and the opposing team would already be scared. (③) A few years ago, Cuba altered that uniform style, modernizing it and perhaps conforming to other countries' style; interestingly, the national team has declined since that time. (④) The country that ruled international baseball for decades has not been on top since that uniform change. (⑤) Traditions are important for a team; while a team brand or image can adjust to keep up with present times, if it abandons or neglects its roots, negative effects can surface.

35. 35)글의 흐름으로 보아, 주어진 문장이 들어가기에 <u>가장 적절한</u> 곳은?

☑ **다음 글을 읽고 물음에 답하시오.** (39)

> A few years ago, Cuba altered that uniform style, modernizing it and perhaps conforming to other countries' style; interestingly, the national team has declined since that time.

Between 1940 and 2000, Cuba ruled the world baseball scene. They won 25 of the first 28 World Cups and 3 of 5 Olympic Games. (①) The Cubans were known for wearing uniforms covered in red from head to toe, a strong contrast to the more conservative North American style featuring grey or white pants. (②) Not only were their athletic talents superior, the Cubans appeared even stronger from just the colour of their uniforms. (③) A game would not even start and the opposing team would already be scared. (④) The country that ruled international baseball for decades has not been on top since that uniform change. (⑤) Traditions are important for a team; while a team brand or image can adjust to keep up with present times, if it abandons or neglects its roots, negative effects can surface.

36. 36)글의 흐름으로 보아, 주어진 문장이 들어가기에 <u>가장 적절한</u> 곳은?

☑ **다음 글을 읽고 물음에 답하시오.** (40)

> However, these approaches had to be modified to account for the differences between genetic and cultural transmission.

Many of the first models of cultural evolution drew noticeable connections between culture and genes by using concepts from theoretical population genetics and applying them to culture. (①) Cultural patterns of transmission, innovation, and selection are conceptually likened to genetic processes of transmission, mutation, and selection. (②) For example, we do not expect the

cultural transmission to follow the rules of genetic transmission strictly. (③) If two biological parents have different forms of a cultural trait, their child is not necessarily equally likely to acquire the mother's or father's form of that trait. (④) Further, a child can acquire cultural traits not only from its parents but also from nonparental adults and peers. (⑤) Thus, the frequency of a cultural trait in the population is relevant beyond just the probability that an individual's parents had that trait.

37. 37)글의 흐름으로 보아, 주어진 문장이 들어가기에 <u>가장 적절한</u> 곳은?

☑ **다음 글을 읽고 물음에 답하시오.** (40)

> Further, a child can acquire cultural traits not only from its parents but also from nonparental adults and peers.

Many of the first models of cultural evolution drew noticeable connections between culture and genes by using concepts from theoretical population genetics and applying them to culture. (①) Cultural patterns of transmission, innovation, and selection are conceptually likened to genetic processes of transmission, mutation, and selection. (②) However, these approaches had to be modified to account for the differences between genetic and cultural transmission. (③) For example, we do not expect the cultural transmission to follow the rules of genetic transmission strictly. (④) If two biological parents have different forms of a cultural trait, their child is not necessarily equally likely to acquire the mother's or father's form of that trait. (⑤) Thus, the frequency of a cultural trait in the population is relevant beyond just the probability that an individual's parents had that trait.

38. 38)글의 흐름으로 보아, 주어진 문장이 들어가기에 <u>가장 적절한</u> 곳은?

☑ **다음 글을 읽고 물음에 답하시오.** (40)

Thus, the frequency of a cultural trait in the population is relevant beyond just the probability that an individual's parents had that trait.

Many of the first models of cultural evolution drew noticeable connections between culture and genes by using concepts from theoretical population genetics and applying them to culture. (①) Cultural patterns of transmission, innovation, and selection are conceptually likened to genetic processes of transmission, mutation, and selection. (②) However, these approaches had to be modified to account for the differences between genetic and cultural transmission. (③) For example, we do not expect the cultural transmission to follow the rules of genetic transmission strictly. (④) If two biological parents have different forms of a cultural trait, their child is not necessarily equally likely to acquire the mother's or father's form of that trait. (⑤) Further, a child can acquire cultural traits not only from its parents but also from nonparental adults and peers.

39. 39)글의 흐름으로 보아, 주어진 문장이 들어가기에 <u>가장</u> <u>적절한</u> 곳은?

☑ **다음 글을 읽고 물음에 답하시오.** (41,42)

In the same way, when two or more human individuals are together, their mutual relationships and their arrangement into a group are things which would not be revealed if we confined our attention to each individual separately.

A ball thrown into the air is acted upon by the initial force given it, persisting as inertia of movement and tending to carry it in the same straight line, and by the constant pull of gravity downward, as well as by the resistance of the air. (①) It moves, accordingly, in a curved path. (②) Now the path does not represent the working of any particular force; there is simply the combination of the three elementary forces mentioned; but in a real sense, there is something in the total action besides the isolated action of three forces, namely, their joint action. (③) The significance of group behavior is greatly increased in the case of human beings by the fact that some of the tendencies to action of the individual are related definitely to other persons, and could not be aroused except by other persons acting as stimuli. (④) An individual in complete isolation would not reveal their competitive tendencies, their tendencies towards the opposite sex, their protective tendencies towards children. (⑤) This shows that the traits of human nature do not fully appear until the individual is brought into relationships with other individuals.

40. 40)글의 흐름으로 보아, 주어진 문장이 들어가기에 <u>가장</u> <u>적절한</u> 곳은?

☑ **다음 글을 읽고 물음에 답하시오.** (41,42)

An individual in complete isolation would not reveal their competitive tendencies, their tendencies towards the opposite sex, their protective tendencies towards children.

A ball thrown into the air is acted upon by the initial force given it, persisting as inertia of movement and tending to carry it in the same straight line, and by the constant pull of gravity downward, as well as by the resistance of the air. (①) It moves, accordingly, in a curved path. (②) Now the path does not represent the working of any particular force; there is simply the combination of the three elementary forces mentioned; but in a real sense, there is something in the total action besides the isolated action of three forces, namely, their joint action. (③) In the same way, when two or more human individuals are together, their mutual relationships and their arrangement into a group are things which would not be revealed if we confined our attention to each individual separately. (④) The significance of group behavior is greatly increased in the case of human beings by the fact that some of the tendencies to action of the individual are related definitely to other persons, and could not be aroused except by other persons acting as stimuli. (⑤) This shows that the traits of human nature do not fully appear until the individual is brought into relationships with other individuals.

41. 41)글의 흐름으로 보아, 주어진 문장이 들어가기에 <u>가장 적절한</u> 곳은?

☑ **다음 글을 읽고 물음에 답하시오.** (43,44,45)

When the man got to meet the saint, he confessed that he was very unhappy with life because problems always surrounded him, like workplace tension or worries about his health. He said, "Please give me a solution so that all the problems in my life will end and I can live peacefully".

There once lived a man in a village who was not happy with his life. He was always troubled by one problem or another. One day, a saint with his guards stopped by his village. Many people heard the news and started going to him with their problems. (①) The man also decided to visit the saint. Even after reaching the saint's place in the morning, he didn't get the opportunity to meet him till evening. (②) The saint smiled and said that he would answer the request the next day. But the saint also asked if the man could do a small job for him. (③) He told the man to take care of a hundred camels in his group that night, saying "When all hundred camels sit down, you can go to sleep". The man agreed. The next morning when the saint met that man, he asked if the man had slept well. (④) Tired and sad, the man replied that he couldn't sleep even for a moment. In fact, the man tried very hard but couldn't make all the camels sit at the same time because every time he made one camel sit, another would stand up. (⑤) The saint told him, "You realized that no matter how hard you try, you can't make all the camels sit down. If one problem is solved, for some reason, another will arise like the camels did. So, humans should enjoy life despite these problems".

42. 42)글의 흐름으로 보아, 주어진 문장이 들어가기에 <u>가장 적절한</u> 곳은?

43. 43) 18.

Dear Ms. MacAlpine,
I was so excited to hear that your brand is opening a new shop on Bruns Street next month.

(A) Thank you for reading my letter. Yours sincerely, Grace Braddock

(B) During that time, I've developed strong customer service and sales skills, and now I would like to apply for the sales position in your clothing store. I am available for an interview at your earliest convenience. I look forward to hearing from you.

(C) I have always appreciated the way your brand helps women to feel more stylish and confident. I am writing in response to your ad in the Bruns Journal. I graduated from the Meline School of Fashion and have worked as a sales assistant at LoganMart for the last five years.

44. 44) 19.

I had never seen a beach with such white sand or water that was such a beautiful shade of blue.

(A) Jane waved her hand to point at the beautiful scene before us—and her gold wedding ring went flying off her hand.

(B) I didn't want to lose her wedding ring, so I started looking in the area where I thought it had landed.

(C) Jane and I set up a blanket on the sand while looking forward to our ten days of honeymooning on an exotic island. "Look!"

(D) I tried to see where it went, but the sun hit my eyes and I lost track of it.

(E) However, the sand was so fine and I realized that anything heavy, like gold, would quickly sink and might never be found again.

45. 45) 20.

Unfortunately, many people don't take personal responsibility for their own growth.

(A) Instead, they simply run the race laid out for them. They do well enough in school to keep advancing. Maybe they manage to get a good job at a well-run company.

(B) But so many think and act as if their learning journey ends with college. They have checked all the boxes in the life that was laid out for them and now lack a road map describing the right ways to move forward and continue to grow.

(C) In truth, that's when the journey really begins. When school is finished, your growth becomes voluntary.

(D) Like healthy eating habits or a regular exercise program, you need to commit to it and devote thought, time, and energy to it. Otherwise, it simply won't happen—and your life and career are likely to stop progressing as a result.

46. 46) 21.

Many people take the commonsense view that color is an objective property of things, or of the light that bounces off them.

(A) They say there is no such thing as color; there are only the people who see it. Both positions are, in a way, correct.

(B) Color is objective and subjective—"the place," as Paul Cézanne put it, "where our brain and the universe meet." Color is created when light from the world is registered by the eyes and interpreted by the brain.

(C) They say a tree's leaves are green because they reflect green light—a greenness that is just as real as the leaves. Others argue that color doesn't inhabit the physical world at all but exists only in the eye or mind of the viewer. They maintain that if a tree fell in a forest and no one was there to see it, its leaves would be colorless—and so would everything else.

47. 47) 22.

When writing a novel, research for information needs to be done.

(A) The details that matter are those that reveal the human experience.

(B) Often, a polite letter will earn you permission to visit a particular location and record all the details that you need. But remember that you will drive your readers to boredom if you think that you need to pack everything you discover into your work.

(C) The thing is that some kinds of fiction demand a higher level of detail: crime fiction, for example, or scientific thrillers. The information is never hard to find; one website for authors even organizes trips to police stations, so that crime writers can get it right.

(D) The crucial thing is telling a story, finding the characters, the tension, and the conflict—not the train timetable or the building blueprint.

48. 48) 23.

Nearly everything has to go through your mouth to get to the rest of you, from food and air to bacteria and viruses.

(A) The microorganisms in an unhealthy mouth can enter the bloodstream and travel anywhere in the body, posing serious health risks.

(B) A healthy mouth can help your body get what it needs and prevent it from harm—with adequate space for air to travel to your lungs, and healthy teeth and gums that prevent harmful microorganisms from entering your bloodstream. From the moment you are created, oral health affects every aspect of your life.

(C) What happens in the mouth is usually just the tip of the iceberg and a reflection of what is happening in other parts of the body. Poor oral health can be a cause of a disease that affects the entire body.

49. 49) 24.

Kids tire of their toys, college students get sick of cafeteria food, and sooner or later most of us lose interest in our favorite TV shows.

(A) The bottom line is that we humans are easily bored. But why should this be true?

(B) It's the neural equivalent of turning off a front door light to see the fireflies.

(C) The answer lies buried deep in our nerve cells, which are designed to reduce their initial excited response to stimuli each time they occur. At the same time, these neurons enhance their responses to things that change—especially things that change quickly.

(D) We probably evolved this way because our ancestors got more survival value, for example, from attending to what was moving in a tree (such as a puma) than to the tree itself. Boredom in reaction to an unchanging environment turns down the level of neural excitation so that new stimuli (like our ancestor's hypothetical puma threat) stand out more.

50. 50) 26.

Frederick Douglass was born into slavery at a farm in Maryland.

(A) He became a leader of the Underground Railroad—a network of people, places, and routes that helped enslaved people escape to the north. He assisted other runaway slaves until they could safely get to other areas in the north.

(B) His full name at birth was Frederick Augustus Washington Bailey. He changed his name to Frederick Douglass after he successfully escaped from slavery in 1838.

(C) He wrote several autobiographies describing his experiences as a slave. In addition to all this, he became the first African-American candidate for vice president of the United States.

(D) As a slave, he had taught himself to read and write and he spread that knowledge to other slaves as well. Once free, he became a well-known abolitionist and strong believer in equality for all people including Blacks, Native Americans, women, and recent immigrants.

51. 51) 29.

Some countries have proposed tougher guidelines for determining brain death when transplantation—transferring organs to others—is under consideration.

(A) As a matter of consistency, at least, criteria for diagnosing the deaths of organ donors should be exactly the same as for those for whom immediate burial or cremation is intended.

(B) They certainly maintain mistaken beliefs that diagnosing brain death is an unreliable process lacking precision.

(C) In several European countries, there are legal requirements which specify that a whole team of doctors must agree over the diagnosis of death in the case of a potential donor. The reason for these strict regulations for diagnosing brain death in potential organ donors is, no doubt, to ease public fears of a premature diagnosis of brain death for the purpose of obtaining organs.

(D) But it is questionable whether these requirements reduce public suspicions as much as they create them.

52. 52) 30.

The term minimalism gives a negative impression to some people who think that it is all about sacrificing valuable possessions.

(A) So, the question arising here is that if minimalism will hurt one's emotions, why become a minimalist? The answer is very simple; the assumption of the question is fundamentally wrong.

(B) Minimalism does not hurt emotions. You might feel a bit sad while getting rid of a useless item but sooner than later, this feeling will be overcome by the joy of clarity.

(C) Minimalists never argue that you should leave every convenience of the modern era. They are of the view that you only need to eliminate stuff that is unused or not going to be used in the near future.

(D) This insecurity naturally stems from their attachment to their possessions. It is difficult to distance oneself from something that has been around for quite some time. Being an emotional animal, human beings give meaning to the things around them.

53. 53) 31.

A remarkable characteristic of the visual system is that it has the ability of adapting itself.

(A) Fortunately, Stratton could reverse the perception, and he did not have to wear reversing glasses for the rest of his life.

(B) Psychologist George M. Stratton made this clear in an impressive self-experiment.

(C) With time, however, his visual system adjusted to the new stimuli from reality, and he was able to act normally in his environment again, even seeing it upright when he concentrated. As he took off his reversing glasses, he was again confronted with problems: he used the wrong hand when he wanted to reach for something, for example.

(D) For him, everything returned to normal after one day.

(E) Stratton wore reversing glasses for several days, which literally turned the world upside down for him. In the beginning, this caused him great difficulties: just putting food in his mouth with a fork was a challenge for him.

54. 54) 32.

Participants in a study were asked to answer questions like "Why does the moon have phases?"

(A) But those who used the internet in the first part of the study rated themselves as more knowledgeable than those who hadn't, even about questions they hadn't searched online for.

(B) These questions were unrelated to the ones asked during the first part of the study, so participants who used the internet had absolutely no advantage over those who hadn't. You would think that both sets of participants would be equally sure or unsure about how well they could answer the new questions.

(C) Half the participants were told to search for the answers on the internet, while the other half weren't allowed to do so. Then, in the second part of the study, all of the participants were presented with a new set of questions, such as "Why does Swiss cheese have holes?"

(D) The study suggests that having access to unrelated information was enough to pump up their intellectual confidence.

55. 55) 33.

Anthropologist Gregory Bateson suggests that we tend to understand the world by focusing in on particular features within it.

(A) We can pay attention to the varied behavior of individual animals, look at what unites them into a single species, or look at them as part of bigger ecological patterns. Every possible perspective involves emphasizing certain aspects and ignoring others.

(B) Take platypuses. We might zoom in so closely to their fur that each hair appears different.

(C) We might also zoom out to the extent where it appears as a single, uniform object. We might take the platypus as an individual, or we might treat it as part of a larger unit such as a species or an ecosystem.

(D) It's possible to move between many of these perspectives, although we may need some additional tools and skills to zoom in on individual pieces of hair or zoom out to entire ecosystems. Crucially, however, we can only take up one perspective at a time.

56. 56) 34.

Plato's realism includes all aspects of experience but is most easily explained by considering the nature of mathematical and geometrical objects such as circles.

(A) Plato's extraordinary answer was that the world we see is a poor reflection of a deeper unseen reality of Forms, or universals, where perfect cats chase perfect mice in perfect circles around perfect rocks. Plato believed that the Forms or universals are the true reality that exists in an invisible but perfect world beyond our senses.

(B) He asked the question, what is a circle? You might indicate a particular example carved into stone or drawn in the sand. However, Plato would point out that, if you looked closely enough, you would see that neither it, nor indeed any physical circle, was perfect.

(C) They all possessed flaws, and all were subject to change and decayed with time. So how can we talk about perfect circles if we cannot actually see or touch them?

57. 57) 35.

In statistics, the law of large numbers describes a situation where having more data is better for making predictions.

(A) According to it, the more often an experiment is conducted, the closer the average of the results can be expected to match the true state of the world. For instance, on your first encounter with the game of roulette, you may have beginner's luck after betting on 7.

(B) Both casinos and insurance industries rely on the law of large numbers to balance individual losses.

(C) But the more often you repeat this bet, the closer the relative frequency of wins and losses is expected to approach the true chance of winning, meaning that your luck will at some point fade away. Similarly, car insurers collect large amounts of data to figure out the chances that drivers will cause accidents, depending on their age, region, or car brand.

58. 58) 36.

The adolescent brain is not fully developed until its early twenties.

(A) This means the way the adolescents' decision-making circuits integrate and process information may put them at a disadvantage. One of their brain regions that matures later is the prefrontal cortex, which is the control center, tasked with thinking ahead and evaluating consequences. It is the area of the brain responsible for preventing you from sending off an initial angry text and modifying it with kinder words.

(B) Due to these differences, there is an imbalance between feeling-based decision-making ruled by the more mature limbic system and logical-based decision-making by the not-yet-mature prefrontal cortex. This may explain why some teens are more likely to make bad decisions.

(C) On the other hand, the limbic system matures earlier, playing a central role in processing emotional responses. Because of its earlier development, it is more likely to influence decision-making. Decision-making in the adolescent brain is led by emotional factors more than the perception of consequences.

59. 59) 37.

Despite the remarkable progress in deep-learning based facial recognition approaches in recent years, in terms of identification performance, they still have limitations.

(A) These limitations relate to the database used in the learning stage. If the selected database does not contain enough instances, the result may be systematically affected.

(B) For example, the performance of a facial biometric system may decrease if the person to be identified was enrolled over 10 years ago. The factor to consider is that this person may experience changes in the texture of the face, particularly with the appearance of wrinkles and sagging skin.

(C) These changes may be highlighted by weight gain or loss. To counteract this problem, researchers have developed models for face aging or digital de-aging.

(D) It is used to compensate for the differences in facial characteristics, which appear over a given time period.

60. 60) 38.

The decline in the diversity of our food is an entirely human-made process.

(A) The biggest loss of crop diversity came in the decades that followed the Second World War. In an attempt to save millions from extreme hunger, crop scientists found ways to produce grains such as rice and wheat on an enormous scale. And thousands of traditional varieties were replaced by a small number of new super-productive ones.

(B) The strategy worked spectacularly well, at least to begin with. Because of it, grain production tripled, and between 1970 and 2020 the human population more than doubled.

(C) Leaving the contribution of that strategy to one side, the danger of creating more uniform crops is that they are more at risk when it comes to disasters. Specifically, a global food system that depends on just a narrow selection of plants has a greater chance of not being able to survive diseases, pests and climate extremes.

61. 61) 39.

Between 1940 and 2000, Cuba ruled the world baseball scene.

(A) The country that ruled international baseball for decades has not been on top since that uniform change.

(B) Traditions are important for a team; while a team brand or image can adjust to keep up with present times, if it abandons or neglects its roots, negative effects can surface.

(C) They won 25 of the first 28 World Cups and 3 of 5 Olympic Games. The Cubans were known for wearing uniforms covered in red from head to toe, a strong contrast to the more conservative North American style featuring grey or white pants.

(D) Not only were their athletic talents superior, the Cubans appeared even stronger from just the colour of their uniforms. A game would not even start and the opposing team would already be scared.

(E) A few years ago, Cuba altered that uniform style, modernizing it and perhaps conforming to other countries' style; interestingly, the national team has declined since that time.

62. 62) 40.

Many of the first models of cultural evolution drew noticeable connections between culture and genes by using concepts from theoretical population genetics and applying them to culture.

(A) For example, we do not expect the cultural transmission to follow the rules of genetic transmission strictly.

(B) Further, a child can acquire cultural traits not only from its parents but also from nonparental adults and peers; thus, the frequency of a cultural trait in the population is relevant beyond just the probability that an individual's parents had that trait.

(C) If two biological parents have different forms of a cultural trait, their child is not necessarily equally likely to acquire the mother's or father's form of that trait.

(D) Cultural patterns of transmission, innovation, and selection are conceptually likened to genetic processes of transmission, mutation, and selection. However, these approaches had to be modified to account for the differences between genetic and cultural transmission.

63. 63) 41~42.

A ball thrown into the air is acted upon by the initial force given it, persisting as inertia of movement and tending to carry it in the same straight line, and by the constant pull of gravity downward, as well as by the resistance of the air.

(A) It moves, accordingly, in a curved path. Now the path does not represent the working of any particular force; there is simply the combination of the three elementary forces mentioned; but in a real sense, there is something in the total action besides the isolated action of three forces, namely, their joint action.

(B) This shows that the traits of human nature do not fully appear until the individual is brought into relationships with other individuals.

(C) An individual in complete isolation would not reveal their competitive tendencies, their tendencies towards the opposite sex, their protective tendencies towards children.

(D) The significance of group behavior is greatly increased in the case of human beings by the fact that some of the tendencies to action of the individual are related definitely to other persons, and could not be aroused except by other persons acting as stimuli.

(E) In the same way, when two or more human individuals are together, their mutual relationships and their arrangement into a group are things which would not be revealed if we confined our attention to each individual separately.

64. 64) 43~45.

There once lived a man in a village who was not happy with his life.

(A) The saint told him, "You realized that no matter how hard you try, you can't make all the camels sit down. If one problem is solved, for some reason, another will arise like the camels did. So, humans should enjoy life despite these problems."

(B) But the saint also asked if the man could do a small job for him. He told the man to take care of a hundred camels in his group that night, saying "When all hundred camels sit down, you can go to sleep." The man agreed.

(C) He was always troubled by one problem or another. One day, a saint with his guards stopped by his village. Many people heard the news and started going to him with their problems. The man also decided to visit the saint.

(D) Even after reaching the saint's place in the morning, he didn't get the opportunity to meet him till evening. When the man got to meet the saint, he confessed that he was very unhappy with life because problems always surrounded him, like workplace tension or worries about his health. He said, "Please give me a solution so that all the problems in my life will end and I can live peacefully." The saint smiled and said that he would answer the request the next day.

(E) The next morning when the saint met that man, he asked if the man had slept well. Tired and sad, the man replied that he couldn't sleep even for a moment. In fact, the man tried very hard but couldn't make all the camels sit at the same time because every time he made one camel sit, another would stand up.

2023 고1 11월 모의고사

❶ voca ❷ text ❸ [/] ❹ _____ ❺ quiz 1 ❻ quiz 2 ❼ quiz 3 ❽ quiz 4 ❾ quiz 5

1. ¹⁾밑줄 친 부분 중, 어법, 혹은 문맥상 어색한 곳을 고르시오. 18.

Dear Ms. MacAlpine,

I was so ① **excited** to hear that your brand is opening a new shop on Bruns Street next month. I have always ② **appreciated** the way your brand helps women to feel more stylish and confident. I am writing in response to your ad in the Bruns Journal. I ③ **graduated** the Meline School of Fashion and have worked as a sales assistant at LoganMart for the last five years. ④ **During** that time, I've developed strong customer service and sales skills, and now I would like to apply ⑤ **for** the sales position in your clothing store. I am available for an interview at your earliest convenience. I look forward to hearing from you. Thank you for reading my letter.

Yours sincerely,

Grace Braddock

2. ²⁾밑줄 친 부분 중, 어법, 혹은 문맥상 어색한 곳을 고르시오. 19.

I had never ① **seen** a beach with such white sand or water ② **that** was such a beautiful shade of blue. Jane and I set up a blanket on the sand ③ **during** looking forward to our ten days of honeymooning on an exotic island. "Look"! Jane waved her hand to point at the beautiful scene before us—and her gold wedding ring went flying off her hand. I tried to see where it went, but the sun hit my eyes and I lost track of ④ **it** . I didn't want to lose her wedding ring, so I started looking in the area where I thought it had landed. However, the sand was so fine and I realized that anything heavy, like gold, would quickly sink and might never ⑤ **be found** again.

3. ³⁾밑줄 친 부분 중, 어법, 혹은 문맥상 어색한 곳을 고르시오. 20.

Unfortunately, many people don't take ① **personal** responsibility for their own growth. Instead, they simply run the race laid out for them. They do ② **well** enough in school to keep advancing. Maybe they manage to get a good job at a well-run company. But so many think and act as if their learning journey ③ **ends** with college. They have checked all the boxes in the life that was laid out for them and now lack a road map describing the right ways to move forward and continue to grow. In truth, that's when the journey really begins. When school is finished, your growth becomes voluntary. Like healthy eating habits or a regular exercise program, you need to commit to it and devote thought, time, and energy to it. Otherwise, it simply won't ④ **be happened**—and your life and career are likely to stop ⑤ **progressing** as a result.

4. ⁴⁾밑줄 친 부분 중, 어법, 혹은 문맥상 어색한 곳을 고르시오. 21.

Many people take the commonsense view that color is an ① **objective** property of things, or of the light that bounces off them. They say a tree's leaves are green because they ② **reflect** green light—a greenness that is just as real as the leaves. Others argue that color doesn't ③ **inhibit** the physical world at all but exists only in the eye or mind of the viewer. They maintain that if a tree fell in a forest and no one was there to see it, its leaves would be colorless—and so ④ **would everything else**. They say there is no such thing as color; there are only the people who see it. Both positions are, in a way, correct. Color is objective and subjective—"the place", as Paul Cézanne put it, "where our brain and the universe meet". Color is created when light from the world is ⑤ **registered** by the eyes and interpreted by the brain.

5. 5)밑줄 친 부분 중, 어법, 혹은 문맥상 어색한 곳을 고르시오. 22.

When writing a novel, research for information needs to be done. The thing is that some kinds of fiction demand a higher level of detail: crime fiction, for example, or scientific thrillers. The information is never hard ① **to find** ; one website for authors even organizes trips to police stations, so that crime writers can get it right. Often, a polite letter will earn you ② **permission** to visit a particular location and ③ **records** all the details that you need. But remember that you will drive your readers to boredom if you think that you need to pack everything ④ **that** you discover into your work. The details that ⑤ **matter** are those that reveal the human experience. The crucial thing is telling a story, finding the characters, the tension, and the conflict—not the train timetable or the building blueprint.

6. 6)밑줄 친 부분 중, 어법, 혹은 문맥상 어색한 곳을 고르시오. 23.

Nearly everything ① **has** to go through your mouth to get to the rest of you, from food and air to bacteria and viruses. A healthy mouth can help your body ② **getting** ③ **what** it needs and prevent it from harm—with adequate space for air to travel to your lungs, and healthy teeth and gums that prevent harmful microorganisms from entering your bloodstream. From the moment you are created, oral health affects every aspect of your life. What happens in the mouth is usually just the tip of the iceberg and a reflection of what is happening in other parts of the body. Poor oral health can be a cause of a disease that ④ **affects** the entire body. The microorganisms in an unhealthy mouth can ⑤ **enter** the bloodstream and travel anywhere in the body, posing serious health risks.

7. 7)밑줄 친 부분 중, 어법, 혹은 문맥상 어색한 곳을 고르시오. 24.

Kids tire of their toys, college students get sick of cafeteria food, and sooner or later most of us lose interest in our favorite TV shows. The bottom line is that we humans are easily ① **boring** . But why should this be true? The answer ② **lies** buried deep in our nerve cells, which are designed to ③ **reduce** their initial excited response to stimuli each time they ④ **occur** . At the same time, these neurons enhance their responses to things that change—especially things that change quickly . We probably evolved this way because our ancestors got more survival value, for example, from attending to what was moving in a tree (such as a puma) than to the tree itself. Boredom in reaction to an unchanging environment turns ⑤ **down** the level of neural excitation so that new stimuli (like our ancestor's hypothetical puma threat) stand out more. It's the neural equivalent of turning off a front door light to see the fireflies.

8. 8)밑줄 친 부분 중, 어법, 혹은 문맥상 어색한 곳을 고르시오. 26.

Frederick Douglass was born into slavery at a farm in Maryland. His full name at birth was Frederick Augustus Washington Bailey. He changed his name to Frederick Douglass after ① **he** successfully escaped from slavery in 1838. He became a leader of the Underground Railroad —a network of people, places, and routes that helped enslaved people escape to the north. He assisted other runaway slaves until they could safely get to other areas in the north. As a slave, he had taught himself to read and write and he ② **spread** that knowledge to other ③ **slave** as well. Once free, he became a well-known abolitionist and strong believer in equality for all people ④ **including** Blacks, Native Americans, women, and recent immigrants. He wrote several autobiographies ⑤ **describing** his experiences as a slave. In addition to all this, he became the first African-American candidate for vice president of the United States.

9. 9)밑줄 친 부분 중, 어법, 혹은 문맥상 어색한 곳을 고르시오. 29.

Some countries have proposed tougher guidelines for determining brain death when ① **transplantation**—② **transferring** organs to others—is under consideration. In several European countries, there are legal requirements which specify that a whole team of doctors must ③ **be agreed** over the diagnosis of death in the case of a potential donor. The reason for these strict regulations for diagnosing brain death in potential organ donors is , no doubt, to ease public fears of a premature diagnosis of brain death for the purpose of obtaining organs. But it is questionable whether these requirements ④ **reduce** public suspicions as much as they create them. They certainly maintain mistaken beliefs that diagnosing brain death is an unreliable process lacking precision. As a matter of consistency, at least, criteria for diagnosing the deaths of organ donors should be exactly the same as for those ⑤ **for whom** immediate burial or cremation is intended.

10. 10)밑줄 친 부분 중, 어법, 혹은 문맥상 어색한 곳을 고르시오. 30.

The term minimalism gives a negative impression to some people who think that it is all about ① **sacrificing** valuable possessions. This insecurity naturally stems from their ② **detachment** to their possessions. It is difficult to distance oneself from something that has been around for quite some time. ③ **Being** an emotional animal, human beings give meaning to the things around them. So, the question ④ **arising** here is that if minimalism will hurt one's emotions, why become a minimalist? The answer is very simple; the assumption of the question is fundamentally wrong. Minimalism does not hurt emotions. You might feel a bit sad while getting rid of a useless item but sooner than later, this feeling will be ⑤ **overcome** by the joy of clarity . Minimalists never argue that you should leave every convenience of the modern era. They are of the view that you only need to eliminate stuff that is unused or not going to be used in the near future.

11. 11)밑줄 친 부분 중, 어법, 혹은 문맥상 어색한 곳을 고르시오. 31.

A remarkable characteristic of the visual system is that it has the ability of adapting itself. Psychologist George M. Stratton made this ① **clear** in an impressive self-experiment. Stratton wore reversing glasses for several days, which literally turned the world upside down for him. In the beginning, this caused ② **him** great difficulties: just putting food in his mouth with a fork was a challenge for him. With time, however, his visual system adjusted to the new stimuli from reality , and he was able to act normally in his environment again, even seeing ③ **it** upright when he concentrated. As he took off his reversing glasses, he was again confronted ④ **with problems**: he used the wrong hand when he wanted to reach for something, for example. Fortunately, Stratton could reverse the ⑤ **reality** , and he did not have to wear reversing glasses for the rest of his life. For him, everything returned to normal after one day.

12. 12)밑줄 친 부분 중, 어법, 혹은 문맥상 어색한 곳을 고르시오. 32.

Participants in a study were asked to answer questions like "Why does the moon have phases"? Half the participants ① **were** told to search for the answers on the internet, while the other half weren't allowed to do so. Then, in the second part of the study, all of the participants were presented with a new set of questions, such as "Why does Swiss cheese have holes"? These questions were unrelated to the ones asked ② **during** the first part of the study, so participants who used the internet had absolutely no advantage over those who ③ **hadn't** . You would think that both sets of participants would be equally sure or unsure about how well they could answer the new questions. But those who used the internet in the first part of the study rated ④ **itself** as more knowledgeable than those who hadn't , even about questions they hadn't searched ⑤ **online**. The study suggests that having access to unrelated information was enough to pump up their intellectual confidence.

13. 13)**밑줄 친 부분 중, 어법, 혹은 문맥상 어색한 곳을 고르시오.** 33.

Anthropologist Gregory Bateson suggests ① **which** we tend to understand the world by focusing in on particular features within it . Take platypuses. We might zoom in so closely to their fur ② **that** each hair appears different . We might also zoom out to the extent ③ **where** it appears as a single, uniform object. We might take the platypus as an individual, or we might treat it as part of a larger unit such as a species or an ecosystem. It's possible to move between many of these ④ **perspectives** , although we may need some additional tools and skills to zoom in on individual pieces of hair or zoom out to entire ecosystems. Crucially, ⑤ **however** , we can only take up one perspective at a time. We can pay attention to the varied behavior of individual animals, look at what unites them into a single species, or look at them as part of bigger ecological patterns. Every possible perspective involves emphasizing certain aspects and ignoring others.

14. 14)**밑줄 친 부분 중, 어법, 혹은 문맥상 어색한 곳을 고르시오.** 34.

Plato's realism ① **concludes** all aspects of experience but is most easily explained by considering the nature of mathematical and ② **geometrical** objects such as circles. He asked the question, what is a circle? You might indicate a particular example carved into stone or drawn in the sand. However, Plato would point out that , if you looked closely enough, you would see that neither it, nor indeed any physical circle, was perfect. They all possessed flaws , and all were subject to change and decayed with time. So how can we talk about perfect circles if we cannot actually see or touch them? Plato's extraordinary answer was ③ **that** the world we see is a poor reflection of a deeper ④ **unseen** reality of Forms, or universals, ⑤ **where** perfect cats chase perfect mice in perfect circles around perfect rocks. Plato believed that the Forms or universals are the true reality that exists in an invisible but perfect world beyond our senses.

15. 15)**밑줄 친 부분 중, 어법, 혹은 문맥상 어색한 곳을 고르시오.** 35.

In statistics, the law of large numbers ① **describing** a situation ② **where** having more data is better for making predictions. According to it, the ③ **more** often an experiment is conducted, the closer the average of the results can be expected to match the true state of the world. For instance, on your first encounter with the game of roulette, you may have beginner's luck after betting on 7. But the more often you repeat this bet, the closer the ④ **relative** frequency of wins and losses is expected to approach the true chance of winning, meaning that your luck will at some point fade away. Similarly, car insurers collect large amounts of data to figure out the chances that drivers will cause ⑤ **accidents** , depending on their age, region, or car brand. Both casinos and insurance industries rely on the law of large numbers to balance individual losses.

16. 16)**밑줄 친 부분 중, 어법, 혹은 문맥상 어색한 곳을 고르시오.** 36.

The adolescent brain is not fully developed until its early twenties. This means ① **the way** the adolescents' decision-making circuits integrate and process information may put them at a disadvantage . One of their brain regions that matures later is the prefrontal cortex, which is the control center, tasked with thinking ahead and evaluating consequences. It is the area of the brain responsible for preventing you from sending off an initial angry text and modifying it with kinder words. On the other hand, the limbic system matures earlier, playing a central role in processing emotional responses. ② **Because** its earlier development, it is more likely to influence decision-making. Decision-making in the adolescent brain is led by emotional factors more than the perception of consequences. Due to these differences, there is an ③ **imbalance** between feeling-based decision-making ruled by the more mature limbic system and logical-based decision-making by the ④ **not-yet-mature** prefrontal cortex. This may explain ⑤ **why** some teens are more likely to make bad decisions.

113

17. 17)밑줄 친 부분 중, 어법, 혹은 문맥상 어색한 곳을 고르시오. 37.

Despite the remarkable ① **progress** in deep-learning based facial recognition approaches in recent years, in terms of identification performance, they still have limitations. These limitations relate to the database used in the learning stage. If the selected database does not contain enough instances, the result may be systematically affected . For example, the performance of a facial biometric system may ② **decrease** if the person to be identified was enrolled over 10 years ago. The factor to consider is that this person may experience changes in the texture of the face, particularly with the appearance of wrinkles and sagging skin. These changes may be ③ **highlighted** by weight gain or loss. To counteract this problem, researchers have developed models for face aging or digital de-aging. It is used to ④ **compensating** for the differences in facial characteristics, which ⑤ **appear** over a given time period.

18. 18)밑줄 친 부분 중, 어법, 혹은 문맥상 어색한 곳을 고르시오. 38.

The decline in the diversity of our food is an entirely human-made ① **process** . The biggest loss of crop diversity came in the decades that ② **was followed by** the Second World War. In an attempt to save millions from extreme hunger, crop scientists found ways to produce grains such as rice and wheat on an enormous scale. And thousands of traditional varieties were replaced by a small number of new super-productive ones . The strategy worked spectacularly well, at least to begin with. Because of it, grain production tripled, and between 1970 and 2020 the human population more than doubled. Leaving the contribution of that strategy to one side, the danger of creating more ③ **uniform** crops ④ **is** that they are more at risk when it comes to disasters. Specifically, a global food system that depends on just a narrow selection of plants has a greater chance of ⑤ **not being** able to survive diseases, pests and climate extremes.

19. 19)밑줄 친 부분 중, 어법, 혹은 문맥상 어색한 곳을 고르시오. 39.

Between 1940 and 2000, Cuba ruled the world baseball scene. They won 25 of the first 28 World Cups and 3 of 5 Olympic Games. The Cubans were known ① **for** wearing uniforms ② **covered** in red from head to toe, a strong contrast to the more conservative North American style ③ **featuring** grey or white pants. Not only were their athletic talents superior, the Cubans appeared even stronger from just the colour of their uniforms. A game would not even start and the opposing team would already be scared. A few years ago, Cuba altered that uniform style, modernizing it and perhaps ④ **conforming** to other countries' style; interestingly, the national team has declined since that time. The country that ruled international baseball for decades has not been on top since ⑤ **which** uniform change. Traditions are important for a team; while a team brand or image can adjust to keep up with present times, if it abandons or neglects its roots, negative effects can surface .

20. 20)밑줄 친 부분 중, 어법, 혹은 문맥상 어색한 곳을 고르시오. 40.

Many of the first models of cultural ① **revolution** drew noticeable connections between culture and genes by using concepts from theoretical population genetics and ② **applying** them to culture. Cultural patterns of transmission, innovation, and selection are conceptually ③ **likened** to genetic processes of transmission, mutation, and selection. However, these approaches had to be modified to account for the differences between genetic and cultural transmission. For example, we do not expect the cultural transmission to follow the rules of genetic transmission strictly. If two biological parents have different forms of a cultural trait, their child is ④ **not necessarily** equally likely to acquire the mother's or father's form of that trait. Further, a child can ⑤ **acquire** cultural traits not only from its parents but also from nonparental adults and peers; thus, the frequency of a cultural trait in the population is relevant beyond just the probability that an individual's parents had that trait.

21. 21)밑줄 친 부분 중, 어법, 혹은 문맥상 어색한 곳을 고르시오. 41~42.

A ball thrown into the air is acted upon by the initial force given it, ① **persisting** as inertia of movement and ② **tending** to carry it in the same straight line, and by the constant ③ **pull** of gravity downward, as well as by the resistance of the air. It moves, accordingly, in a curved path. Now the path does not represent the working of any particular force; there is simply the combination of the three elementary forces mentioned ; but in a real sense, there is something in the total action besides the isolated action of three forces, namely, their joint action. In the same way, when two or more human individuals are together, their mutual relationships and their arrangement into a group ④ **is** things which would not be ⑤ **revealed** if we confined our attention to each individual separately. The significance of group behavior is greatly increased in the case of human beings by the fact that some of the tendencies to action of the individual are related definitely to other persons, and could not be aroused except by other persons acting as stimuli. An individual in complete isolation would not reveal their competitive tendencies, their tendencies towards the opposite sex, their protective tendencies towards children. This shows that the traits of human nature do not fully appear until the individual is brought into relationships with other individuals.

22. 22)밑줄 친 부분 중, 어법, 혹은 문맥상 어색한 곳을 고르시오. 43~45.

There once lived a man in a village who was not happy with his life. He was always troubled by one problem or another. One day, a saint with his guards stopped by his village. Many people heard the news and started going to him with their problems. The man also decided to visit the saint. Even after reaching the saint's place in the morning, he didn't get the opportunity to meet him till evening. When the man got to meet the saint, he confessed that he was very unhappy with life because problems always surrounded him, like workplace tension or worries about his health. He said, "Please give me a solution so that all the problems in my life will end and I can live peacefully". The saint smiled and said ① **that** he would answer the request the next day. But the saint also asked if the man could do a small job for him. He told the man to ② **take** care of a hundred camels in his group that night, ③ **saying** "When all hundred camels sit down, you can go to sleep". The man agreed. The next morning when the saint met that man, he asked if the man had slept well. ④ **Tired** and sad, the man replied that he couldn't sleep even for a moment. In fact, the man tried very hard but couldn't make all the camels sit at the same time because every time he made one camel sit, another would stand up. The saint told him, "You realized that no matter how hard you try, you can't make all the camels sit down. If one problem is solved, for some reason, another will ⑤ **raise** like the camels did . So, humans should enjoy life despite these problems".

2023 고1 11월 모의고사

❶ voca | ❷ text | ❸ [/] | ❹ ＿＿ | ❺ quiz 1 | ❻ quiz 2 | ❼ quiz 3 | ❽ quiz 4 | ❾ quiz 5

1. 1)밑줄 친 ⓐ~ⓕ 중 어법, 혹은 문맥상 어휘의 사용이 어색한 것끼리 짝지어진 것을 고르시오. 18.

Dear Ms. MacAlpine, / I was so ⓐ **exciting** to hear that your brand is opening a new shop on Bruns Street next month. I have always ⓑ **been appreciated** the way your brand helps women to feel more stylish and confident. I am writing in response to your ad in the Bruns Journal. I ⓒ **graduated** the Meline School of Fashion and have worked as a sales assistant at LoganMart for the last five years. ⓓ **During** that time, I've developed strong customer service and sales skills, and now I would like to apply ⓔ **for** the sales position in your clothing store. I am available for an interview at your earliest convenience. I look forward to ⓕ **hear** from you. Thank you for reading my letter.
Yours sincerely, Grace Braddock

① ⓓ, ⓕ   ② ⓐ, ⓓ, ⓔ   ③ ⓑ, ⓓ, ⓔ
④ ⓓ, ⓔ, ⓕ   ⑤ ⓐ, ⓑ, ⓒ, ⓕ

2. 2)밑줄 친 ⓐ~ⓗ 중 어법, 혹은 문맥상 어휘의 사용이 어색한 것끼리 짝지어진 것을 고르시오. 19.

I had never ⓐ **been seen** a beach with such white sand or water ⓑ **that** was such a beautiful shade of blue. Jane and I set up a blanket on the sand ⓒ **while** looking forward to our ten days of honeymooning on an exotic island. "Look"! Jane ⓓ **waved** her hand to point at the beautiful scene before us—and her gold wedding ring went flying off her hand. I tried to see ⓔ **what** it went, but the sun hit my eyes and I lost track of ⓕ **it** . I didn't want to lose her wedding ring, so I started looking in the area ⓖ **which** I thought it had landed. However, the sand was so fine and I realized that anything heavy, like gold, would quickly sink and might never ⓗ **find it** again.

① ⓐ, ⓓ, ⓔ   ② ⓒ, ⓓ, ⓔ   ③ ⓓ, ⓕ, ⓗ
④ ⓐ, ⓔ, ⓖ, ⓗ   ⑤ ⓑ, ⓓ, ⓕ, ⓖ

3. 3)밑줄 친 ⓐ~ⓘ 중 어법, 혹은 문맥상 어휘의 사용이 어색한 것끼리 짝지어진 것을 고르시오. 20.

Unfortunately, many people don't take ⓐ **personal** responsibility for their own growth. Instead, they simply run the race ⓑ **laid** out for them. They do ⓒ **well** enough in school to keep advancing. Maybe they manage to get a good job at a well-run company. But so many think and act as if their learning journey ⓓ **ends** with college. They have checked all the boxes in the life that was ⓔ **lain** out for them and now lack a road map ⓕ **describing** the right ways to move forward and continue to grow. In truth, that's when the journey really begins. When school is finished, your growth becomes ⓖ **voluntary** . Like healthy eating habits or a regular exercise program, you need to commit to it and devote thought, time, and energy to it. Otherwise, it simply won't ⓗ **be happened**—and your life and career are likely to stop ⓘ **progressing** as a result.

① ⓔ, ⓗ   ② ⓕ, ⓗ   ③ ⓐ, ⓒ, ⓔ
④ ⓑ, ⓓ, ⓖ   ⑤ ⓐ, ⓑ, ⓖ, ⓗ

4. ⁴⁾밑줄 친 ⓐ~ⓘ 중 어법, 혹은 문맥상 어휘의 사용이 어색한 것끼리 짝지어진 것을 고르시오. ²¹.

Many people take the commonsense view that color is an ⓐ **subjective** property of things, or of the light that ⓑ **bounces** off them. They say a tree's leaves are green because they ⓒ **absorb** green light—a greenness that is just as ⓓ **real** as the leaves. Others argue that color doesn't ⓔ **inhabit** the physical world at all but exists only in the eye or mind of the viewer. They maintain that if a tree fell in a forest and no one was there to see it, its leaves would be ⓕ **colorless**—and so ⓖ **would everything else**. They say there is no such thing as color; there are only the people who see it. Both positions are, in a way, correct. Color is objective and subjective—"the place", as Paul Cézanne put it, "ⓗ **where** our brain and the universe meet". Color is created when light from the world is ⓘ **registered** by the eyes and interpreted by the brain.

① ⓐ, ⓒ   ② ⓐ, ⓔ   ③ ⓐ, ⓔ, ⓗ
④ ⓑ, ⓒ, ⓖ   ⑤ ⓐ, ⓑ, ⓓ, ⓗ

5. ⁵⁾밑줄 친 ⓐ~ⓛ 중 어법, 혹은 문맥상 어휘의 사용이 어색한 것끼리 짝지어진 것을 고르시오. ²².

When ⓐ **writes** a novel, research for information needs to be done. The thing is that some kinds of fiction ⓑ **demands** a higher level of detail: crime fiction, for example, or scientific thrillers. The information is never hard ⓒ **to find** ; one website for authors even ⓓ **organizes** trips to police stations, so that crime writers can get it right. Often, a polite letter will earn you ⓔ **permission** to visit a particular location and ⓕ **record** all the details that you need. But remember ⓖ **that** you will drive your readers to ⓗ **boredom** if you ⓘ **think** that you need to pack everything ⓙ **what** you discover into your work. The details that ⓚ **matter** are those that ⓛ **reveal** the human experience. The crucial thing is telling a story, finding the characters, the tension, and the conflict—not the train timetable or the building blueprint.

① ⓐ, ⓒ   ② ⓐ, ⓑ, ⓙ   ③ ⓐ, ⓙ, ⓛ
④ ⓑ, ⓙ, ⓛ   ⑤ ⓑ, ⓒ, ⓔ, ⓙ

6. ⁶⁾밑줄 친 ⓐ~ⓛ 중 어법, 혹은 문맥상 어휘의 사용이 어색한 것끼리 짝지어진 것을 고르시오. ²³.

Nearly everything ⓐ **has** to go through your mouth to get to the rest of you, from food and air to bacteria and viruses. A ⓑ **healthy** mouth can help your body ⓒ **get** ⓓ **what** it needs and prevent it ⓔ **to** harm—with adequate space for air to travel to your lungs, and healthy teeth and gums that prevent harmful microorganisms from ⓕ **entrance** your bloodstream. From the moment you are created, oral health ⓖ **effects** every ⓗ **aspect** of your life. What happens in the mouth is usually just the tip of the iceberg and a reflection of what is happening in other ⓘ **parts** of the body. Poor oral health can be a cause of a disease that ⓙ **affects** the entire body. The microorganisms in an unhealthy mouth can ⓚ **enter** the bloodstream and travel anywhere in the body, ⓛ **posed** serious health risks.

① ⓑ, ⓔ, ⓘ   ② ⓐ, ⓒ, ⓕ, ⓚ   ③ ⓐ, ⓕ, ⓘ, ⓛ
④ ⓓ, ⓔ, ⓚ, ⓛ   ⑤ ⓔ, ⓕ, ⓖ, ⓛ

7. ⁷⁾밑줄 친 ⓐ~ⓡ 중 어법, 혹은 문맥상 어휘의 사용이 어색한 것끼리 짝지어진 것을 고르시오. ²⁴.

Kids ⓐ **tire** of their toys, college students get sick of cafeteria food, and sooner or later most of us ⓑ **lose** interest in our favorite TV shows. The bottom line is that we humans are easily ⓒ **bored** . But why should this be true? The answer ⓓ **lies** buried deep in our nerve cells, ⓔ **which** are designed to ⓕ **reduce** their initial excited response to stimuli each time they ⓖ **occur** . At the same time, these neurons enhance their responses to things that ⓗ **change**—especially things that ⓘ **change** ⓙ **quickly** . We probably ⓚ **evolved** this way ⓛ **because** our ancestors got more survival value, for example, from ⓜ **attending** what was moving in a tree (such as a puma) than to the tree itself. ⓝ **Excitement** in reaction to an unchanging environment turns ⓞ **down** the level of neural excitation so that new stimuli (like our ancestor's hypothetical puma threat) ⓟ **stand** out more. It's the neural ⓠ **equivalent** of turning ⓡ **on** a front door light to see the fireflies.

① ⓓ, ⓡ   ② ⓛ, ⓡ   ③ ⓐ, ⓘ, ⓚ
④ ⓘ, ⓜ, ⓡ   ⑤ ⓜ, ⓝ, ⓡ

8. 8)밑줄 친 ⓐ~ⓘ 중 어법, 혹은 문맥상 어휘의 사용이 어색한 것끼리 짝지어진 것을 고르시오. 26.

Frederick Douglass was born into slavery at a farm in Maryland. His full name at birth was Frederick Augustus Washington Bailey. He changed his name to Frederick Douglass after ⓐ **he** successfully escaped from slavery in 1838. He became a leader of the Underground Railroad —a network of people, places, and routes ⓑ **that** helped ⓒ **enslave** people ⓓ **escaping** to the north. He assisted other runaway slaves until they could safely get to other areas in the north. As a slave, he had taught ⓔ **himself** to read and write and he ⓕ **spreads** that knowledge to other ⓖ **slave** as well. Once free, he became a well-known abolitionist and strong believer in equality for all people ⓗ **including** Blacks, Native Americans, women, and recent immigrants. He wrote several autobiographies ⓘ **describing** his experiences as a slave. In addition to all this, he became the first African-American candidate for vice president of the United States.

① ⓓ, ⓗ   ② ⓐ, ⓔ, ⓕ   ③ ⓒ, ⓔ, ⓕ
④ ⓐ, ⓒ, ⓓ, ⓖ   ⑤ ⓒ, ⓓ, ⓕ, ⓖ

9. 9)밑줄 친 ⓐ~ⓝ 중 어법, 혹은 문맥상 어휘의 사용이 어색한 것끼리 짝지어진 것을 고르시오. 29.

Some countries have proposed ⓐ **tougher** guidelines for determining brain death when ⓑ **transportation**—ⓒ **transferring** organs to others—is under consideration. In several European countries, there are legal requirements which ⓓ **specific** that a whole team of doctors must ⓔ **agree** over the diagnosis of death in the case of a potential donor. The reason for these strict ⓕ **regulations** for diagnosing brain death in potential organ donors ⓖ **are** , no doubt, to ⓗ **ease** public fears of a premature diagnosis of brain death for the purpose of obtaining organs. But it is questionable ⓘ **whether**

these requirements ⓙ **gain** public suspicions as much as they create them. They certainly ⓚ **maintain** mistaken beliefs ⓛ **that** diagnosing brain death is an unreliable process ⓜ **lacking** precision. As a matter of consistency, at least, criteria for diagnosing the deaths of organ donors should be exactly the same as for those ⓝ **for whom** immediate burial or cremation is intended.

① ⓑ, ⓔ, ⓚ   ② ⓑ, ⓗ, ⓚ   ③ ⓑ, ⓓ, ⓖ, ⓙ
④ ⓑ, ⓘ, ⓙ, ⓜ   ⑤ ⓓ, ⓕ, ⓖ, ⓜ

10. 10)밑줄 친 ⓐ~ⓝ 중 어법, 혹은 문맥상 어휘의 사용이 어색한 것끼리 짝지어진 것을 고르시오. 30.

The term minimalism gives a negative impression to some people who think ⓐ **that** it is all about ⓑ **maintaining** valuable possessions. This ⓒ **security** naturally stems from their ⓓ **attachment** to their possessions. It is difficult to ⓔ **distance** oneself from something that has been around for quite some time. ⓕ **Be** an emotional animal, human beings give meaning to the things around them. So, the question ⓖ **arising** here is that ⓗ **if** minimalism will hurt one's emotions, why become a minimalist? The answer is very simple; the ⓘ **assumption** of the question is fundamentally wrong. Minimalism does not hurt emotions. You might feel a bit sad while getting rid of a useless item but ⓙ **sooner than later**, this feeling will be ⓚ **overcome** by the joy of ⓛ **clarity** . Minimalists never argue that you should leave every convenience of the modern era. They are of the view ⓜ **that** you only need to ⓝ **eliminate** stuff that is unused or not going to be used in the near future.

① ⓐ, ⓒ   ② ⓑ, ⓒ, ⓕ   ③ ⓑ, ⓒ, ⓘ
④ ⓒ, ⓓ, ⓙ   ⑤ ⓓ, ⓘ, ⓙ

11. 11)**밑줄 친 ⓐ~ⓘ 중 어법, 혹은 문맥상 어휘의 사용이 어색한 것끼리 짝지어진 것을 고르시오.** 31.

A remarkable characteristic of the visual system is that it has the ability of ⓐ **adapting** itself. Psychologist George M. Stratton made this ⓑ **clearly** in an impressive self-experiment. Stratton wore reversing glasses for several days, which literally turned the world upside down for him. In the beginning, this caused ⓒ **him** great difficulties: just putting food in his mouth with a ⓓ **pork** was a challenge for him. With time, however, his visual system adjusted to the new stimuli from ⓔ **habit** , and he was able to act normally in his environment again, even seeing ⓕ **it** upright when he concentrated. As he took ⓖ **off** his reversing glasses, he was again confronted ⓗ **problems**: he used the wrong hand when he wanted to reach for something, for example. Fortunately, Stratton could reverse the ⓘ **perception** , and he did not have to wear reversing glasses for the rest of his life. For him, everything returned to normal after one day.

① ⓐ, ⓕ   ② ⓑ, ⓓ, ⓖ   ③ ⓐ, ⓒ, ⓖ, ⓘ
④ ⓑ, ⓓ, ⓔ, ⓗ   ⑤ ⓑ, ⓔ, ⓕ, ⓗ

12. 12)**밑줄 친 ⓐ~ⓙ 중 어법, 혹은 문맥상 어휘의 사용이 어색한 것끼리 짝지어진 것을 고르시오.** 32.

Participants in a study were asked to ⓐ **answer** questions like "Why does the moon have phases"? Half the participants ⓑ **were** told to search for the answers on the internet, while the other half weren't allowed to ⓒ **be** so. Then, in the second part of the study, all of the participants were presented with a new set of questions, such as "Why does Swiss cheese ⓓ **have** holes"? These questions were ⓔ **related** to the ones ⓕ **asking** ⓖ **while** the first part of the study, so participants who ⓗ **used** the internet had absolutely no advantage over those who ⓘ **hadn't** . You would think ⓙ **that** both sets of participants would be equally sure

or unsure about how well they could answer the new questions. But those who used the internet in the first part of the study rated ⓚ **themselves** as more knowledgeable than those who ⓛ **hadn't** , even about questions they hadn't searched ⓜ **online**. The study suggests that ⓝ **having** access to unrelated information was enough to pump ⓞ **up** their intellectual confidence.

① ⓐ, ⓔ, ⓞ   ② ⓒ, ⓛ, ⓞ   ③ ⓔ, ⓕ, ⓗ
④ ⓒ, ⓔ, ⓕ, ⓖ   ⑤ ⓒ, ⓕ, ⓖ, ⓘ

13. 13)**밑줄 친 ⓐ~ⓝ 중 어법, 혹은 문맥상 어휘의 사용이 어색한 것끼리 짝지어진 것을 고르시오.** 33.

Anthropologist Gregory Bateson suggests ⓐ **that** we tend to understand the world by focusing in on particular features within ⓑ **them** . Take platypuses. We might zoom in so ⓒ **closely** to their fur ⓓ **that** each hair appears ⓔ **different** . We might also zoom out to the extent ⓕ **where** it appears as a single, uniform object. We might take the platypus as an individual, or we might treat it as part of a ⓖ **larger** unit such as a species or an ecosystem. It's possible to move between many of these ⓗ **perspectives** , ⓘ **although** we may need some additional tools and skills to zoom in on individual pieces of hair or zoom out to entire ecosystems. Crucially, ⓙ **on the other hand** , we can only take up one perspective at a time. We can pay attention to the varied behavior of individual animals, look at ⓚ **what** unites them into a single species, or look at them as part of bigger ecological patterns. Every possible ⓛ **perspective** ⓜ **involves** emphasizing certain aspects and ⓝ **ignoring** others.

① ⓑ, ⓗ   ② ⓑ, ⓙ   ③ ⓗ, ⓚ
④ ⓒ, ⓕ, ⓙ   ⑤ ⓑ, ⓖ, ⓛ, ⓜ

14. ¹⁴⁾**밑줄 친 ⓐ~ⓜ 중 어법, 혹은 문맥상 어휘의 사용이 어색한 것끼리 짝지어진 것을 고르시오.** 34.

Plato's realism ⓐ **includes** all aspects of experience but is most easily explained by considering the nature of mathematical and ⓑ **geometrical** objects such as circles. He asked the question, what is a circle? You might indicate a particular example ⓒ **carved** into stone or drawn in the sand. However, Plato would point out ⓓ **which** , if you looked closely enough, you would see ⓔ **which** neither it, nor indeed any physical circle, was perfect. They all possessed ⓕ **flaws** , and all were subject to change and ⓖ **decayed** with time. So how can we talk about perfect circles if we cannot actually see or touch them? Plato's extraordinary answer was ⓗ **what** the world we see is a ⓘ **poor** reflection of a deeper ⓙ **unseen** reality of Forms, or universals, ⓚ **where** perfect cats chase perfect mice in perfect circles around perfect rocks. Plato believed that the Forms or universals are the true reality that ⓛ **is existed** in an ⓜ **invisible** but perfect world beyond our senses.

① ⓑ, ⓒ, ⓙ   ② ⓑ, ⓔ, ⓛ   ③ ⓖ, ⓙ, ⓛ
④ ⓓ, ⓔ, ⓗ, ⓛ   ⑤ ⓓ, ⓗ, ⓙ, ⓛ

15. ¹⁵⁾**밑줄 친 ⓐ~ⓚ 중 어법, 혹은 문맥상 어휘의 사용이 어색한 것끼리 짝지어진 것을 고르시오.** 35.

In statistics, the law of large numbers ⓐ **describes** a situation ⓑ **where** having more data is better for making predictions. According to it, the ⓒ **more** often an experiment is conducted, the ⓓ **closer** the average of the results can be expected to ⓔ **match** the true state of the world. For instance, on your first encounter with the game of roulette, you may have beginner's luck after ⓕ **betting** on 7. But the more often you repeat this bet, the closer the ⓖ **relevant** frequency of wins and losses is expected to ⓗ **approach to** the true chance of winning, meaning that your luck will at some point fade away. Similarly, car insurers collect large amounts of data to figure out the chances that ⓘ **drives** will cause ⓙ **accidents** , depending on their age, region, or car brand. Both casinos and insurance industries rely on the law of large numbers to ⓚ **compensate** individual losses.

① ⓒ, ⓖ, ⓚ   ② ⓓ, ⓔ, ⓗ   ③ ⓕ, ⓖ, ⓘ   ④ ⓓ, ⓖ, ⓘ, ⓚ   ⑤ ⓖ, ⓗ, ⓘ, ⓚ

16. ¹⁶⁾**밑줄 친 ⓐ~ⓜ 중 어법, 혹은 문맥상 어휘의 사용이 어색한 것끼리 짝지어진 것을 고르시오.** 36.

The adolescent brain is not fully developed until its early twenties. This means ⓐ **the way** the adolescents' decision-making circuits integrate and ⓑ **procedure** information may put them at a ⓒ **disadvantage** . One of their brain regions that ⓓ **matures** later is the prefrontal cortex, ⓔ **that** is the control center, tasked with thinking ahead and evaluating consequences. It is the area of the brain responsible for preventing you from sending off an initial angry text and modifying it with kinder words. On the other hand, the limbic system matures earlier, playing a ⓕ **central** role in processing emotional responses. ⓖ **Because of** its earlier development, it is more likely to influence decision-making. Decision-making in the adolescent brain is led by ⓗ **emotional** factors more than the perception of consequences. Due ⓘ **to** these differences, there is an ⓙ **imbalance** between feeling-based decision-making ruled by the more mature limbic system and ⓚ **logical-based** decision-making by the ⓛ **not-yet-mature** prefrontal cortex. This may explain ⓜ **why** some teens are more likely to make bad decisions.

① ⓑ, ⓔ   ② ⓑ, ⓛ   ③ ⓔ, ⓛ
④ ⓔ, ⓙ   ⑤ ⓐ, ⓑ, ⓖ, ⓛ

17. 17)**밑줄 친 ⓐ~ⓙ 중 어법, 혹은 문맥상 어휘의 사용이 어색한 것끼리 짝지어진 것을 고르시오.** 37.

ⓐ **Despite** the remarkable ⓑ **progress** in deep-learning based facial recognition approaches in recent years, in terms of ⓒ **identification** performance, they still have limitations. These limitations ⓓ **related** to the database used in the learning stage. If the selected database does not contain enough instances, the result may be systematically ⓔ **affected** . For example, the performance of a facial biometric system may ⓕ **increase** if the person to ⓖ **be identified** was enrolled over 10 years ago. The factor to consider is that this person may experience changes in the texture of the face, particularly with the appearance of wrinkles and sagging skin. These changes may be ⓗ **highlighted** by weight gain or loss. To counteract this problem, researchers have developed models for face aging or digital de-aging. It is used to ⓘ **compensating** for the differences in facial characteristics, which ⓙ **appears** over a given time period.

① ⓒ, ⓓ, ⓘ   ② ⓔ, ⓕ, ⓙ   ③ ⓐ, ⓑ, ⓕ, ⓙ
④ ⓐ, ⓓ, ⓔ, ⓕ   ⑤ ⓓ, ⓕ, ⓘ, ⓙ

18. 18)**밑줄 친 ⓐ~ⓚ 중 어법, 혹은 문맥상 어휘의 사용이 어색한 것끼리 짝지어진 것을 고르시오.** 38.

The decline in the diversity of our food is an entirely human-made ⓐ **process** . The biggest loss of crop diversity came in the decades that ⓑ **followed** the Second World War. In an attempt to save millions from extreme hunger, crop scientists found ways to produce grains such as rice and wheat on an enormous scale. And thousands of traditional ⓒ **varieties** were replaced by a ⓓ **small** number of new super-productive ⓔ **ones** . The strategy worked spectacularly well, at least to begin with. Because of it, grain production tripled, and

between 1970 and 2020 the human population more than doubled. ⓕ **Leaving** the contribution of that strategy to one side, the danger of creating more ⓖ **various** crops ⓗ **are** that they are more at risk when it comes to disasters. Specifically, a global food system that depends on just a ⓘ **narrow** selection of plants has a greater chance of ⓙ **not being** able to ⓚ **survive** diseases, pests and climate extremes.

① ⓐ, ⓕ   ② ⓒ, ⓖ   ③ ⓓ, ⓖ
④ ⓔ, ⓗ   ⑤ ⓖ, ⓗ

19. 19)**밑줄 친 ⓐ~ⓘ 중 어법, 혹은 문맥상 어휘의 사용이 어색한 것끼리 짝지어진 것을 고르시오.** 39.

Between 1940 and 2000, Cuba ruled the world baseball scene. They won 25 of the first 28 World Cups and 3 of 5 Olympic Games. The Cubans were known ⓐ **for** wearing uniforms ⓑ **covered** in red from head to toe, a strong contrast to the more conservative North American style ⓒ **featuring** grey or white pants. Not only ⓓ **were** their athletic talents superior, the Cubans appeared even stronger from just the colour of their uniforms. A game would not even start and the opposing team would already be scared. A few years ago, Cuba altered that uniform style, modernizing it and perhaps ⓔ **confirming** to other countries' style; interestingly, the national team has declined since that time. The country that ruled international baseball for decades ⓕ **have** not been on top since ⓖ **that** uniform change. Traditions are important for a team; while a team brand or image can ⓗ **adjust** to keep up with present times, if it abandons or neglects its roots, ⓘ **positive** effects can surface .

① ⓒ, ⓘ   ② ⓑ, ⓕ, ⓗ   ③ ⓑ, ⓕ, ⓘ
④ ⓓ, ⓖ, ⓗ   ⑤ ⓔ, ⓕ, ⓘ

20. 20)밑줄 친 ⓐ~ⓗ 중 어법, 혹은 문맥상 어휘의 사용이 어색한 것끼리 짝지어진 것을 고르시오. 40.

Many of the first models of cultural ⓐ **evolution** drew noticeable connections between culture and genes by using concepts from theoretical population genetics and ⓑ **applying** them to culture. Cultural patterns of transmission, innovation, and selection are conceptually ⓒ **liked** to genetic processes of transmission, mutation, and selection. However, these approaches had to be ⓓ **modified** to ⓔ **account for** the differences between genetic and cultural transmission. For example, we do not expect the cultural transmission to follow the rules of genetic transmission strictly. If two biological parents have different forms of a cultural trait, their child is ⓕ **not necessarily** equally likely to ⓖ **require** the mother's or father's form of that trait. Further, a child can ⓗ **enquire** cultural traits not only from its parents but also from nonparental adults and peers; thus, the frequency of a cultural trait in the population is relevant beyond just the probability that an individual's parents had that trait.

① ⓐ, ⓔ, ⓗ   ② ⓐ, ⓕ, ⓖ   ③ ⓑ, ⓓ, ⓕ
④ ⓒ, ⓔ, ⓗ   ⑤ ⓒ, ⓖ, ⓗ

21. 21)밑줄 친 ⓐ~ⓟ 중 어법, 혹은 문맥상 어휘의 사용이 어색한 것끼리 짝지어진 것을 고르시오. 41~42.

A ball ⓐ **thrown** into the air is ⓑ **acted** upon by the ⓒ **initial** force given it, ⓓ **persisting** as inertia of movement and ⓔ **tending** to carry it in the same straight line, and by the constant ⓕ **pull** of gravity downward, as well as by the ⓖ **resistant** of the air. It moves, accordingly, in a curved path. Now the path does not represent the working of any particular force; there is simply the combination of the three elementary forces ⓗ **mentioned** ; but in a real sense, there is something in the total action ⓘ **besides** the ⓙ **isolated** action of three forces, namely, their joint action. In the same way, when two or more human individuals are together, their mutual relationships and their arrangement into a group ⓚ **are** things which would not be ⓛ **revealed** if we ⓜ **defined** our attention to each individual separately. The significance of group behavior is greatly ⓝ **increased** in the case of human beings by the fact that some of the tendencies to action of the individual are ⓞ **unrelated** definitely to other persons, and could not be aroused except by other persons acting as stimuli. An individual in complete isolation would not reveal their competitive tendencies, their tendencies towards the opposite sex, their protective tendencies towards children. This shows that the traits of human nature ⓟ **do not** fully appear until the individual is brought into relationships with other individuals.

① ⓒ, ⓞ   ② ⓛ, ⓞ   ③ ⓒ, ⓓ, ⓜ
④ ⓖ, ⓜ, ⓞ   ⑤ ⓛ, ⓜ, ⓞ

22. 22)밑줄 친 ⓐ~ⓝ 중 어법, 혹은 문맥상 어휘의 사용이 어색한 것끼리 짝지어진 것을 고르시오. 43~45.

There once lived a man in a village who was not happy with his life. He was always ⓐ **troubled by** one problem or another. One day, a saint with his guards stopped by his village. Many people heard the news and started going to him with their problems. The man also decided ⓑ **to visit** the saint. Even after ⓒ **reaching** the saint's place in the morning, he didn't get the opportunity to meet him till evening. When the man got to meet the saint, he confessed that he was very unhappy with life ⓓ **because** problems always surrounded him, like workplace tension or worries about his health. He said, "Please give me a solution so that all the problems in my life will end and I can live peacefully". The saint smiled and said ⓔ **that** he would answer the request the next day. But the saint also asked if the man could do a small job for him. He told the man to ⓕ **take** care of a hundred camels in his group that night, ⓖ **said** "When all hundred camels sit down, you can go to sleep". The man agreed. The next morning when the saint met that man, he asked if the man had slept well. ⓗ **Tired** and sad, the man replied that he couldn't sleep even for a moment. In fact, the man tried very ⓘ **hard** but couldn't make all the camels sit at the same time because every time he made one camel sit, another would stand up. The saint told him, "You realized that no matter how ⓙ **hard** you try, you can't make all the camels ⓚ **sit** down. If one problem is solved, for some reason, another will ⓛ **arise** like the camels ⓜ **did** . So, humans should enjoy life ⓝ **though** these problems".

① ⓓ, ⓖ   ② ⓖ, ⓚ   ③ ⓖ, ⓜ

④ ⓖ, ⓝ   ⑤ ⓑ, ⓜ, ⓝ

2023 고1 11월 모의고사

❶ voca | ❷ text | ❸ [/] | ❹ ___ | ❺ quiz 1 | ❻ quiz 2 | ❼ quiz 3 | ⑧ quiz 4 | ❾ quiz 5

1. 1)**밑줄 부분 중 어법, 혹은 문맥상 어휘의 쓰임이 어색한 것을 올바르게 고쳐 쓰시오. (4개)** 18.

Dear Ms. MacAlpine,

I was so ① **excited** to hear that your brand is opening a new shop on Bruns Street next month. I have always ② **been appreciated** the way your brand helps women to feel more stylish and confident. I am writing in response to your ad in the Bruns Journal. I ③ **graduated** the Meline School of Fashion and have worked as a sales assistant at LoganMart for the last five years. ④ **While** that time, I've developed strong customer service and sales skills, and now I would like to apply ⑤ **for** the sales position in your clothing store. I am available for an interview at your earliest convenience. I look forward to ⑥ **hear** from you. Thank you for reading my letter.

Yours sincerely,

Grace Braddock

기호   어색한 표현   올바른 표현

( ) _____ ⇨ _____

( ) _____ ⇨ _____

( ) _____ ⇨ _____

( ) _____ ⇨ _____

2. 2)**밑줄 부분 중 어법, 혹은 문맥상 어휘의 쓰임이 어색한 것을 올바르게 고쳐 쓰시오. (3개)** 19.

I had never ① **been seen** a beach with such white sand or water ② **what** was such a beautiful shade of blue. Jane and I set up a blanket on the sand ③ **while** looking forward to our ten days of honeymooning on an exotic island. "Look"! Jane ④ **waved** her hand to point at the beautiful scene before us—and her gold wedding ring went flying off her hand. I tried to see ⑤ **where** it went, but the sun hit my eyes and I lost track of ⑥ **it** . I didn't want to lose her wedding ring, so I started looking in the area ⑦ **where** I thought it had landed. However, the sand was so fine and I realized that anything heavy, like gold, would quickly sink and might never ⑧ **find it** again.

기호   어색한 표현   올바른 표현

( ) _____ ⇨ _____

( ) _____ ⇨ _____

( ) _____ ⇨ _____

3. ³⁾밑줄 부분 중 어법, 혹은 문맥상 어휘의 쓰임이 어색한 것을 올바르게 고쳐 쓰시오. (4개) ²⁰·

Unfortunately, many people don't take ① **personal** responsibility for their own growth. Instead, they simply run the race ② **lie** out for them. They do ③ **well** enough in school to keep advancing. Maybe they manage to get a good job at a well-run company. But so many think and act as if their learning journey ④ **ends** with college. They have checked all the boxes in the life that was ⑤ **laid** out for them and now lack a road map ⑥ **describes** the right ways to move forward and continue to grow. In truth, that's when the journey really begins. When school is finished, your growth becomes ⑦ **mandatory** . Like healthy eating habits or a regular exercise program, you need to commit to it and devote thought, time, and energy to it. Otherwise, it simply won't ⑧ **be happened**—and your life and career are likely to stop ⑨ **progressing** as a result.

기호	어색한 표현		올바른 표현
( )	_____	⇨	_____
( )	_____	⇨	_____
( )	_____	⇨	_____
( )	_____	⇨	_____

4. ⁴⁾밑줄 부분 중 어법, 혹은 문맥상 어휘의 쓰임이 어색한 것을 올바르게 고쳐 쓰시오. (6개) ²¹·

Many people take the commonsense view that color is an ① **subjective** property of things, or of the light that ② **takes** off them. They say a tree's leaves are green because they ③ **absorb** green light—a greenness that is just as ④ **real** as the leaves. Others argue that color doesn't ⑤ **inhibit** the physical world at all but exists only in the eye or mind of the viewer. They maintain that if a tree fell in a forest and no one was there to see it, its leaves would be ⑥ **colorful**—and so ⑦ **everything else would**. They say there is no such thing as color; there are only the people who see it. Both positions are, in a way, correct. Color is objective and subjective—"the place", as Paul Cézanne put it, "⑧ **where** our brain and the universe meet". Color is created when light from the world is ⑨ **registered** by the eyes and interpreted by the brain.

기호	어색한 표현		올바른 표현
( )	_____	⇨	_____
( )	_____	⇨	_____
( )	_____	⇨	_____
( )	_____	⇨	_____
( )	_____	⇨	_____
( )	_____	⇨	_____

5. 5)밑줄 부분 중 어법, 혹은 문맥상 어휘의 쓰임이 어색한 것을 올바르게 고쳐 쓰시오. **(1개)** 22.

When ① **writing** a novel, research for information needs to be done. The thing is that some kinds of fiction ② **demand** a higher level of detail: crime fiction, for example, or scientific thrillers. The information is never hard ③ **finding** ; one website for authors even ④ **organizes** trips to police stations, so that crime writers can get it right. Often, a polite letter will earn you ⑤ **permission** to visit a particular location and ⑥ **record** all the details that you need. But remember ⑦ **that** you will drive your readers to ⑧ **boredom** if you ⑨ **think** that you need to pack everything ⑩ **that** you discover into your work. The details that ⑪ **matter** are those that ⑫ **reveal** the human experience. The crucial thing is telling a story, finding the characters, the tension, and the conflict—not the train timetable or the building blueprint.

기호	어색한 표현	올바른 표현
( )	_____ ⇨	_____

6. 6)밑줄 부분 중 어법, 혹은 문맥상 어휘의 쓰임이 어색한 것을 올바르게 고쳐 쓰시오. **(11개)** 23.

Nearly everything ① **have** to go through your mouth to get to the rest of you, from food and air to bacteria and viruses. A ② **healthful** mouth can help your body ③ **get** ④ **that** it needs and prevent it ⑤ **to** harm—with adequate space for air to travel to your lungs, and healthy teeth and gums that prevent harmful microorganisms from ⑥ **entrance** your bloodstream. From the moment you are created, oral health ⑦ **effects** every ⑧ **aspects** of your life. What happens in the mouth is usually just the tip of the iceberg and a reflection of what is happening in other ⑨ **part** of the body. Poor oral health can be a cause of a disease that ⑩ **effects** the entire body. The microorganisms in an unhealthy mouth can ⑪ **enter into** the bloodstream and travel anywhere in the body, ⑫ **posed** serious health risks.

기호	어색한 표현	올바른 표현
( )	_____ ⇨	_____
( )	_____ ⇨	_____
( )	_____ ⇨	_____
( )	_____ ⇨	_____
( )	_____ ⇨	_____
( )	_____ ⇨	_____
( )	_____ ⇨	_____
( )	_____ ⇨	_____
( )	_____ ⇨	_____
( )	_____ ⇨	_____
( )	_____ ⇨	_____

7. 7)밑줄 부분 중 어법, 혹은 문맥상 어휘의 쓰임이 어색한 것을 올바르게 고쳐 쓰시오. (4개) 24.

Kids ① **tire** of their toys, college students get sick of cafeteria food, and sooner or later most of us ② **lose** interest in our favorite TV shows. The bottom line is that we humans are easily ③ **bored** . But why should this be true? The answer ④ **lies** buried deep in our nerve cells, ⑤ **which** are designed to ⑥ **reduce** their initial excited response to stimuli each time they ⑦ **are occurred** . At the same time, these neurons enhance their responses to things that ⑧ **change**—especially things that ⑨ **change** ⑩ **consistently** . We probably ⑪ **evolved** this way ⑫ **because** our ancestors got more survival value, for example, from ⑬ **attending to** what was moving in a tree (such as a puma) than to the tree itself. ⑭ **Boredom** in reaction to an unchanging environment turns ⑮ **down** the level of neural excitation so that new stimuli (like our ancestor's hypothetical puma threat) ⑯ **stands** out more. It's the neural ⑰ **equivalent** of turning ⑱ **on** a front door light to see the fireflies.

기호	어색한 표현		올바른 표현
( )	_____	⇨	_____
( )	_____	⇨	_____
( )	_____	⇨	_____
( )	_____	⇨	_____

8. 8)밑줄 부분 중 어법, 혹은 문맥상 어휘의 쓰임이 어색한 것을 올바르게 고쳐 쓰시오. (8개) 26.

Frederick Douglass was born into slavery at a farm in Maryland. His full name at birth was Frederick Augustus Washington Bailey. He changed his name to Frederick Douglass after ① **his** successfully escaped from slavery in 1838. He became a leader of the Underground Railroad—a network of people, places, and routes ② **where** helped ③ **enslave** people ④ **escaping** to the north. He assisted other runaway slaves until they could safely get to other areas in the north. As a slave, he had taught ⑤ **him** to read and write and he ⑥ **spreads** that knowledge to other ⑦ **slave** as well. Once free, he became a well-known abolitionist and strong believer in equality for all people ⑧ **include** Blacks, Native Americans, women, and recent immigrants. He wrote several autobiographies ⑨ **describing** his experiences as a slave. In addition to all this, he became the first African-American candidate for vice president of the United States.

기호	어색한 표현		올바른 표현
( )	_____	⇨	_____
( )	_____	⇨	_____
( )	_____	⇨	_____
( )	_____	⇨	_____
( )	_____	⇨	_____
( )	_____	⇨	_____
( )	_____	⇨	_____
( )	_____	⇨	_____

9. 9)**밑줄 부분 중 어법, 혹은 문맥상 어휘의 쓰임이 어색한 것을 올바르게 고쳐 쓰시오. (1개)** [29.]

Some countries have proposed ① **tougher** guidelines for determining brain death when ② **transplantation**—③ **transacting** organs to others—is under consideration. In several European countries, there are legal requirements which ④ **specify** that a whole team of doctors must ⑤ **agree** over the diagnosis of death in the case of a potential donor. The reason for these strict ⑥ **regulations** for diagnosing brain death in potential organ donors ⑦ **is** , no doubt, to ⑧ **ease** public fears of a premature diagnosis of brain death for the purpose of obtaining organs. But it is questionable ⑨ **whether** these requirements ⑩ **reduce** public suspicions as much as they create them. They certainly ⑪ **maintain** mistaken beliefs ⑫ **that** diagnosing brain death is an unreliable process ⑬ **lacking** precision. As a matter of consistency, at least, criteria for diagnosing the deaths of organ donors should be exactly the same as for those ⑭ **for whom** immediate burial or cremation is intended.

기호   어색한 표현   올바른 표현

( ) _____ ⇨ _____

10. 10)**밑줄 부분 중 어법, 혹은 문맥상 어휘의 쓰임이 어색한 것을 올바르게 고쳐 쓰시오. (9개)** [30.]

The term minimalism gives a negative impression to some people who think ① **that** it is all about ② **maintaining** valuable possessions. This ③ **security** naturally stems from their ④ **detachment** to their possessions. It is difficult to ⑤ **distant** oneself from something that has been around for quite some time. ⑥ **Be** an emotional animal, human beings give meaning to the things around them. So, the question ⑦ **raising** here is that ⑧ **if** minimalism will hurt one's emotions, why become a minimalist? The answer is very simple; the ⑨ **assumption** of the question is fundamentally wrong. Minimalism does not hurt emotions. You might feel a bit sad while getting rid of a useless item but ⑩ **sooner than later**, this feeling will be ⑪ **overseen** by the joy of ⑫ **obscurity** . Minimalists never argue that you should leave every convenience of the modern era. They are of the view ⑬ **which** you only need to ⑭ **eliminate** stuff that is unused or not going to be used in the near future.

기호   어색한 표현   올바른 표현

( ) _____ ⇨ _____

( ) _____ ⇨ _____

( ) _____ ⇨ _____

( ) _____ ⇨ _____

( ) _____ ⇨ _____

( ) _____ ⇨ _____

( ) _____ ⇨ _____

( ) _____ ⇨ _____

( ) _____ ⇨ _____

11. 11)밑줄 부분 중 어법, 혹은 문맥상 어휘의 쓰임이 어색한 것을 올바르게 고쳐 쓰시오. (1개) 31.

A remarkable characteristic of the visual system is that it has the ability of ① **adapting** itself. Psychologist George M. Stratton made this ② **clear** in an impressive self-experiment. Stratton wore reversing glasses for several days, which literally turned the world upside down for him. In the beginning, this caused ③ **him** great difficulties: just putting food in his mouth with a ④ **fork** was a challenge for him. With time, however, his visual system adjusted to the new stimuli from ⑤ **habit** , and he was able to act normally in his environment again, even seeing ⑥ **it** upright when he concentrated. As he took ⑦ **off** his reversing glasses, he was again confronted ⑧ **with problems**: he used the wrong hand when he wanted to reach for something, for example. Fortunately, Stratton could reverse the ⑨ **perception** , and he did not have to wear reversing glasses for the rest of his life. For him, everything returned to normal after one day.

기호   어색한 표현   올바른 표현

(   ) _____ ⇨ _____

12. 12)밑줄 부분 중 어법, 혹은 문맥상 어휘의 쓰임이 어색한 것을 올바르게 고쳐 쓰시오. (1개) 32.

Participants in a study were asked to ① **answer** questions like "Why does the moon have phases"? Half the participants ② **was** told to search for the answers on the internet, while the other half weren't allowed to ③ **do** so. Then, in the second part of the study, all of the participants were presented with a new set of questions, such as "Why does Swiss cheese ④ **have** holes"? These questions were ⑤ **unrelated** to the ones ⑥ **asked** ⑦ **during** the first part of the study, so participants who ⑧ **used** the internet had absolutely no advantage over those who ⑨ **hadn't** . You would think ⑩ **that** both sets of participants would be equally sure or unsure about how well they could answer the new questions. But those who used the internet in the first part of the study rated ⑪ **themselves** as more knowledgeable than those who ⑫ **hadn't** , even about questions they hadn't searched ⑬ **online**. The study suggests that ⑭ **having** access to unrelated information was enough to pump ⑮ **up** their intellectual confidence.

기호   어색한 표현   올바른 표현

(   ) _____ ⇨ _____

13. ¹³⁾**밑줄 부분 중 어법, 혹은 문맥상 어휘의 쓰임이 어색한 것을 올바르게 고쳐 쓰시오. (13개)** ^{33.}

Anthropologist Gregory Bateson suggests ① **which** we tend to understand the world by focusing in on particular features within ② **them** . Take platypuses. We might zoom in so ③ **close** to their fur ④ **which** each hair appears ⑤ **differently** . We might also zoom out to the extent ⑥ **which** it appears as a single, uniform object. We might take the platypus as an individual, or we might treat it as part of a ⑦ **smaller** unit such as a species or an ecosystem. It's possible to move between many of these ⑧ **prospects** , ⑨ **despite** we may need some additional tools and skills to zoom in on individual pieces of hair or zoom out to entire ecosystems. Crucially, ⑩ **on the other hand** , we can only take up one perspective at a time. We can pay attention to the varied behavior of individual animals, look at ⑪ **what** unites them into a single species, or look at them as part of bigger ecological patterns. Every possible ⑫ **perspectives** ⑬ **involve** emphasizing certain aspects and ⑭ **embracing** others.

기호   어색한 표현   올바른 표현

( ) _____ ⇨ _____

( ) _____ ⇨ _____

( ) _____ ⇨ _____

( ) _____ ⇨ _____

( ) _____ ⇨ _____

( ) _____ ⇨ _____

( ) _____ ⇨ _____

( ) _____ ⇨ _____

( ) _____ ⇨ _____

( ) _____ ⇨ _____

( ) _____ ⇨ _____

( ) _____ ⇨ _____

( ) _____ ⇨ _____

14. ¹⁴⁾**밑줄 부분 중 어법, 혹은 문맥상 어휘의 쓰임이 어색한 것을 올바르게 고쳐 쓰시오. (2개)** ^{34.}

Plato's realism ① **includes** all aspects of experience but is most easily explained by considering the nature of mathematical and ② **geographical** objects such as circles. He asked the question, what is a circle? You might indicate a particular example ③ **carved** into stone or drawn in the sand. However, Plato would point out ④ **that** , if you looked closely enough, you would see ⑤ **that** neither it, nor indeed any physical circle, was perfect. They all possessed ⑥ **flaws** , and all were subject to change and ⑦ **decayed** with time. So how can we talk about perfect circles if we cannot actually see or touch them? Plato's extraordinary answer was ⑧ **that** the world we see is a ⑨ **perfect** reflection of a deeper ⑩ **unseen** reality of Forms, or universals, ⑪ **where** perfect cats chase perfect mice in perfect circles around perfect rocks. Plato believed that the Forms or universals are the true reality that ⑫ **exists** in an ⑬ **invisible** but perfect world beyond our senses.

기호   어색한 표현   올바른 표현

( ) _____ ⇨ _____

( ) _____ ⇨ _____

15. 15)**밑줄 부분 중 어법, 혹은 문맥상 어휘의 쓰임이 어색한 것을 올바르게 고쳐 쓰시오. (6개)** 35.

In statistics, the law of large numbers ① **describing** a situation ② **where** having more data is better for making predictions. According to it, the ③ **less** often an experiment is conducted, the ④ **closer** the average of the results can be expected to ⑤ **match** the true state of the world. For instance, on your first encounter with the game of roulette, you may have beginner's luck after ⑥ **bidding** on 7. But the more often you repeat this bet, the closer the ⑦ **relevant** frequency of wins and losses is expected to ⑧ **approach to** the true chance of winning, meaning that your luck will at some point fade away. Similarly, car insurers collect large amounts of data to figure out the chances that ⑨ **drivers** will cause ⑩ **to accidents** , depending on their age, region, or car brand. Both casinos and insurance industries rely on the law of large numbers to ⑪ **balance** individual losses.

기호	어색한 표현		올바른 표현
( )	_____	⇨	_____
( )	_____	⇨	_____
( )	_____	⇨	_____
( )	_____	⇨	_____
( )	_____	⇨	_____
( )	_____	⇨	_____

16. 16)**밑줄 부분 중 어법, 혹은 문맥상 어휘의 쓰임이 어색한 것을 올바르게 고쳐 쓰시오. (1개)** 36.

The adolescent brain is not fully developed until its early twenties. This means ① **the way** the adolescents' decision-making circuits integrate and ② **process** information may put them at a ③ **disadvantage** . One of their brain regions that ④ **matures** later is the prefrontal cortex, ⑤ **which** is the control center, tasked with thinking ahead and evaluating consequences. It is the area of the brain responsible for preventing you from sending off an initial angry text and modifying it with kinder words. On the other hand, the limbic system matures earlier, playing a ⑥ **central** role in processing emotional responses. ⑦ **Because of** its earlier development, it is more likely to influence decision-making. Decision-making in the adolescent brain is led by ⑧ **emotional** factors more than the perception of consequences. Due ⑨ **to** these differences, there is an ⑩ **imbalance** between feeling-based decision-making ruled by the more mature limbic system and ⑪ **emotion-based** decision-making by the ⑫ **not-yet-mature** prefrontal cortex. This may explain ⑬ **why** some teens are more likely to make bad decisions.

기호	어색한 표현		올바른 표현
( )	_____	⇨	_____

17. 17)**밑줄 부분 중 어법, 혹은 문맥상 어휘의 쓰임이 어색한 것을 올바르게 고쳐 쓰시오. (3개)** 37.

① **Despite** the remarkable ② **process** in deep-learning based facial recognition approaches in recent years, in terms of ③ **identification** performance, they still have limitations. These limitations ④ **relate** to the database used in the learning stage. If the selected database does not contain enough instances, the result may be systematically ⑤ **effected** . For example, the performance of a facial biometric system may ⑥ **decrease** if the person to ⑦ **identify** was enrolled over 10 years ago. The factor to consider is that this person may experience changes in the texture of the face, particularly with the appearance of wrinkles and sagging skin. These changes may be ⑧ **highlighted** by weight gain or loss. To counteract this problem, researchers have developed models for face aging or digital de-aging. It is used to ⑨ **compensate** for the differences in facial characteristics, which ⑩ **appear** over a given time period.

기호	어색한 표현		올바른 표현
( )	_____	⇨	_____
( )	_____	⇨	_____
( )	_____	⇨	_____

18. 18)**밑줄 부분 중 어법, 혹은 문맥상 어휘의 쓰임이 어색한 것을 올바르게 고쳐 쓰시오. (8개)** 38.

The decline in the diversity of our food is an entirely human-made ① **process** . The biggest loss of crop diversity came in the decades that ② **was followed by** the Second World War. In an attempt to save millions from extreme hunger, crop scientists found ways to produce grains such as rice and wheat on an enormous scale. And thousands of traditional ③ **variety** were replaced by a ④ **large** number of new super-productive ⑤ **one** . The strategy worked spectacularly well, at least to begin with. Because of it, grain production tripled, and between 1970 and 2020 the human population more than doubled. ⑥ **Left** the contribution of that strategy to one side, the danger of creating more ⑦ **various** crops ⑧ **are** that they are more at risk when it comes to disasters. Specifically, a global food system that depends on just a ⑨ **narrow** selection of plants has a greater chance of ⑩ **being** able to ⑪ **survive** diseases, pests and climate extremes.

기호	어색한 표현		올바른 표현
( )	_____	⇨	_____
( )	_____	⇨	_____
( )	_____	⇨	_____
( )	_____	⇨	_____
( )	_____	⇨	_____
( )	_____	⇨	_____
( )	_____	⇨	_____
( )	_____	⇨	_____

19. 19)밑줄 부분 중 어법, 혹은 문맥상 어휘의 쓰임이 어색한 것을 올바르게 고쳐 쓰시오. (6개) 39.

Between 1940 and 2000, Cuba ruled the world baseball scene. They won 25 of the first 28 World Cups and 3 of 5 Olympic Games. The Cubans were known ① **for** wearing uniforms ② **covered** in red from head to toe, a strong contrast to the more conservative North American style ③ **featured** grey or white pants. Not only ④ **did** their athletic talents superior, the Cubans appeared even stronger from just the colour of their uniforms. A game would not even start and the opposing team would already be scared. A few years ago, Cuba altered that uniform style, modernizing it and perhaps ⑤ **confirming** to other countries' style; interestingly, the national team has declined since that time. The country that ruled international baseball for decades ⑥ **have** not been on top since ⑦ **that** uniform change. Traditions are important for a team; while a team brand or image can ⑧ **adopt** to keep up with present times, if it abandons or neglects its roots, ⑨ **positive** effects can surface .

기호	어색한 표현		올바른 표현
( )	_____	⇨	_____
( )	_____	⇨	_____
( )	_____	⇨	_____
( )	_____	⇨	_____
( )	_____	⇨	_____
( )	_____	⇨	_____

20. 20)밑줄 부분 중 어법, 혹은 문맥상 어휘의 쓰임이 어색한 것을 올바르게 고쳐 쓰시오. (4개) 40.

Many of the first models of cultural ① **evolution** drew noticeable connections between culture and genes by using concepts from theoretical population genetics and ② **applying** them to culture. Cultural patterns of transmission, innovation, and selection are conceptually ③ **liked** to genetic processes of transmission, mutation, and selection. However, these approaches had to be ④ **codified** to ⑤ **account for** the differences between genetic and cultural transmission. For example, we do not expect the cultural transmission to follow the rules of genetic transmission strictly. If two biological parents have different forms of a cultural trait, their child is ⑥ **not** equally likely to ⑦ **require** the mother's or father's form of that trait. Further, a child can ⑧ **acquire** cultural traits not only from its parents but also from nonparental adults and peers; thus, the frequency of a cultural trait in the population is relevant beyond just the probability that an individual's parents had that trait.

기호	어색한 표현		올바른 표현
( )	_____	⇨	_____
( )	_____	⇨	_____
( )	_____	⇨	_____
( )	_____	⇨	_____

21. 21)**밑줄 부분 중 어법, 혹은 문맥상 어휘의 쓰임이 어색한 것을 올바르게 고쳐 쓰시오. (12개)** 41~42.

A ball ① **is thrown** into the air is ② **acting** upon by the ③ **initiative** force given it, ④ **persists** as inertia of movement and ⑤ **tend** to carry it in the same straight line, and by the constant ⑥ **push** of gravity downward, as well as by the ⑦ **resistance** of the air. It moves, accordingly, in a curved path. Now the path does not represent the working of any particular force; there is simply the combination of the three elementary forces ⑧ **mentioning** ; but in a real sense, there is something in the total action ⑨ **besides** the ⑩ **isolated** action of three forces, namely, their joint action. In the same way, when two or more human individuals are together, their mutual relationships and their arrangement into a group ⑪ **is** things which would not be ⑫ **relieved** if we ⑬ **defined** our attention to each individual separately. The significance of group behavior is greatly ⑭ **weakened** in the case of human beings by the fact that some of the tendencies to action of the individual are ⑮ **unrelated** definitely to other persons, and could not be aroused except by other persons acting as stimuli. An individual in complete isolation would not reveal their competitive tendencies, their tendencies towards the opposite sex, their protective tendencies towards children. This shows that the traits of human nature ⑯ **do not** fully appear until the individual is brought into relationships with other individuals.

기호	어색한 표현		올바른 표현
(　　)	＿＿＿＿＿＿＿	⇨	＿＿＿＿＿＿＿
(　　)	＿＿＿＿＿＿＿	⇨	＿＿＿＿＿＿＿
(　　)	＿＿＿＿＿＿＿	⇨	＿＿＿＿＿＿＿
(　　)	＿＿＿＿＿＿＿	⇨	＿＿＿＿＿＿＿
(　　)	＿＿＿＿＿＿＿	⇨	＿＿＿＿＿＿＿
(　　)	＿＿＿＿＿＿＿	⇨	＿＿＿＿＿＿＿
(　　)	＿＿＿＿＿＿＿	⇨	＿＿＿＿＿＿＿
(　　)	＿＿＿＿＿＿＿	⇨	＿＿＿＿＿＿＿
(　　)	＿＿＿＿＿＿＿	⇨	＿＿＿＿＿＿＿
(　　)	＿＿＿＿＿＿＿	⇨	＿＿＿＿＿＿＿
(　　)	＿＿＿＿＿＿＿	⇨	＿＿＿＿＿＿＿
(　　)	＿＿＿＿＿＿＿	⇨	＿＿＿＿＿＿＿

22. 22)밑줄 부분 중 어법, 혹은 문맥상 어휘의 쓰임이 어색한 것을 올바르게 고쳐 쓰시오. (13개) 43~45.

There once lived a man in a village who was not happy with his life. He was always ① **troubling** one problem or another. One day, a saint with his guards stopped by his village. Many people heard the news and started going to him with their problems. The man also decided ② **visiting** the saint. Even after ③ **reaching at** the saint's place in the morning, he didn't get the opportunity to meet him till evening. When the man got to meet the saint, he confessed that he was very unhappy with life ④ **because of** problems always surrounded him, like workplace tension or worries about his health. He said, "Please give me a solution so that all the problems in my life will end and I can live peacefully". The saint smiled and said ⑤ **which** he would answer the request the next day. But the saint also asked if the man could do a small job for him. He told the man to ⑥ **taking** care of a hundred camels in his group that night, ⑦ **saying** "When all hundred camels sit down, you can go to sleep". The man agreed. The next morning when the saint met that man, he asked if the man had slept well. ⑧ **Tiring** and sad, the man replied that he couldn't sleep even for a moment. In fact, the man tried very ⑨ **hardly** but couldn't make all the camels sit at the same time because every time he made one camel sit, another would stand up. The saint told him, "You realized that no matter how ⑩ **hardly** you try, you can't make all the camels ⑪ **sat** down. If one problem is solved, for some reason, another will ⑫ **raise** like the camels ⑬ **were** . So, humans should enjoy life ⑭ **though** these problems".

기호	어색한 표현		올바른 표현
( )	_____	⇨	_____
( )	_____	⇨	_____
( )	_____	⇨	_____
( )	_____	⇨	_____
( )	_____	⇨	_____
( )	_____	⇨	_____
( )	_____	⇨	_____
( )	_____	⇨	_____
( )	_____	⇨	_____
( )	_____	⇨	_____
( )	_____	⇨	_____
( )	_____	⇨	_____
( )	_____	⇨	_____

2023 고1 11월 모의고사

❶ voca   ❷ text   ❸ [/]   ❹ ____   ❺ quiz 1   ❻ quiz 2   ❼ quiz 3   ❽ quiz 4   ❾ quiz 5

18

☑ **다음 글을 읽고 물음에 답하시오.** (18.)

Dear Ms. MacAlpine, ⓐ I was so exciting to hear what your brand is opening a new shop on Bruns Street next month. ⓑ I have always appreciated the way how your brand helps women to feeling more stylish and confident. I am writing in response to your ad in the Bruns Journal. I ^{~를 졸업하다} _____ the Meline School of Fashion and have worked as a sales ^{조수} _____ at LoganMart for the last five years. ⓒ While that time, I've developed strong customer service and sales skills, and now I would have liked to apply for the sales position in your clothing store. I am available for an interview at your earliest convenience. (가) 당신에게서 듣는 것을 기대하겠습니다. Thank you for reading my letter. Yours sincerely, Grace Braddock

1. ¹⁾힌트를 참고하여 각 빈칸에 알맞은 단어를 쓰시오.

2. ²⁾밑줄 친 ⓐ~ⓒ에서, 어법 혹은 문맥상 어색한 부분을 찾아 올바르게 고쳐 쓰시오.

   ⓐ   잘못된 표현   바른 표현

   (   ) ⇨ (   )
   (   ) ⇨ (   )

   ⓑ   잘못된 표현   바른 표현

   (   ) ⇨ (   )
   (   ) ⇨ (   )

   ⓒ   잘못된 표현   바른 표현

   (   ) ⇨ (   )
   (   ) ⇨ (   )

3. ³⁾위 글에 주어진 (가)의 한글과 같은 의미를 가지도록, 각각의 주어진 단어들을 알맞게 배열하시오.

(가) from / to / you. / I / hearing / forward / look

19

☑ **다음 글을 읽고 물음에 답하시오.** (19.)

ⓐ I had never seen a beach with so white sand or water what was such a beautiful shade of blue. ⓑ Jane and I set up a blanket on the sand during looking forward to our ten days of honeymooning on an exotic island. "Look"! Jane waved her hand to point at the beautiful scene before us—and her gold wedding ring went flying off her hand. (가) 나는 그것이 어디로 갔는지 보려고 했지만, 햇빛이 눈에 들어와 그것의 가던 방향을 놓쳤다. ⓒ I didn't want to lose her wedding ring, so I started looking in the area where I thought it landed. ⓓ However, the sand was so fine and I realized that anything heavy, like gold, would quickly sink and might never found again.

4. 4)밑줄 친 ⓐ~ⓓ에서, 어법 혹은 문맥상 어색한 부분을 찾아 올바르게 고쳐 쓰시오.

ⓐ   잘못된 표현   바른 표현

(   ) ⇨ (   )

(   ) ⇨ (   )

ⓑ   잘못된 표현   바른 표현

(   ) ⇨ (   )

(   ) ⇨ (   )

ⓒ   잘못된 표현   바른 표현

(   ) ⇨ (   )

ⓓ   잘못된 표현   바른 표현

(   ) ⇨ (   )

5. 5)위 글에 주어진 (가)의 한글과 같은 의미를 가지도록, 각각의 주어진 단어들을 알맞게 배열하시오.

(가) and / my / I / sun / lost track of / it / see / eyes / went, / I / hit / it. / where / but / tried / to / the

20

☑ **다음 글을 읽고 물음에 답하시오.** (20.)

Unfortunately, many people don't take ^{개인적인} _____ responsibility for their own growth. Instead, they simply run the race laid out for them. They do well enough in school to keep advancing. ⓐ <u>Maybe they manage to getting a good job at a well-run company.</u> (가) 하지만 아주 많은 사람들이 마치 그들의 배움의 여정이 대학으로 끝나는 것처럼 착각하고 행동한다. ⓑ <u>They have checked all the boxes in the life that was laid out for them and now lack a road map describes the right ways to move forward and continue to grow.</u> In truth, that's when the journey really begins. When school is finished, your growth becomes voluntary. ⓒ <u>Like healthily eating habits or a regular exercise program, you need to commit to it and devoting thought, time, and energy to it.</u> Otherwise, it simply won't happen—and your life and career are likely to stop progressing as a result.

6. ⁶⁾힌트를 참고하여 각 <u>빈칸에 알맞은</u> 단어를 쓰시오.

7. ⁷⁾밑줄 친 ⓐ~ⓒ에서, 어법 혹은 문맥상 어색한 부분을 찾아 올바르게 고쳐 쓰시오.

  ⓐ   잘못된 표현   바른 표현

  (   ) ⇨ (   )

  ⓑ   잘못된 표현   바른 표현

  (   ) ⇨ (   )

  ⓒ   잘못된 표현   바른 표현

  (   ) ⇨ (   )

  (   ) ⇨ (   )

8. ⁸⁾위 글에 주어진 (가)의 한글과 같은 의미를 가지도록, 각각의 주어진 단어들을 알맞게 배열하시오.

(가) as if / journey / and / think / with / their / ends / college. / act / many / so / But / learning

21

☑ **다음 글을 읽고 물음에 답하시오.** (21.)

Many people take the commonsense view that color is an ^{객관적인} _____ property of things, or of the light that bounces off them. They say a tree's leaves are green because they reflect green light—a greenness that is just as real as the leaves. Others argue that color doesn't inhabit the physical world at all but exists only in the eye or mind of the viewer. They maintain that if a tree fell in a forest and no one was there to see it, its leaves would be colorless —and so would everything else. (가) 그들은 색깔 같은 것은 없고 그것을 보는 사람들만 있다고 말한다. Both positions are, in a way, correct. Color is objective and subjective—"the place", as Paul Cézanne put it, "where our brain and the universe meet". ⓐ <u>Color is created when light from the world registers by the eyes and interpreted by the brain.</u>

9. 9)힌트를 참고하여 각 빈칸에 알맞은 단어를 쓰시오.

10. 10)밑줄 친 @에서, 어법 혹은 문맥상 어색한 부분을 찾아 올바르게 고쳐 쓰시오.

  @ 잘못된 표현   바른 표현
  (   ) ⇨ (   )

11. 11)위 글에 주어진 (가)의 한글과 같은 의미를 가지도록, 각각의 주어진 단어들을 알맞게 배열하시오.

(가) thing / only / there / who / such / see / is / as / there / the people / it. / no / They say / color; / are

22

☑ **다음 글을 읽고 물음에 답하시오.** (22.)

When writing a novel, research for information needs to be done. @ The thing is what some kinds of fiction demands a higher level of detail: crime fiction, for example, or scientific thrillers. The information is never hard to find; one website for authors even organizes trips to police stations, so that crime writers can get it right. ⓑ Often, a polite letter will earn you permission to visit a particular location and recording all the details that you need. (가) 하지만 만약 여러분이 발견한 모든 것을 작품에 담아야 한다고 생각할 경우 여러분은 독자들을 지루하게 만들 것이라는 것을 기억하라. The details that matter are those that reveal the human experience. The ^{중요한} _____ thing is telling a story, finding the characters, the tension, and the conflict—not the train timetable or the building blueprint.

12. 12)힌트를 참고하여 각 빈칸에 알맞은 단어를 쓰시오.

13. 13)밑줄 친 @~ⓑ에서, 어법 혹은 문맥상 어색한 부분을 찾아 올바르게 고쳐 쓰시오.

  @ 잘못된 표현   바른 표현
  (   ) ⇨ (   )
  (   ) ⇨ (   )
  ⓑ 잘못된 표현   바른 표현
  (   ) ⇨ (   )

14. 14)위 글에 주어진 (가)의 한글과 같은 의미를 가지도록, 각각의 주어진 단어들을 알맞게 배열하시오.

(가) you / boredom / you / pack / discover / to / you / think that / need / readers / drive / to / everything / your / your / you / work. / remember that / But / will / if / into

23

☑ **다음 글을 읽고 물음에 답하시오.** (23.)

ⓐ <u>Nearly everything have to go through your mouth to get to rest of you, from food and air to bacteria and viruses.</u> ⓑ <u>A healthy mouth can help your body get that it needs and prevent them from harm—with adequate space for air to travel to your lungs, and healthy teeth and gums that prevent harmful microorganisms from entering your bloodstream.</u> (가) <u>여러분이 생겨난 순간부터 구강 건강은 여러분의 삶의 모든 측면에 영향을 미친다.</u> What happens in the mouth is usually just the tip of the iceberg and a reflection of what is happening in other parts of the body. Poor oral health can be a cause of a disease that affects the ^{전체의} _____ body. ⓒ <u>The microorganisms in an unhealthy mouth can enter the bloodstream and travels anywhere in the body, posing serious health risks.</u>

15. 15)힌트를 참고하여 각 <u>빈칸에 알맞은</u> 단어를 쓰시오.

16. 16)밑줄 친 ⓐ~ⓒ에서, 어법 혹은 문맥상 어색한 부분을 찾아 올바르게 고쳐 쓰시오.

   ⓐ   잘못된 표현   바른 표현

   (   ) ⇨ (   )

   (   ) ⇨ (   )

   ⓑ   잘못된 표현   바른 표현

   (   ) ⇨ (   )

   (   ) ⇨ (   )

   ⓒ   잘못된 표현   바른 표현

   (   ) ⇨ (   )

17. 17)위 글에 주어진 (가)의 한글과 같은 의미를 가지도록, 각각의 주어진 단어들을 알맞게 배열하시오.

(가) your / moment / of / life. / every / are / created, / the / you / oral health / affects / From / aspect

24

☑ **다음 글을 읽고 물음에 답하시오.** (24.)

Kids ^{~에 싫증나다} _____ their toys, college students get sick of cafeteria food, and sooner or later most of us lose interest in our favorite TV shows. (가) 요점은 우리 인간이 쉽게 지루해한다는 것이다. But why should this be true? The answer lies buried deep in our nerve cells, which are designed to reduce their ^{초기의} _____ excited response to stimuli each time they occur. At the same time, these neurons enhance their responses to things that change—especially things that change quickly. ⓐ <u>We probably evolved this way because our ancestors got more survival value, for example, from attending to that was moving in a tree (such as a puma) than to the tree itself.</u> Boredom in reaction to an unchanging environment turns down the level of neural excitation so that new stimuli (like our ancestor's hypothetical puma threat) stand out more. It's the ^{신경의} _____ equivalent of turning off a front door light to see the fireflies.

18. 18)힌트를 참고하여 각 <u>빈칸에 알맞은</u> 단어를 쓰시오.

19. 19)밑줄 친 ⓐ에서, 어법 혹은 문맥상 어색한 부분을 찾아 올바르게 고쳐 쓰시오.

    ⓐ   잘못된 표현   바른 표현

    (   ) ⇨ (   )

    (   ) ⇨ (   )

    (   ) ⇨ (   )

20. 20)위 글에 주어진 (가)의 한글과 같은 의미를 가지도록, 각각의 주어진 단어들을 알맞게 배열하시오.

(가) humans / that / easily / we / is / are / The bottom line / bored.

26

☑ **다음 글을 읽고 물음에 답하시오.** (26.)

Frederick Douglass was born into slavery at a farm in Maryland. His full name at birth was Frederick Augustus Washington Bailey. He changed his name to Frederick Douglass after he ^{성공적으로} _____ escaped from slavery in 1838. He became a leader of the Underground Railroad—a network of people, places, and routes that helped enslaved people escape to the north. ⓐ <u>He assisted another runaway slaves until they could safely get to other areas in the north.</u> ⓑ <u>As a slave, he taught himself to read and write and he spread that knowledge to other slaves as well.</u> Once free, he became a well-known abolitionist and strong believer in equality for all people including Blacks, Native Americans, women, and recent ^{이민자들} _____. He wrote several autobiographies describing his experiences as a slave. (가) <u>이 모든 것에 더하여 그는 미국의 첫 아프리카계 미국인 부통령 후보가 되었다.</u>

21. 21)힌트를 참고하여 각 <u>빈칸에 알맞은</u> 단어를 쓰시오.

22. 22)밑줄 친 ⓐ~ⓑ에서, 어법 혹은 문맥상 어색한 부분을 찾아 올바르게 고쳐 쓰시오.

    ⓐ   잘못된 표현   바른 표현

    (   ) ⇨ (   )

    ⓑ   잘못된 표현   바른 표현

    (   ) ⇨ (   )

23. 23)위 글에 주어진 (가)의 한글과 같은 의미를 가지도록, 각각의 주어진 단어들을 알맞게 배열하시오.

(가) candidate / for / he / States. / this, / the / the / vice / president / first / of / became / United / In   addition   to / all / African-American

29

☑ **다음 글을 읽고 물음에 답하시오.** ^(29.)

Some countries have proposed tougher guidelines for determining brain death when transplantation—transferring organs to others—is under consideration. In several European countries, there are legal requirements which ^{명시하다} _____ that a whole team of doctors must agree over the diagnosis of death in the case of a ^{잠재적인} _____ donor. The reason for these strict regulations for diagnosing brain death in potential organ donors is, no doubt, to ease public fears of a premature diagnosis of brain death for the purpose of obtaining organs. (가) 하지만 이러한 요건들이 대중의 의심을 만들어 내는 만큼 그것을 줄여 주는지는 의문이다. ⓐ They certainly maintain mistaken beliefs that diagnosing brain death is an unreliable process lacked precision. ⓑ As a matter of consistency, at least, criteria for diagnosing the deaths of organ donors should be exactly the same as for that for whom immediate burial or cremation is intended.

24. ²⁴⁾힌트를 참고하여 각 <u>빈칸에 알맞은</u> 단어를 쓰시오.

25. ²⁵⁾밑줄 친 ⓐ~ⓑ에서, 어법 혹은 문맥상 어색한 부분을 찾아 올바르게 고쳐 쓰시오.

   ⓐ   잘못된 표현   바른 표현

   (   ) ⇨ (   )

   ⓑ   잘못된 표현   바른 표현

   (   ) ⇨ (   )

26. ²⁶⁾위 글에 주어진 (가)의 한글과 같은 의미를 가지도록, 각각의 주어진 단어들을 알맞게 배열하시오.

(가) suspicions / these   requirements / public / as / create / But / as / they / it / whether / is / them. / much / reduce / questionable

30

☑ **다음 글을 읽고 물음에 답하시오.** ^(30.)

The term minimalism gives a negative impression to some people who think that it is all about ^{희생하다} _____ valuable possessions. This insecurity naturally stems from their attachment to their possessions. It is difficult to distance oneself from something that has been around for quite some time. Being an emotional animal, human beings give meaning to the things around them. So, the question arising here is that if minimalism will hurt one's emotions, why become a minimalist? ⓐ <u>The answer is very simple; the assumption of the question is fundamental wrong.</u> Minimalism does not hurt emotions. ⓑ <u>You might feel a bit sad during getting rid of a useless item but sooner than later, this feeling will be overcoming by the joy of clarity.</u> (가) <u>미니멀리스트는 여러분이 현대의 모든 편의를 버려야 한다고 주장하지 않는다.</u> They are of the view that you only need to ^{제거하다} _____ stuff that is unused or not going to be used in the near future.

27. 27)힌트를 참고하여 각 빈칸에 알맞은 단어를 쓰시오.

28. 28)밑줄 친 ⓐ~ⓑ에서, 어법 혹은 문맥상 어색한 부분을 찾아 올바르게 고쳐 쓰시오.

ⓐ　　잘못된 표현　　　　　　바른 표현

(　　　　　　　) ⇨ (　　　　　　　)

ⓑ　　잘못된 표현　　　　　　바른 표현

(　　　　　　　) ⇨ (　　　　　　　)

(　　　　　　　) ⇨ (　　　　　　　)

29. 29)위 글에 주어진 (가)의 한글과 같은 의미를 가지도록, 각각의 주어진 단어들을 알맞게 배열하시오.

(가) convenience / that / argue / never / you / of / leave / should / every / the modern era. / Minimalists

31

☑ **다음 글을 읽고 물음에 답하시오.** (31.)

A remarkable characteristic of the visual system is that it has the ability of ^{적용하다} _____ itself. Psychologist George M. Stratton made this clear in an ^{인상적인} _____ self-experiment. ⓐ Stratton wore reversed glasses for several days, which literal turned the world upside down for him. In the beginning, this caused him great difficulties: just putting food in his mouth with a fork was a ^{어려움} _____ for him. With time, however, his visual system ^{적용하다} _____ to the new stimuli from reality, and he was able to act normally in his environment again, even seeing it upright when he concentrated. (가) 반전 안경을 벗었을 때 그는 다시 문제에 직면했다.: he used the wrong hand when he wanted to reach for something, for example. (나) 다행히 Stratton은 지각을 뒤집을 수 있었고 평생 반전 안경을 착용하지 않아도 되었다. For him, everything returned to normal after one day.

30. 30)힌트를 참고하여 각 빈칸에 알맞은 단어를 쓰시오.

31. 31)밑줄 친 ⓐ에서, 어법 혹은 문맥상 어색한 부분을 찾아 올바르게 고쳐 쓰시오.

ⓐ　　잘못된 표현　　　　　　바른 표현

(　　　　　　　) ⇨ (　　　　　　　)

(　　　　　　　) ⇨ (　　　　　　　)

32. 32)위 글에 주어진 (가) ~ (나)의 한글과 같은 의미를 가지도록, 각각의 주어진 단어들을 알맞게 배열하시오.

(가) was / he / reversing glasses, / problems / he / As / took off / confronted with / again / his

(나) could / reversing glasses / the / did / and / the rest / life. / Fortunately, / not / for / of / Stratton / his / wear / he / have to / perception, / reverse

32

☑ **다음 글을 읽고 물음에 답하시오.** (32.)

Participants in a study were asked to answer questions like "Why does the moon have phases"? ⓐ <u>Half the participants told to search for the answers on the internet, during other half weren't allowed to do so.</u> ⓑ <u>Then, in the second part of the study, all of the participants presented with a new set of questions, such as "Why does Swiss cheese have holes"?</u> ⓒ <u>These questions were unrelated to the ones asked while the first part of the study, so participants who used the internet had absolutely no advantage over those who hadn't.</u> You would think that both sets of participants would be equally sure or unsure about how well they could answer the new questions. ⓓ <u>But those who used the internet in the first part of the study rated them as more knowledgeable than those who hadn't, even about questions they hadn't searched online for.</u> (가) <u>이 연구는 관련 없는 정보에 접근하는 것이 그들의 지적 자신감을 부풀리기에 충분했다는 것을 시사한다.</u>

33. 33)밑줄 친 ⓐ~ⓓ에서, 어법 혹은 문맥상 어색한 부분을 찾아 올바르게 고쳐 쓰시오.

ⓐ	잘못된 표현	바른 표현	잘못된 표현	바른 표현
	( ) ⇨ ( )		( ) ⇨ ( )	
	( ) ⇨ ( )			

ⓑ	잘못된 표현	바른 표현
	( ) ⇨ ( )	

ⓒ	잘못된 표현	바른 표현	잘못된 표현	바른 표현
	( ) ⇨ ( )		( ) ⇨ ( )	
	( ) ⇨ ( )			

ⓓ	잘못된 표현	바른 표현
	( ) ⇨ ( )	

34. 34)위 글에 주어진 (가)의 한글과 같은 의미를 가지도록, 각각의 주어진 단어들을 알맞게 배열하시오.

(가) information / that / to / access / intellectual / unrelated / having / pump up / The study / suggests / was / their / enough to / confidence.

33

☑ **다음 글을 읽고 물음에 답하시오.** (33.)

^{인류학자} _____ Gregory Bateson suggests that we tend to understand the world by focusing in on particular features within it. Take platypuses. ⓐ <u>We might zoom in so close to their fur that each hair appears different.</u> ⓑ <u>We might also zoom out to the extent which it appears as a single, uniform object.</u> We might take the platypus as an individual, or we might treat it as part of a larger unit such as a species or an ecosystem. It's possible to move between many of these ^{관점} _____, although we may need some additional tools and skills to zoom in on individual pieces of hair or zoom out to ^{전체의} _____ ecosystems. (가) <u>그러나 결정적으로 우리는 한 번에 하나의 관점만 취할 수 있다.</u> We can pay attention to the varied behavior of individual animals, look at what unites them into a single species, or look at them as part of bigger ecological patterns. ⓒ <u>Every possible perspective involve emphasizing certain aspects and ignoring other.</u>

35. 35)힌트를 참고하여 각 빈칸에 알맞은 단어를 쓰시오.

36. 36)밑줄 친 ⓐ~ⓒ에서, 어법 혹은 문맥상 어색한 부분을 찾아 올바르게 고쳐 쓰시오.

    ⓐ   잘못된 표현   바른 표현

    (   ) ⇨ (   )

    ⓑ   잘못된 표현   바른 표현

    (   ) ⇨ (   )

    (   ) ⇨ (   )

    ⓒ   잘못된 표현   바른 표현

    (   ) ⇨ (   )

    (   ) ⇨ (   )

37. 37)위 글에 주어진 (가)의 한글과 같은 의미를 가지도록, 각각의 주어진 단어들을 알맞게 배열하시오.

(가) perspective / can / at / take up / time. / however, / only / Crucially, / we / one / a

34

☑ **다음 글을 읽고 물음에 답하시오.** (34.)

Plato's realism includes all aspects of experience but is most easily explained by considering the nature of 수학적인 _____ and 기하학적인 _____ objects such as circles. ⓐ He asked the question, what is a circle? You might indicate a particular example carving into stone or drawn in the sand. ⓑ However, Plato would point out that, if you look closely enough, you would see that neither it, nor indeed any physical circle, was perfect. (가) 그것들 모두는 결함을 가지고 있었고, 모두 변화의 영향을 받고 시간이 지남에 따라 쇠하였다. So how can we talk about perfect circles if we cannot actually see or touch them? Plato's 비범한 _____ answer was that the world we see is a poor 반영물 _____ of a deeper unseen reality of Forms, or universals, where perfect cats chase perfect mice in perfect circles around perfect rocks. (나) 플라톤은 '형상' 또는 '보편자'가 보이지 않지만 우리의 감각을 넘어서는 완벽한 세계에 존재하는 진정한 실재라고 믿었다.

38. 38)힌트를 참고하여 각 빈칸에 알맞은 단어를 쓰시오.

39. 39)밑줄 친 ⓐ~ⓑ에서, 어법 혹은 문맥상 어색한 부분을 찾아 올바르게 고쳐 쓰시오.

    ⓐ   잘못된 표현   바른 표현

    (   ) ⇨ (   )

    (   ) ⇨ (   )

    ⓑ   잘못된 표현   바른 표현

    (   ) ⇨ (   )

40. ⁴⁰⁾위 글에 주어진 (가) ~ (나)의 한글과 같은 의미를 가지도록, 각각의 주어진 단어들을 알맞게 배열하시오.

(가) all / change / were subject to / and / time. / flaws, / They / with / decayed / all / possessed / and

(나) are / reality / senses. / perfect / or / universals / the / exists / invisible / an / the / Forms / world / that / believed / but / true / our / in / beyond / Plato / that

35

☑ **다음 글을 읽고 물음에 답하시오.** ⁽³⁵·⁾

ⓐ In statistics, the law of large numbers describes a situation where having more data is better for making predictions. According to it, the more often an experiment is conducted, the closer the average of the results can be expected to match the true ^{상태} _____ of the world. For instance, on your first encounter with the game of roulette, you may have beginner's luck after betting on 7. But the more often you repeat this bet, the closer the ^{상대적인} _____ frequency of wins and losses is expected to approach the true chance of winning, meaning that your luck will at some point fade away. ⓑ Similarly, car insurers collect large amounts of data to figure out the chances that drivers will cause accidents, depend on their age, region, or car brand. (가) 카지노와 보험 산업 모두 개별 손실의 균형을 맞추기 위해 대수의 법칙에 의존한다.

41. ⁴¹⁾힌트를 참고하여 각 빈칸에 알맞은 단어를 쓰시오.

42. ⁴²⁾밑줄 친 ⓐ~ⓑ에서, 어법 혹은 문맥상 어색한 부분을 찾아 올바르게 고쳐 쓰시오.

   ⓐ   잘못된 표현   바른 표현

   (   ) ⇨ (   )

   ⓑ   잘못된 표현   바른 표현

   (   ) ⇨ (   )

43. ⁴³⁾위 글에 주어진 (가)의 한글과 같은 의미를 가지도록, 각각의 주어진 단어들을 알맞게 배열하시오.

(가) rely on / the law / balance / losses. / of / industries / Both / insurance / numbers / casinos / to / individual / large / and

36

☑ **다음 글을 읽고 물음에 답하시오.** (36.)

The adolescent brain is not fully developed ^{~까지} _____ its early twenties. This means the way the adolescents' decision-making circuits ^{통합하다} _____ and ^{처리하다} _____ information may put them at a disadvantage. ⓐ <u>One of their brain regions that mature later is the prefrontal cortex, which is the control center, tasking with thinking ahead and evaluating consequences.</u> It is the area of the brain responsible for preventing you from sending off an initial angry text and ^{수정하다} _____ it with kinder words. On the other hand, the limbic system matures earlier, playing a central role in processing emotional responses. ⓑ <u>Because its earlier development, it is more likely to influence decision-making.</u> Decision-making in the adolescent brain is led by emotional factors more than the perception of consequences. Due to these differences, there is an imbalance between feeling-based decision-making ruled by the more mature limbic system and logical-based decision-making by the not-yet-mature prefrontal cortex. (가) <u>이것은 왜 일부 십 대들이 그릇된 결정을 내릴 가능성이 더 높은지를 설명해 줄 수 있다.</u>

44. ⁴⁴⁾힌트를 참고하여 각 <u>빈칸에 알맞은</u> 단어를 쓰시오.

45. ⁴⁵⁾밑줄 친 ⓐ~ⓑ에서, 어법 혹은 문맥상 어색한 부분을 찾아 올바르게 고쳐 쓰시오.

   ⓐ   잘못된 표현   바른 표현

   (   ) ⇨ (   )
   (   ) ⇨ (   )

   ⓑ   잘못된 표현   바른 표현

   (   ) ⇨ (   )

46. ⁴⁶⁾위 글에 주어진 (가)의 한글과 같은 의미를 가지도록, 각각의 주어진 단어들을 알맞게 배열하시오.

(가) bad / more / This / likely / explain / some / teens / are / decisions. / why / make / to / may

37

☑ **다음 글을 읽고 물음에 답하시오.** (37.)

ⓐ Although the remarkable progress in deep-learning based facial recognition approaches in recent years, in terms of identification performance, they still have limitations. These limitations relate to the database used in the learning stage. (가) 선택된 데이터베이스가 충분한 사례를 포함하지 않으면 그 결과가 시스템적으로 영향을 받을 수 있다. For example, the performance of a facial biometric system may decrease if the person to be identified was enrolled over 10 years ago. The factor to consider is that this person may experience changes in the texture of the face, particularly with the appearance of wrinkles and sagging skin. These changes may be highlighted by weight gain or loss. To ^{대응하다} _____ this problem, researchers have developed models for face aging or digital de-aging. It is used to ^{보완하다} _____ for the differences in facial characteristics, which appear over a given time period.

47. 47)힌트를 참고하여 각 빈칸에 알맞은 단어를 쓰시오.

48. 48)밑줄 친 ⓐ에서, 어법 혹은 문맥상 어색한 부분을 찾아 올바르게 고쳐 쓰시오.

　　ⓐ　　　　잘못된 표현　　　　　　　바른 표현

　　(　　　　　　　　) ⇨ (　　　　　　　　)

49. 49)위 글에 주어진 (가)의 한글과 같은 의미를 가지도록, 각각의 주어진 단어들을 알맞게 배열하시오.

(가) contain / not / systematically / the selected database / affected. / enough / instances, / be / If / does / the result / may

38

☑ **다음 글을 읽고 물음에 답하시오.** (38.)

(가) 우리 음식의 다양성의 감소는 전적으로 인간이 만든 과정이다. ⓐ The biggest loss of crop diversity came in the decades that following the Second World War. In an attempt to save millions from ^{극도의} _____ hunger, crop scientists found ways to produce grains such as rice and wheat on an enormous scale. And thousands of traditional varieties were ^{대체하다} _____ by a small number of new super-productive ones. The strategy worked spectacularly well, at least to begin with. ⓑ Because it, grain production tripled, and between 1970 and 2020 the human population more than doubled. Leaving the contribution of that strategy to one side, the danger of creating more ^{획일적인} _____ crops is that they are more at risk when it comes to disasters. ^{특히} _____, a global food system that depends on just a narrow selection of plants has a greater chance of not being able to survive diseases, pests and climate extremes.

50. ⁵⁰⁾힌트를 참고하여 각 <u>빈칸에 알맞은</u> 단어를 쓰시오.

51. ⁵¹⁾밑줄 친 ⓐ~ⓑ에서, 어법 혹은 문맥상 어색한 부분을 찾아 올바르게 고쳐 쓰시오.

　　ⓐ　　　잘못된 표현　　　　　　바른 표현

　　（　　　　　　　）⇨（　　　　　　　　　）

　　ⓑ　　　잘못된 표현　　　　　　바른 표현

　　（　　　　　　　）⇨（　　　　　　　　　）

52. ⁵²⁾위 글에 주어진 (가)의 한글과 같은 의미를 가지도록, 각각의 주어진 단어들을 알맞게 배열하시오.

(가) process. / in / the diversity / an / human-made / food / entirely / of / The / decline / our / is

39

☑ **다음 글을 읽고 물음에 답하시오.** ⁽³⁹·⁾

Between 1940 and 2000, Cuba ^지배하다 _____ the world baseball scene. They won 25 of the first 28 World Cups and 3 of 5 Olympic Games. The Cubans were known for wearing uniforms covered in red from head to toe, a strong contrast to the more ^보수적인 _____ North American style featuring grey or white pants. (가) 쿠바인들의 운동 재능이 뛰어났을 뿐만 아니라 그들은 그들의 유니폼의 색깔만으로도 훨씬 더 강하게 보였다. ⓐ <u>A game would not even start and the opposed team would already be scared.</u> ⓑ <u>few years ago, Cuba altered that uniform style, modernizing it and perhaps conforming to other countries' style; interestingly, the national team has declined since that time.</u> The country that ruled international baseball for decades has not been on top since that uniform change. Traditions are important for a team; while a team brand or image can adjust to keep up with present times, if it abandons or neglects its roots, negative effects can surface.

53. ⁵³⁾힌트를 참고하여 각 <u>빈칸에 알맞은</u> 단어를 쓰시오.

54. ⁵⁴⁾밑줄 친 ⓐ~ⓑ에서, 어법 혹은 문맥상 어색한 부분을 찾아 올바르게 고쳐 쓰시오.

　　ⓐ　　　잘못된 표현　　　　　　바른 표현

　　（　　　　　　　）⇨（　　　　　　　　　）

　　ⓑ　　　잘못된 표현　　　　　　바른 표현

　　（　　　　　　　）⇨（　　　　　　　　　）

　　（　　　　　　　）⇨（　　　　　　　　　）

55. ⁵⁵⁾위 글에 주어진 (가)의 한글과 같은 의미를 가지도록, 각각의 주어진 단어들을 알맞게 배열하시오.

(가) the / from / appeared / just / even / of / superior, / were / talents / their / colour / the　　Cubans / stronger / Not　　only / athletic / uniforms. / their

40

☑ **다음 글을 읽고 물음에 답하시오.** (40.)

Many of the first models of cultural evolution drew ^{주목할 만한} _____ connections between culture and genes by using concepts from theoretical population genetics and applying them to culture. ⓐ <u>Cultural patterns of transmission, innovation, and selection are conceptually likened to genetically processes of transmission, mutation, and selection.</u> (가) <u>그러나 이러한 접근법은 유전자의 전달과 문화 전파 사이의 차이점을 설명하기 위해 수정되어야만 했다.</u> ⓑ <u>For example, we do not expect the cultural transmission to follow the rules of genetic transmission strict.</u> If two biological parents have different forms of a cultural trait, their child is not necessarily equally likely to acquire the mother's or father's form of that trait. ^{더욱이} _____, a child can acquire cultural traits not only from its parents but also from nonparental adults and peers; thus, the frequency of a cultural trait in the population is relevant beyond just the ^{확률} _____ that an individual's parents had that trait.

56. ⁵⁶⁾힌트를 참고하여 각 <u>빈칸에 알맞은</u> 단어를 쓰시오.

57. ⁵⁷⁾밑줄 친 ⓐ~ⓑ에서, 어법 혹은 문맥상 어색한 부분을 찾아 올바르게 고쳐 쓰시오.

    ⓐ   잘못된 표현   바른 표현

   (   ) ⇨ (   )

    ⓑ   잘못된 표현   바른 표현

   (   ) ⇨ (   )

58. ⁵⁸⁾위 글에 주어진 (가)의 한글과 같은 의미를 가지도록, 각각의 주어진 단어들을 알맞게 배열하시오.

(가) be / cultural / these / approaches / had / and / account / transmission. / modified / for / to / to / However, / genetic / the differences / between

41~42

☑ **다음 글을 읽고 물음에 답하시오.** (41~42.)

A ball thrown into the air is acted upon by the ^{초기의} _____ force given it, persisting as inertia of movement and tending to carry it in the same straight line, and by the constant pull of gravity downward, as well as by the ^{저항} _____ of the air. ⓐ <u>It moves, accordingly, in a curving path.</u> Now the path does not represent the working of any particular force; there is simply the combination of the three elementary forces mentioned; but in a real sense, there is something in the total action ^{~외에} _____ the isolated action of three forces, namely, their joint action. ⓑ <u>In the same way, when two or more human individuals are together, their mutual relationships and their arrangement into a group are things which would not reveal if we confined our attention to each individual separately.</u> ⓒ <u>The significance of group behavior is greatly increased in the case of human beings by the fact that some of the tendencies to action of the individual related definitely to the other persons, and could not be aroused except by the other persons acting as stimuli.</u> An individual in complete isolation would not reveal their competitive tendencies, their tendencies towards the opposite sex, their protective tendencies towards children. (가) <u>이것은 개인이 다른 개인과의 관계에 관여될 때까지는 인간 본성의 특성이 완전히 나타나지 않는다는 것을 보여 준다.</u>

59. ⁵⁹⁾힌트를 참고하여 각 빈칸에 알맞은 단어를 쓰시오.

60. ⁶⁰⁾밑줄 친 ⓐ~ⓒ에서, 어법 혹은 문맥상 어색한 부분을 찾아 올바르게 고쳐 쓰시오.

ⓐ   잘못된 표현   바른 표현

(   ) ⇨ (   )

ⓑ   잘못된 표현   바른 표현

(   ) ⇨ (   )

ⓒ   잘못된 표현   바른 표현

(   ) ⇨ (   )

(   ) ⇨ (   )

(   ) ⇨ (   )

61. ⁶¹⁾위 글에 주어진 (가)의 한글과 같은 의미를 가지도록, 각각의 주어진 단어들을 알맞게 배열하시오.

(가) that / other / with / into / the   traits / is / brought / shows / of / fully / appear / until / relationships / individuals. / human / nature / This / do / not / the individual

43~45

☑ **다음 글을 읽고 물음에 답하시오.** (43~45.)

ⓐ <u>There once lived a man in a village who was not happy with his life. He was always troubled by one problem or the other.</u> One day, a saint with his guards stopped by his village. Many people heard the news and started going to him with their problems. The man also decided to visit the saint. Even after reaching the saint's place in the morning, he didn't get the opportunity to meet him till evening. ⓑ <u>When the man got to meet the saint, he confessed what he was very unhappy with life because of problems always surrounded him, like workplace tension or worries about his health.</u> ⓒ <u>He said, "Please give me a solution so that all the problems in my life will end and I can live peaceful".</u> The saint smiled and said that he would answer the request the next day. But the saint also asked if the man could do a small job for him. He told the man to take care of a hundred camels in his group that night, saying "When all hundred camels sit down, you can go to sleep". The man agreed. The next morning when the saint met that man, he asked if the man had slept well. (가) 피곤해하고 슬퍼하면서 남자는 한순간도 잠을 자지 못했다고 대답했다. (나) 사실 그 남자는 아주 열심히 노력했지만 그가 낙타 한 마리를 앉힐 때마다 다른 낙타 한 마리가 일어섰기 때문에 모든 낙타를 동시에 앉게 할 수 없었다. The saint told him, "You realized that no matter how hard you try, you can't make all the camels sit down. ⓓ <u>If one problem is solved, for some reason, the other will arise like the camels did.</u> So, humans should enjoy life despite these problems".

62. 62)밑줄 친 ⓐ~ⓓ에서, 어법 혹은 문맥상 어색한 부분을 찾아 올바르게 고쳐 쓰시오.

   ⓐ   잘못된 표현   바른 표현

     (   ) ⇨ (   )

   ⓑ   잘못된 표현   바른 표현

     (   ) ⇨ (   )

     (   ) ⇨ (   )

   ⓒ   잘못된 표현   바른 표현

     (   ) ⇨ (   )

   ⓓ   잘못된 표현   바른 표현

     (   ) ⇨ (   )

63. 63)위 글에 주어진 (가) ~ (나)의 한글과 같은 의미를 가지도록, 각각의 주어진 단어들을 알맞게 배열하시오.

(가) even / replied / the man / and / a moment. / for / he / that / sad, / couldn't / sleep / Tired

(나) sit, / the / but / every / the / make / at / made / he / time / In fact, / tried / the man / would / up. / one / all / sit / couldn't / stand / very / camels / time / camel / same / hard / another / because

정답

WORK BOOK

———

2023년 고1 11월 모의고사 내신대비용 WorkBook & 변형문제

Answer Keys

Prac 1 Answers

1) that
2) have
3) confident
4) assistant
5) During
6) convenience
7) hearing
8) that
9) while
10) flying
11) to see
12) had
13) so
14) be found
15) are
16) nonetheless
17) that
18) Doing
19) acceptance
20) compassion
21) more
22) accept
23) that
24) to see
25) acceptance
26) over
27) dreamed of
28) alter
29) influence
30) being
31) less
32) act
33) emerges
34) conceived
35) access
36) that
37) forward
38) demand
39) to find
40) organizes
41) so that
42) permission
43) to
44) that
45) reveal
46) finding
47) get
48) prevent
49) from entering
50) are created
51) oral
52) aspect
53) what
54) travel
55) posing
56) lose
57) that
58) lies
59) are designed
60) enhance
61) evolved
62) because
63) what
64) unchanging
65) turns
66) so that
67) more
68) was born

69) successfully
70) enslaved
71) other
72) himself
73) including
74) immigrants
75) autobiographies
76) describing
77) have
78) is
79) that
80) potential
81) is
82) premature
83) questionable
84) them
85) mistaken
86) diagnosing
87) unreliable
88) those
89) immediate
90) sacrificing
91) attachment
92) oneself
93) fundamentally
94) while
95) be overcome
96) leave
97) eliminate
98) be used
99) itself
100) impressive
101) reversing
102) adjusted
103) normally
104) confronted
105) reverse
106) were asked
107) the other
108) the other
109) ones
110) over
111) equally
112) themselves
113) hadn't
114) having
115) Anthropologist
116) closely
117) different
118) extent
119) although
120) Crucially
121) take up
122) varied
123) unites
124) perspective
125) includes
126) carved
127) closely
128) possessed
129) decayed
130) poor
131) invisible
132) beyond
133) describes
134) where
135) is conducted
136) relative
137) is

138) meaning
139) Similarly
140) that
141) to balance
142) until
143) process
144) a disadvantage
145) matures
146) tasked
147) from
148) playing
149) more
150) Due
151) more
152) used
153) selected
154) affected
155) decrease
156) be identified
157) sagging
158) be highlighted
159) have
160) is used
161) entirely
162) followed
163) from
164) were replaced
165) Because of
166) Leaving
167) is
168) at
169) has
170) greater
171) ruled
172) were known
173) conservative
174) were
175) superior
176) opposing
177) altered
178) conforming
179) has
180) that
181) abandons
182) neglects
183) from
184) applying
185) be modified
186) to follow
187) acquire
188) its
189) relevant
190) is acted
191) isolated
192) mutual
193) increased
194) are
195) complete
196) other
197) with
198) another
199) because
200) surrounded
201) so that
202) saying
203) another
204) arise

Prac 1 Answers

1) that
2) have
3) confident
4) assistant
5) During
6) convenience
7) hearing
8) that
9) while
10) flying
11) to see
12) had
13) so
14) be found
15) are
16) nonetheless
17) that
18) Doing
19) acceptance
20) compassion
21) more
22) accept
23) that
24) to see
25) acceptance
26) over
27) dreamed of
28) alter
29) influence
30) being
31) less
32) act
33) emerges
34) conceived
35) access
36) that
37) forward
38) demand
39) to find
40) organizes
41) so that
42) permission
43) to
44) that
45) reveal
46) finding
47) get
48) prevent
49) from entering
50) are created
51) oral
52) aspect
53) what
54) travel
55) posing
56) lose
57) that
58) lies
59) are designed
60) enhance
61) evolved
62) because
63) what
64) unchanging
65) turns
66) so that
67) more

68) was born
69) successfully
70) enslaved
71) other
72) himself
73) including
74) immigrants
75) autobiographies
76) describing
77) have
78) is
79) that
80) potential
81) is
82) premature
83) questionable
84) them
85) mistaken
86) diagnosing
87) unreliable
88) those
89) immediate
90) sacrificing
91) attachment
92) oneself
93) fundamentally
94) while
95) be overcome
96) leave
97) eliminate
98) be used
99) itself
100) impressive
101) reversing
102) adjusted
103) normally
104) confronted
105) reverse
106) were asked
107) the other
108) the other
109) ones
110) over
111) equally
112) themselves
113) hadn't
114) having
115) Anthropologist
116) closely
117) different
118) extent
119) although
120) Crucially
121) take up
122) varied
123) unites
124) perspective
125) includes
126) carved
127) closely
128) possessed
129) decayed
130) poor
131) invisible
132) beyond
133) describes
134) where
135) is conducted
136) relative

137) is
138) meaning
139) Similarly
140) that
141) to balance
142) until
143) process
144) a disadvantage
145) matures
146) tasked
147) from
148) playing
149) more
150) Due
151) more
152) used
153) selected
154) affected
155) decrease
156) be identified
157) sagging
158) be highlighted
159) have
160) is used
161) entirely
162) followed
163) from
164) were replaced
165) Because of
166) Leaving
167) is
168) at
169) has
170) greater
171) ruled
172) were known
173) conservative
174) were
175) superior
176) opposing
177) altered
178) conforming
179) has
180) that
181) abandons
182) neglects
183) from
184) applying
185) be modified
186) to follow
187) acquire
188) its
189) relevant
190) is acted
191) isolated
192) mutual
193) increased
194) are
195) complete
196) other
197) with
198) another
199) because
200) surrounded
201) so that
202) saying
203) another
204) arise

1) that
2) have
3) appreciated
4) in
5) response
6) to
7) last
8) During
9) available
10) had
11) seen
12) while
13) exotic
14) lost
15) track
16) of
17) had
18) landed.
19) fine
20) be
21) found
22) personal
23) Instead,
24) laid
25) out
26) keep
27) advancing
28) manage
29) to
30) as
31) if
32) ends
33) have
34) checked
35) lack
36) describing
37) voluntary
38) devote
39) Otherwise
40) objective
41) reflect
42) as
43) as
44) Others
45) inhabit
46) if
47) fell
48) colorless
49) positions
50) objective
51) subjective
52) put
53) registered
54) interpreted
55) demand
56) to
57) find
58) even
59) so
60) that
61) permission
62) record
63) drive
64) that
65) matter

66) those
67) crucial
68) everything
69) the
70) rest
71) what
72) prevent
73) from
74) entering
75) every
76) What
77) other
78) affects
79) posing
80) sooner
81) or
82) later
83) bottom
84) line
85) easily
86) lies
87) their
88) that
89) because
90) from
91) unchanging
92) so
93) that
94) neural
95) was
96) born
97) into
98) successfully
99) enslaved
100) escape
101) other
102) As
103) taught
104) himself
105) that
106) Once
107) equality
108) describing
109) candidate
110) have
111) proposed
112) others
113) legal
114) potential
115) these
116) ease
117) premature
118) questionable
119) as
120) as
121) that
122) criteria
123) whom
124) impression
125) sacrificing
126) stems
127) from
128) distance
129) that
130) emotional
131) arising
132) become
133) simple
134) hurt

135) overcome
136) every
137) eliminate
138) visual
139) adapting
140) impressive
141) reversing
142) literally
143) beginning
144) challenge
145) adjusted
146) normally
147) confronted
148) with
149) reach
150) the
151) rest
152) returned
153) Participants
154) Half
155) while
156) the
157) other
158) all
159) presented
160) during
161) advantage
162) equally
163) those
164) themselves
165) having
166) access
167) to
168) intellectual
169) tend
170) to
171) Take
172) so
173) that
174) appears
175) where
176) individual
177) although
178) additional
179) entire
180) take
181) up
182) what
183) emphasizing
184) ignoring
185) but
186) what
187) indicate
188) point
189) out
190) neither
191) nor
192) were
193) subject
194) to
195) extraordinary
196) reflection
197) where
198) that
199) where
200) According
201) to
202) encounter
203) the

204) more
205) the
206) closer
207) chance
208) fade
209) away
210) Similarly
211) depending
212) rely
213) on
214) adolescent
215) integrate
216) disadvantage
217) matures
218) which
219) responsible
220) for
221) earlier
222) Because
223) of
224) led
225) between
226) and
227) more
228) Despite
229) still
230) used
231) contain
232) affected
233) For
234) example
235) identified
236) enrolled
237) changes
238) highlighted
239) counteract
240) compensate
241) for
242) diversity
243) that
244) extreme
245) enormous scale
246) traditional
247) strategy
248) at
249) least
250) contribution
251) uniform
252) Specifically
253) narrow
254) greater
255) ruled
256) contrast
257) conservative
258) Not
259) only
260) even
261) opposing
262) A
263) few
264) declined
265) since
266) while
267) abandons
268) neglects
269) drew
270) applying
271) conceptually
272) these

273) account
274) for
275) strictly
276) not
277) necessarily
278) nonparental
279) relevant
280) probability
281) initial
282) constant
283) resistance
284) curved
285) represent
286) elementary
287) besides
288) when
289) mutual
290) each
291) that
292) other
293) acting
294) isolation
295) protective
296) brought
297) into
298) another
299) stopped
300) by
301) with
302) opportunity
303) confessed
304) surrounded
305) like
306) solution
307) could
308) saying
309) had
310) slept
311) every
312) made
313) another
314) another
315) despite

Prac 2 Answers

1) that
2) have
3) appreciated
4) in
5) response
6) to
7) last
8) During
9) available
10) had
11) seen
12) while
13) exotic
14) lost
15) track
16) of
17) had
18) landed.
19) fine
20) be
21) found
22) personal
23) Instead,
24) laid
25) out
26) keep
27) advancing
28) manage
29) to
30) as
31) if
32) ends
33) have
34) checked
35) lack
36) describing
37) voluntary
38) devote
39) Otherwise
40) objective
41) reflect
42) as
43) as
44) Others
45) inhabit
46) if
47) fell
48) colorless
49) positions
50) objective
51) subjective
52) put
53) registered
54) interpreted
55) demand
56) to
57) find
58) even
59) so
60) that
61) permission
62) record
63) drive
64) that
65) matter

66) those
67) crucial
68) everything
69) the
70) rest
71) what
72) prevent
73) from
74) entering
75) every
76) What
77) other
78) affects
79) posing
80) sooner
81) or
82) later
83) bottom
84) line
85) easily
86) lies
87) their
88) that
89) because
90) from
91) unchanging
92) so
93) that
94) neural
95) was
96) born
97) into
98) successfully
99) enslaved
100) escape
101) other
102) As
103) taught
104) himself
105) that
106) Once
107) equality
108) describing
109) candidate
110) have
111) proposed
112) others
113) legal
114) potential
115) these
116) ease
117) premature
118) questionable
119) as
120) as
121) that
122) criteria
123) whom
124) impression
125) sacrificing
126) stems
127) from
128) distance
129) that
130) emotional
131) arising
132) become
133) simple
134) hurt

135) overcome
136) every
137) eliminate
138) visual
139) adapting
140) impressive
141) reversing
142) literally
143) beginning
144) challenge
145) adjusted
146) normally
147) confronted
148) with
149) reach
150) the
151) rest
152) returned
153) Participants
154) Half
155) while
156) the
157) other
158) all
159) presented
160) during
161) advantage
162) equally
163) those
164) themselves
165) having
166) access
167) to
168) intellectual
169) tend
170) to
171) Take
172) so
173) that
174) appears
175) where
176) individual
177) although
178) additional
179) entire
180) take
181) up
182) what
183) emphasizing
184) ignoring
185) but
186) what
187) indicate
188) point
189) out
190) neither
191) nor
192) were
193) subject
194) to
195) extraordinary
196) reflection
197) where
198) that
199) where
200) According
201) to
202) encounter
203) the

204) more
205) the
206) closer
207) chance
208) fade
209) away
210) Similarly
211) depending
212) rely
213) on
214) adolescent
215) integrate
216) disadvantage
217) matures
218) which
219) responsible
220) for
221) earlier
222) Because
223) of
224) led
225) between
226) and
227) more
228) Despite
229) still
230) used
231) contain
232) affected
233) For
234) example
235) identified
236) enrolled
237) changes
238) highlighted
239) counteract
240) compensate
241) for
242) diversity
243) that
244) extreme
245) enormous scale
246) traditional
247) strategy
248) at
249) least
250) contribution
251) uniform
252) Specifically
253) narrow
254) greater
255) ruled
256) contrast
257) conservative
258) Not
259) only
260) even
261) opposing
262) A
263) few
264) declined
265) since
266) while
267) abandons
268) neglects
269) drew
270) applying
271) conceptually
272) these

273) account
274) for
275) strictly
276) not
277) necessarily
278) nonparental
279) relevant
280) probability
281) initial
282) constant
283) resistance
284) curved
285) represent
286) elementary
287) besides
288) when
289) mutual
290) each
291) that
292) other
293) acting
294) isolation
295) protective
296) brought
297) into
298) another
299) stopped
300) by
301) with
302) opportunity
303) confessed
304) surrounded
305) like
306) solution
307) could
308) saying
309) had
310) slept
311) every
312) made
313) another
314) another
315) despite

Answer Keys

quiz 1 Answers

1) ③
2) ③
3) ⑤
4) ①
5) ⑥
6) ②
7) ⑤
8) ④
9) ④
10) ①
11) ③
12) ②
13) ②
14) ⑥
15) ②
16) ③
17) ⑥
18) ③
19) ④
20) ③
21) ⑤
22) ③
23) ④
24) ②
25) ③
26) ③
27) ④
28) ⑤
29) ②
30) ⑤
31) ④
32) ⑤
33) ③
34) ⑤
35) ②
36) ④
37) ②
38) ⑤
39) ⑥
40) ③
41) ⑤
42) ②
43) (C)-(B)-(A)
44) (C)-(A)-(D)-(B)-(E)
45) (A)-(B)-(C)-(D)
46) (C)-(A)-(B)
47) (C)-(B)-(A)-(D)
48) (B)-(C)-(A)
49) (A)-(C)-(D)-(B)
50) (B)-(A)-(D)-(C)
51) (C)-(D)-(B)-(A)
52) (D)-(A)-(B)-(C)
53) (B)-(E)-(C)-(A)-(D)
54) (C)-(B)-(A)-(D)
55) (B)-(C)-(D)-(A)
56) (B)-(C)-(A)
57) (A)-(C)-(B)
58) (A)-(C)-(B)
59) (A)-(B)-(C)-(D)
60) (A)-(B)-(C)
61) (C)-(D)-(E)-(A)-(B)
62) (D)-(A)-(C)-(B)
63) (A)-(E)-(D)-(C)-(B)
64) (C)-(D)-(B)-(E)-(A)

quiz 2 Answers

1) [정답] ③
graduated ⇨ graduated from

2) [정답] ③
during ⇨ while

3) [정답] ④
be happened ⇨ happen

4) [정답] ③
inhibit ⇨ inhabit

5) [정답] ③
records ⇨ record

6) [정답] ②
getting ⇨ get

7) [정답] ①
boring ⇨ bored

8) [정답] ③
slave ⇨ slaves

9) [정답] ③
be agreed ⇨ agree

10) [정답] ②
detachment ⇨ attachment

11) [정답] ⑤
reality ⇨ perception

12) [정답] ④
itself ⇨ themselves

13) [정답] ①
which ⇨ that

14) [정답] ①
concludes ⇨ includes

15) [정답] ①
describing ⇨ describes

16) [정답] ②
Because ⇨ Because of

17) [정답] ④
compensating ⇨ compensate

18) [정답] ②
was followed by ⇨ followed

19) [정답] ⑤

which ⇨ that

20) [정답] ①
revolution ⇨ evolution

21) [정답] ④
is ⇨ are

22) [정답] ⑤
raise ⇨ arise

quiz 3 Answers

1) [정답] ⑤ ⓐ, ⓑ, ⓒ, ⓕ
ⓐ exciting ⇨ excited
ⓑ been appreciated ⇨ appreciated
ⓒ graduated ⇨ graduated from
ⓕ hear ⇨ hearing

2) [정답] ④ ⓐ, ⓔ, ⓖ, ⓗ
ⓐ been seen ⇨ seen
ⓔ what ⇨ where
ⓖ which ⇨ where
ⓗ find it ⇨ be found

3) [정답] ① ⓔ, ⓗ
ⓔ lain ⇨ laid
ⓗ be happened ⇨ happen

4) [정답] ① ⓐ, ⓒ
ⓐ subjective ⇨ objective
ⓒ absorb ⇨ reflect

5) [정답] ② ⓐ, ⓑ, ⓙ
ⓐ writes ⇨ writing
ⓑ demands ⇨ demand
ⓙ what ⇨ that

6) [정답] ⑤ ⓔ, ⓕ, ⓖ, ⓛ
ⓔ to ⇨ from
ⓕ entrance ⇨ entering
ⓖ effects ⇨ affects
ⓛ posed ⇨ posing

7) [정답] ⑤ ⓜ, ⓝ, ⓡ
ⓜ attending ⇨ attending to
ⓝ Excitement ⇨ Boredom
ⓡ on ⇨ off

8) [정답] ⑤ ⓒ, ⓓ, ⓕ, ⓖ
ⓒ enslave ⇨ enslaved
ⓓ escaping ⇨ escape
ⓕ spreads ⇨ spread
ⓖ slave ⇨ slaves

9) [정답] ③ ⓑ, ⓓ, ⓖ, ⓙ

ⓑ transportation ⇨ transplantation
ⓓ specific ⇨ specify
ⓖ are ⇨ is
ⓙ gain ⇨ reduce

10) [정답] ② ⓑ, ⓒ, ⓕ
ⓑ maintaining ⇨ sacrificing
ⓒ security ⇨ insecurity
ⓕ Be ⇨ Being

11) [정답] ④ ⓑ, ⓓ, ⓔ, ⓗ
ⓑ clearly ⇨ clear
ⓓ pork ⇨ fork
ⓔ habit ⇨ reality
ⓗ problems ⇨ with problems

12) [정답] ④ ⓒ, ⓔ, ⓕ, ⓖ
ⓒ be ⇨ do
ⓔ related ⇨ unrelated
ⓕ asking ⇨ asked
ⓖ while ⇨ during

13) [정답] ② ⓑ, ⓙ
ⓑ them ⇨ it
ⓙ on the other hand ⇨ however

14) [정답] ④ ⓓ, ⓔ, ⓗ, ⓛ
ⓓ which ⇨ that
ⓔ which ⇨ that
ⓗ what ⇨ that
ⓛ is existed ⇨ exists

15) [정답] ⑤ ⓖ, ⓗ, ⓘ, ⓚ
ⓖ relevant ⇨ relative
ⓗ approach to ⇨ approach
ⓘ drives ⇨ drivers
ⓚ compensate ⇨ balance

16) [정답] ① ⓑ, ⓔ
ⓑ procedure ⇨ process
ⓔ that ⇨ which

17) [정답] ⑤ ⓓ, ⓕ, ⓘ, ⓙ
ⓓ related ⇨ relate
ⓕ increase ⇨ decrease
ⓘ compensating ⇨ compensate
ⓙ appears ⇨ appear

18) [정답] ⑤ ⓖ, ⓗ
ⓖ various ⇨ uniform
ⓗ are ⇨ is

19) [정답] ⑤ ⓔ, ⓕ, ⓘ
ⓔ confirming ⇨ conforming
ⓕ have ⇨ has
ⓘ positive ⇨ negative

20) [정답] ⑤ ⓒ, ⑨, ⓗ
ⓒ liked ⇨ likened
⑨ require ⇨ acquire
ⓗ enquire ⇨ acquire

21) [정답] ④ ⑨, ⓜ, ⓞ
⑨ resistant ⇨ resistance
ⓜ defined ⇨ confined
ⓞ unrelated ⇨ related

22) [정답] ④ ⑨, ⓝ
⑨ said ⇨ saying
ⓝ though ⇨ despite

---

quiz 4 Answers

1) ② been appreciated ⇨ appreciated
③ graduated ⇨ graduated from
④ While ⇨ During
⑥ hear ⇨ hearing

2) ① been seen ⇨ seen
② what ⇨ that
⑧ find it ⇨ be found

3) ② lie ⇨ laid
⑥ describes ⇨ describing
⑦ mandatory ⇨ voluntary
⑧ be happened ⇨ happen

4) ① subjective ⇨ objective
② takes ⇨ bounces
③ absorb ⇨ reflect
⑤ inhibit ⇨ inhabit
⑥ colorful ⇨ colorless
⑦ everything else would ⇨ would everything else

5) ③ finding ⇨ to find

6) ① have ⇨ has
② healthful ⇨ healthy
④ that ⇨ what
⑤ to ⇨ from
⑥ entrance ⇨ entering
⑦ effects ⇨ affects
⑧ aspects ⇨ aspect
⑨ part ⇨ parts
⑩ effects ⇨ affects
⑪ enter into ⇨ enter
⑫ posed ⇨ posing

7) ⑦ are occurred ⇨ occur
⑩ consistently ⇨ quickly
⑯ stands ⇨ stand
⑱ on ⇨ off

8) ① his ⇨ he
② where ⇨ that
③ enslave ⇨ enslaved
④ escaping ⇨ escape
⑤ him ⇨ himself
⑥ spreads ⇨ spread
⑦ slave ⇨ slaves
⑧ include ⇨ including

9) ③ transacting ⇨ transferring

10) ② maintaining ⇨ sacrificing
③ security ⇨ insecurity
④ detachment ⇨ attachment
⑤ distant ⇨ distance
⑥ Be ⇨ Being
⑦ raising ⇨ arising
⑪ overseen ⇨ overcome
⑫ obscurity ⇨ clarity
⑬ which ⇨ that

11) ⑤ habit ⇨ reality

12) ② was ⇨ were

13) ① which ⇨ that
② them ⇨ it
③ close ⇨ closely
④ which ⇨ that
⑤ differently ⇨ different
⑥ which ⇨ where
⑦ smaller ⇨ larger
⑧ prospects ⇨ perspectives
⑨ despite ⇨ although
⑩ on the other hand ⇨ however
⑫ perspectives ⇨ perspective
⑬ involve ⇨ involves
⑭ embracing ⇨ ignoring

14) ② geographical ⇨ geometrical
⑨ perfect ⇨ poor

15) ① describing ⇨ describes
③ less ⇨ more
⑥ bidding ⇨ betting
⑦ relevant ⇨ relative
⑧ approach to ⇨ approach
⑩ to accidents ⇨ accidents

16) ⑪ emotion-based ⇨ logical-based

17) ② process ⇨ progress
⑤ effected ⇨ affected
⑦ identify ⇨ be identified

18) ② was followed by ⇨ followed

③ variety ⇨ varieties
④ large ⇨ small
⑤ one ⇨ ones
⑥ Left ⇨ Leaving
⑦ various ⇨ uniform
⑧ are ⇨ is
⑩ being ⇨ not being

19) [정답]
③ featured ⇨ featuring
④ did ⇨ were
⑤ confirming ⇨ conforming
⑥ have ⇨ has
⑧ adopt ⇨ adjust
⑨ positive ⇨ negative

20) ③ liked ⇨ likened
④ codified ⇨ modified
⑥ not ⇨ not necessarily
⑦ require ⇨ acquire

21) ① is thrown ⇨ thrown
② acting ⇨ acted
③ initiative ⇨ initial
④ persists ⇨ persisting
⑤ tend ⇨ tending
⑥ push ⇨ pull
⑧ mentioning ⇨ mentioned
⑪ is ⇨ are
⑫ relieved ⇨ revealed
⑬ defined ⇨ confined
⑭ weakened ⇨ increased
⑮ unrelated ⇨ related

22) ① troubling ⇨ troubled by
② visiting ⇨ to visit
③ reaching at ⇨ reaching
④ because of ⇨ because
⑤ which ⇨ that
⑥ taking ⇨ take
⑧ Tiring ⇨ Tired
⑨ hardly ⇨ hard
⑩ hardly ⇨ hard
⑪ sat ⇨ sit
⑫ raise ⇨ arise
⑬ were ⇨ did
⑭ though ⇨ despite

quiz 5 Answers

1) ~를 졸업하다 - graduated from // 조수 - assistant
2) ⓐ exciting ⇨ excited
what ⇨ that
ⓑ the way how ⇨ the way

feeling ⇨ feel
ⓒ While ⇨ During
have liked ⇨ like
3) (가) I look forward to hearing from you.
4) ⓐ so ⇨ such
what ⇨ that
ⓑ during ⇨ while
exotic ⇨ 이국적인
ⓒ landed ⇨ had landed
ⓓ found ⇨ be found
5) (가) I tried to see where it went, but the sun hit my eyes and I lost track of it.
6) 개인적인 - personal
7) ⓐ getting ⇨ get
ⓑ describes ⇨ describing
ⓒ healthily ⇨ healthy
devoting ⇨ devote
8) (가) But so many think and act as if their learning journey ends with college.
9) 객관적인 - objective
10) ⓐ registers ⇨ is registered
11) (가) They say there is no such thing as color; there are only the people who see it.
12) 중요한 - crucial
13) ⓐ what ⇨ that
demands ⇨ demand
ⓑ recording ⇨ record
14) (가) But remember that you will drive your readers to boredom if you think that you need to pack everything you discover into your work.
15) 전체의 - entire
16) ⓐ have ⇨ has
rest ⇨ the rest
ⓑ that ⇨ what
them ⇨ it
ⓒ travels ⇨ travel
17) (가) From the moment you are created, oral health affects every aspect of your life.
18) ~에 싫증나다 - tire of // 초기의 - initial // 신경의 - neural
19) ⓐ evolved ⇨ 진화하다
that ⇨ what
itself ⇨ 그 자체
20) (가) The bottom line is that we humans are easily bored.
21) 성공적으로 - successfully // 이민자들 - immigrants
22) ⓐ another ⇨ other
ⓑ taught ⇨ had taught
23) (가) In addition to all this, he became the first African-American candidate for vice president of the United States.
24) 명시하다 - specify // 잠재적인 - potential
25) ⓐ lacked ⇨ lacking
ⓑ that ⇨ those
26) (가) But it is questionable whether these requirements reduce public suspicions as much as they create them.
27) 희생하다 - sacrificing // 제거하다 - eliminate
28)
ⓐ
fundamental ⇨ fundamentally

ⓑ

during ⇨ while

overcoming ⇨ overcome

29)

(가) Minimalists never argue that you should leave every convenience of the modern era.

30) 적응하다 - adapting // 인상적인 - impressive // 어려움 - challenge // 적응하다 - adjusted

31) ⓐ reversed ⇨ reversing

literal ⇨ literally

32) (가) As he took off his reversing glasses, he was again confronted with problems

(나) Fortunately, Stratton could reverse the perception, and he did not have to wear reversing glasses for the rest of his life.

33) ⓐ told ⇨ were told

during ⇨ while

other ⇨ the other

ⓑ presented ⇨ were presented

ⓒ unrelated ⇨ 관련이 없는

while ⇨ during

advantage ⇨ 이점

ⓓ them ⇨ themselves

34) (가) The study suggests that having access to unrelated information was enough to pump up their intellectual confidence.

35) 인류학자 - Anthropologist // 관점 - perspectives // 전체의 - entire

36) ⓐ close ⇨ closely

ⓑ which ⇨ where

uniform ⇨ 동일한

ⓒ involve ⇨ involves

other ⇨ others

37) (가) Crucially, however, we can only take up one perspective at a time.

38) 수학적인 - mathematical // 기하학적인 - geometrical // 비범한 - extraordinary // 반영물 - reflection

39) ⓐ indicate ⇨ 가리키다

carving ⇨ carved

ⓑ look ⇨ looked

40) (가) They all possessed flaws, and all were subject to change and decayed with time.

(나) Plato believed that the Forms or universals are the true reality that exists in an invisible but perfect world beyond our senses.

41) 상태 - state // 상대적인 - relative

42) ⓐ describes ⇨ describe

ⓑ depend ⇨ depending

43) (가) Both casinos and insurance industries rely on the law of large numbers to balance individual losses.

44) ~까지 - until // 통합하다 - integrate // 처리하다 - process // 수정하다 - modifying

45) ⓐ mature ⇨ matures

tasking ⇨ tasked

ⓑ Because ⇨ Because of

46) (가) This may explain why some teens are more likely to make bad decisions.

47) 대응하다 - counteract // 보완하다 - compensate

48) ⓐ Although ⇨ Despite

49) (가) If the selected database does not contain enough instances, the result may be systematically affected.

50) 극도의 - extreme // 대체하다 - replaced // 획일적인 - uniform // 특히 - Specifically

51) ⓐ following ⇨ followed

ⓑ Because ⇨ Because of

52) (가) The decline in the diversity of our food is an entirely human-made process.

53) 지배하다 - ruled // 보수적인 - conservative

54) ⓐ opposed ⇨ opposing

ⓑ few ⇨ A few

altered ⇨ 바꾸다

55) (가) Not only were their athletic talents superior, the Cubans appeared even stronger from just the colour of their uniforms.

56) 주목할 만한 - noticeable // 더욱이 - Further // 확률 - probability

57) ⓐ genetically ⇨ genetic

ⓑ strict ⇨ strictly

58) (가) However, these approaches had to be modified to account for the differences between genetic and cultural transmission.

59) 초기의 - initial // 저항 - resistance // ~외에 - besides

60) ⓐ curving ⇨ curved

ⓑ reveal ⇨ be revealed

ⓒ related ⇨ are related

the other ⇨ other

the other ⇨ other

61) (가) This shows that the traits of human nature do not fully appear until the individual is brought into relationships with other individuals.

62) ⓐ the other ⇨ another

ⓑ what ⇨ that

because of ⇨ because

ⓒ peaceful ⇨ peacefully

ⓓ the other ⇨ another

63) (가) Tired and sad, the man replied that he couldn't sleep even for a moment.

(나) In fact, the man tried very hard but couldn't make all the camels sit at the same time because every time he made one camel sit, another would stand up.